CliffsNotes™

Thoreau, Emerson, and Transcendentalism

By Leslie Perrin Wilson, M.S., M.A.

IN THIS BOOK

- Examine the Major Tenets of Transcendentalism
- Preview an Introduction to the Times
- Learn about the Life and Background of the Authors
- Explore themes of the writings of Thoreau and Emerson in Major Themes
- Review Selected Chronologies of the authors' writings
- Reinforce what you learn with CliffsNotes Review
- Find additional information to further your study in the Cliffs Notes Resource Center and online at www.cliffsnotes.com

WILEY

Wiley Publishing, Inc.

D0369901

About the Author

Leslie Perrin Wilson earned her B.A. in Latin from Wellesley College, her M.S. from the Simmons College Graduate School of Library and Information Science, and her M.A. in English from Simmons College. She has made her career in special collections and archives and has been Curator of Special Collections of the Concord (Massachusetts) Free Public Library since 1996.

Publisher's Acknowledgments

Editorial

Project Editor: Elizabeth Netedu Kuball
Acquisitions Editor: Gregory W. Tubach

Production

Wiley Indianapolis Composition Services

CliffsNotes™ Thoreau, Emerson, and Transcendentalism
Published by:
Wiley Publishing, Inc.
111 River Street
Hoboken, NJ 07030
www.wiley.com

Table of Contents

How to Use This Book

This CliffsNotes study guide supplements the original literary work, giving you background information about the authors, an introduction to the works, critical commentaries, and a comprehensive index, all for you to use as an educational tool that will allow you to better understand these works. This study guide was written with the assumption that you have read the original works. Reading a literary work doesn't mean that you immediately grasp the major themes and devices used by the author; this study guide will help supplement your reading to be sure you get all you can from the original works. CliffsNotes Review tests your comprehension of the original texts and reinforces learning with questions and answers, practice projects, and more. For further information, check out the CliffsNotes Resource Center.

CliffsNotes provides the following icons to highlight essential elements of particular interest:

Reveals the underlying themes in the work.

Helps you to more easily relate to or discover the depth of a character.

Uncovers elements such as setting, atmosphere, mystery, passion, violence, irony, symbolism, tragedy, foreshadowing, and satire.

Enables you to appreciate the nuances of words and phrases.

Don't Miss Our Web Site

Discover classic literature as well as modern-day treasures by visiting the Cliffs Notes Web site at www.cliffsnotes.com. You can obtain a quick download of a CliffsNotes title, purchase a title in print form, browse our catalog, or view online samples.

You'll also find interactive tools that are fun and informative, links to interesting Web sites, *tips, articles,* and additional resources to help you, *not only for literature, but for test prep, finance, careers, computers, and the Internet too.* See you at www.cliffsnotes.com!

TRANSCEND-ENTALISM: WHAT IS IT?

Introduction

New England Transcendentalism was a religious, philosophical, and literary movement that began to express itself in New England in the 1830s and continued through the 1840s and 1850s. Although Ralph Waldo Emerson, Amos Bronson Alcott, and others among the Transcendentalists lived to old age in the 1880s and beyond, by about 1860 the energy that had earlier characterized Transcendentalism as a distinct movement had subsided. For several reasons, Transcendentalism is not simple to define. Transcendentalism encompassed complex philosophical and religious ideas. Its tenets were tinged with a certain mysticism, which defies concise explanation. Moreover, significant differences of focus and interpretation existed among the Transcendentalists; these differences complicate generalizations about the movement as a whole.

Henry David Thoreau himself pointed out the difficulty of understanding Transcendentalism in his well-known journal entry for March 5, 1853:

> The secretary of the Association for the Advancement of Science requests me . . . to fill the blank against certain questions, among which the most important one was what branch of science I was specially interested in . . . I felt that it would be to make myself the laughing-stock of the scientific community to describe to them that branch of science which specially interests me, inasmuch as they do not believe in a science which deals with the higher law. So I was obliged to speak to their condition and describe to them that poor part of me which alone they can understand. The fact is I am a mystic, a transcendentalist, and a natural philosopher to boot. Now that I think of it, I should have told them at once that I was a transcendentalist. That would have been the shortest way of telling them that they would not understand my explanations.

Transcendentalism clearly eluded succinct definition in Thoreau's time as much as it does in our own.

Moreover, the Transcendentalists were only loosely connected with one another. They were not a cohesive, organized group who shared a formal doctrine. They were distinct and independent individuals who accepted some basic premises about man's place in the universe.

Transcendentalism flourished in the intellectual centers of Boston and Cambridge, Massachusetts, and, because of Ralph Waldo Emerson's presence, in nearby Concord as well. Emerson moved to Concord in 1834 and bought a home on the Cambridge Turnpike in 1835. His essay *Nature*, a systematic exposition of the main principles of Transcendentalism, was published anonymously in 1836. Its publication sparked a period of intense intellectual ferment and literary activity.

Although it was based in part on ancient ideas (the philosophy of Plato, for example), Transcendentalism was in many ways a radical movement, threatening to established religion. Some people opposed Transcendentalism vigorously. One of its most reactionary critics was Harvard professor Andrews Norton, who attacked Emerson's "Divinity School Address" in 1838 and who went on to produce a piece titled *Discourse on the Latest Form of Infidelity* in 1839. (The "latest form of infidelity" to which Norton referred was, of course, Transcendentalism.)

Emerson was, as a high-profile writer, lecturer, and editor of the Transcendental periodical *The Dial*, central among the Transcendentalists. In addition to Emerson and Thoreau, others involved in the movement included: Amos Bronson Alcott (philosopher, educator, and Concordian); Margaret Fuller (early feminist, author, and lecturer; one of the editors of *The Dial*); James Freeman Clarke (Unitarian minister, author, and editor); Theodore Parker (Unitarian minister and abolitionist); Elizabeth Palmer Peabody (teacher and educational reformer, writer, editor, and social reformer; one of the publishers of *The Dial*); George Ripley (Unitarian minister, editor, and founder of the Brook Farm community); Orestes Brownson (editor, reviewer, and contributor of essays to *The Christian Examiner* and to his own *Boston Quarterly Review*); William Henry Channing (Unitarian minister and editor of the *Western Messenger* and other journals); Christopher Pearse Cranch (Unitarian minister, editor of the *Western Messenger*, poet, and artist); Convers Francis (Unitarian minister, biographer of John Eliot, and historian of Watertown); William Henry Furness (Unitarian minister, theologian, and author); Frederic Henry Hedge (Unitarian minister, scholar, author, editor, lecturer, and professor of ecclesiastical history and of German at Harvard); and Jones Very (poet, tutor in Greek at Harvard, and, after he proclaimed himself the second coming of Christ, a resident at McLean's Asylum). These individuals, all of whom devoted serious thought to the major concepts of Transcendentalism, were educated, intellectual people.

Major Tenets

Above all, the Transcendentalists believed in the importance of a direct relationship with God and with nature. Emerson wrote in his essay *Nature* that "The foregoing generations beheld God and Nature face to face; we—through their eyes. Why should not we also enjoy an original relation to the universe?" Theodore Parker spoke of man's relation to God in particular in his powerful sermon "A Discourse of the Transient and Permanent in Christianity" (also known as the "South Boston Sermon, which was delivered in 1841. Parker wrote,

> In an age of corruption, as all ages are, Jesus stood and looked up to God. There was nothing between him and the father of all; no old world . . . no sin or the perverseness of the finite will. . . . He would have us do the same; worship with nothing between us and God; . . . and we never are *Christians* as he was the *Christ*, until we worship, as Jesus did, with nothing between us and the Father of all.

Thoreau, who was born and lived almost his entire life in Concord, went to live at Walden Pond in 1845 to experience nature directly and intensely and to test his Transcendental outlook in the concrete physical world. In the chapter of his book *Walden* titled "Solitude," he wrote of his connection with nature as a very intimate, two-way relationship:

> The indescribable innocence and beneficence of Nature,—of sun and wind and rain, of summer and winter,—such health, such cheer, they afford forever! . . . Shall I not have intelligence with the earth? Am I not partly leaves and vegetable mould myself?

Thoreau's expression of his essential oneness with nature suggests the concept at the very heart of Transcendentalism, that of the Oversoul. The Oversoul formed the encompassing framework within which a direct relationship with God and with nature was so essential to the Transcendentalists. Simply described, the Oversoul was a kind of cosmic unity between man, God, and nature. Emerson wrote an essay titled "The Over-Soul," which was included in the first series of his *Essays* (published in 1841). In it, he described the Oversoul as:

> . . . that great nature in which we rest . . . that Unity, that Over-Soul, within which every man's particular being is contained and made one with all other. . . . We live in succession, in division, in parts, in particles. Meantime within

man is the soul of the whole; the wise silence; the universal beauty, to which every part and particle is equally related; the eternal ONE.

The idea of the Oversoul had roots in the ancient philosophy of Plato, whose writings the Transcendentalists read. To the Transcendentalists, the Oversoul was the divine spirit or mind that was present in each and every man and in all of nature. It was an all-pervading, omniscient, supreme mind. Each particular example of nature or of humanity was a reflection of the divine mind, and the whole of the cosmos could be extrapolated from each particular. In each manifestation of God, man could discover, in encapsulated form, all universal laws at work. The presence of the divine spirit in both nature and the human soul made a direct understanding of God and an openness to the natural world avenues to self-understanding. Self-understanding led to the perception of higher truth.

For some of the Transcendentalists, social activism was a direct consequence of this sense of cosmic unity. If man is intimately connected with and a reflection of God in the way that the Transcendentalists suggested, and if God is good and just, then man is also innately good and just. Evil exists only when man has an imperfect awareness of his essential goodness and godliness. This outlook gave dignity and importance to human activity, as manifestations of the divine, and fostered a belief in man's power to bring about personal improvement and social change in harmony with God's purposes. Out of this belief arose the Transcendentalists' involvement in a variety of reform activities and in social experiments like Brook Farm and Fruitlands, which were utopian communities established in Massachusetts.

As important as this interrelationship between the particular and the cosmic was to the Transcendentalists, the process by which the individual could understand the relationship was equally important. They felt that neither the received dogma of traditional systems of belief nor formal reasoning would give real insight into truth and morality as expressed in the multiple manifestations of the Oversoul. They looked rather to intuitive, as opposed to consciously rational, thought.

James Walker was a Unitarian minister, an editor of *The Christian Examiner*, a Harvard professor of religion and philosophy, and an influence on the Transcendentalists (although not really one of them). In 1834, he published in *The Christian Examiner* an address titled "The Philosophy of Man's Spiritual Nature in Regard to the Foundation of

Faith," in which he described intuitive thought as the Transcendentalists understood it. Walker stated:

> . . . On what evidence does a devout man's conviction of the existence and reality of the *spiritual world* depend? I answer . . . [h]e does not take the facts of his inward experience, and hold to the existence and reality of the spiritual world as a logical deduction from these facts, but as an intuitive suggestion grounded on these facts. He believes in the existence and reality of the spiritual world, just as he believes in his own existence and reality, and just as he believes in the existence and reality of the outward universe,—simply and solely because he is so constituted that with his impressions or perceptions he cannot help it.

Another clear presentation of intuition was written by Francis Bowen, a writer for *The Christian Examiner* and a critic of Transcendentalism, in particular a critic of the emphasis on intuition as opposed to reason. In his review of Emerson's *Nature* in the *Examiner*, Bowen characterized the concept of intuition as expressed by Emerson:

> [Transcendentalism] rejects the aid of observation, and will not trust to experiment. The Baconian mode of discovery is regarded as obsolete; induction is a slow and tedious process, and the results are uncertain and imperfect. General truths are to be attained without the previous examination of particulars, and by the aid of a higher power than the understanding. . . . truths which are *felt* are more satisfactory and certain than those which are *proved*. . . . Hidden meanings, glimpses of spiritual and everlasting truth are found, where former observers sought only for natural facts. The observation of sensible phenomena can lead only to the discovery of insulated, partial, and relative laws; but the consideration of the same phenomena, in a typical point of view, may lead us to infinite and absolute truth,— to a knowledge of the reality of things. . . .

Bowen continued on to draw an unflattering analogy between the validity of the Transcendentalists' "indistinct modes of reflection . . . loose and rambling speculations, mystical forms of expression, and . . . utterance of truths . . . half perceived" and the random luck of the gambler.

In their belief that truth was innate in all of creation and that knowledge of truth was intuitive, the Transcendentalists were heavily influenced by the thoughts and writings of the eighteenth century German philosopher Immanuel Kant. (Kant's *Critique of Pure Reason* was first published in 1781, his *Critique of Practical Reason* in 1788.) Their use of the term *transcendental* came from Kant, who wrote, "I call all knowledge *transcendental* which is concerned, not with objects, but with our mode of knowing objects so far as this is possible *a priori* [that is, independent of reason]."

Reasons for the Rise of the Movement

Transcendentalism flourished at the height of literary and aesthetic Romanticism in Europe and America. Romanticism was marked by a reaction against classical formalism and convention and by an emphasis on emotion, spirituality, subjectivity, and inspiration. Transcendentalism, inspired by English and European Romantic authors, was a form of American Romanticism. Transcendentalism arose when it did for several reasons.

First, it was a humanistic philosophy—it put the individual right at the center of the universe and promoted respect for human capabilities. The movement was in part a reaction against increasing industrialization in the late eighteenth and early nineteenth centuries, and against the dehumanization and materialism that frequently accompanied it. In 1814, progressive mill owner Francis Cabot Lowell introduced the power loom into the American textile industry at his Boston Manufacturing Company in Waltham, Massachusetts. The New England Transcendentalists consequently grew to maturity at a time when the nature of work and the role of labor were undergoing tremendous change before their eyes, and very close to home.

Secondly, in the early nineteenth century, in the period preceding the rise of Transcendentalism, dissatisfaction with the spiritual inadequacy of established religion was on the rise. Some early Unitarian ministers—especially William Ellery Channing (who was the uncle of the Concord poet of the same name)—had turned away from harsh, unforgiving Congregational Calvinism and preached a more humanistic, emotionally expressive, and socially conscious form of religion. Channing and a few others among the early Unitarians had a formative influence on the Transcendentalists.

However, even the liberal Unitarians remained under the sway of the seventeenth century English philosopher John Locke, who had explained knowledge as perceivable only by direct observation through the physical senses. Kant's later presentation of knowledge as intuitive was, of course, in direct opposition to Locke. In this sense, Transcendentalism was a reaction against the extreme rationalism of the Enlightenment.

The dissatisfaction with established religion that affected the Transcendentalists is strongly and clearly expressed in Emerson's 1838 "Divinity School Address," in which Emerson asked,

> In how many churches, by how many prophets, tell me, is man made sensible that he is an infinite Soul; that the earth and heavens are passing into his mind; that he is drinking forever the soul of God? Where now sounds the persuasion, that by its very melody imparadises my heart, and so affirms its own origin in heaven? . . . But now the priest's Sabbath has lost the splendor of nature; it is unlovely; we are glad when it is done; we can make, we do make, even sitting in our pews, a far better, holier, sweeter, for ourselves.

These were critical words, and they drew strong negative response, particularly from Andrews Norton, a Biblical scholar and professor at the Harvard Divinity School, who issued his *Discourse on the Latest Form of Infidelity* in 1839 in response to the ideas Emerson put forth in his address.

Like the "Divinity School Address," Theodore Parker's "A Discourse of the Transient and Permanent in Christianity" expressed rejection of established religion and religious doctrine:

> The stream of Christianity, as men receive it, has caught a stain from every soil it has filtered through, so that now it is not the pure water from the well of life which is offered to our lips, but streams troubled and polluted by man with mire and dirt. If Paul and Jesus could read our books of theological doctrines, would they accept as their teaching what men have vented in their name? Never, till the letters of Paul had faded out of his memory; never, till the words of Jesus had been torn out from the book of life. It is their notions about Christianity men have taught as the only living word of God. They have piled their own rubbish against the temple of Truth where Piety comes up to worship; what wonder the pile seems unshapely and like to fall? But these theological doctrines are fleeting as the leaves on the trees.

Clearly, Emerson and Parker both envisioned true religion as a personal rather than an institutional connection with the divine.

A third reason for the rise of Transcendentalism was the increasing interest in and availability of foreign literature and philosophy after 1800. Americans were traveling and studying in Europe, and some of them brought books back to America when they returned home. The Reverend Joseph Stevens Buckminster traveled to Europe in 1801, studied Biblical scholarship and European methods of Biblical interpretation, and returned home with about three thousand volumes purchased abroad. In 1815, George Ticknor and Edward Everett went to Europe to study. They traveled extensively, studied at the University of Göttingen in Germany (in 1817, Everett because the first American ever to receive a Ph.D. from Göttingen), and returned to America to take up important academic positions at Harvard (Ticknor taught foreign literature, Everett Greek). Emerson, significantly, was one of their students. Ticknor and Everett also brought back large numbers of books—Ticknor for his personal library, Everett for Harvard's library. Charles Follen, a German political refugee, was another influential Harvard teacher. In 1830, the first professor of German literature at Harvard, Follen was very familiar with the writings of Kant.

During this period, too, translations into English from European works began to make foreign thought and writing more available. The Reverend Moses Stuart, a professor at the Andover Theological Seminary, was translating grammars of Greek and Hebrew from German in the early nineteenth century. More significantly, in 1813, Madame de Stäel's *De L'Allemagne* was translated into English under the title *Germany*; a New York edition came out in 1814. (Madame de Stäel was a favorite writer of the Transcendentalists, and was seen as a kind of archetypal intellectual woman.)

At the same time, many in England and America were exposed to German thought and literature through the writings of Coleridge and Carlyle. Coleridge's *Aids to Reflection* (first published in 1825) was edited in 1829 by James Marsh, who added a lengthy introduction elucidating German philosophy for American readers. Carlyle wrote a life of Schiller and translated from Goethe. Between 1838 and 1842, George Ripley edited and published, in fourteen volumes, a set titled *Specimens of Foreign Standard Literature*, which included translations from French and German writings. In 1840, Elizabeth Palmer Peabody opened a circulating library and bookstore on West Street in Boston to supply her comrades with foreign works.

Among the many foreign authors who influenced the Transcendentalists were the Germans Kant, Fichte, Schleiermacher, Hegel, Schelling, Goethe, and Novalis; the French Cousin and Constant; the English writers Coleridge, Carlyle, and Wordsworth; Plato and English Neoplatonic writers; Swedish mystic Emanuel Swedenborg; and the Eastern writings of Confucius and sacred texts of the Vishnu Purana and the Bhagavadgita.

Forms of Expressing Transcendental Philosophy

The Transcendentalists expressed their idealistic philosophy in a variety of ways. They delivered lectures and sermons, and wrote essays, articles, and books. Emerson, Alcott, Ripley, Parker, Brownson, Fuller, Peabody, Channing, Thoreau, Clarke, and others participated in meetings of the Transcendental Club (formed in 1836), which served as a discussion group for crystallizing their views on aspects of religion and philosophy. For four years (1840–1844), they had in the quarterly periodical *The Dial* a vehicle designed specifically for the dissemination of their thoughts. But they also embraced more active, as opposed to strictly verbal and textual, modes of expression.

Teaching and educational reform were major activities to which the Transcendentalists devoted their energies. Because the intuitive nature of knowledge formed such a basic part of their outlook, education was naturally a prime area in which to test their philosophy. Bronson Alcott, a progressive teacher, relied extensively on the power of intuition in the classroom. He ran a school at the Masonic Temple in Boston—the Temple School—from 1834 to 1838. He employed the Socratic dialogue format, or the so-called "conversational" method, in which he asked questions on a designated topic and gave direction to the course of the ensuing discussion. Learning was an interactive process, intended to uncover innate truth and morality rather than to instill these values from without. Alcott served as Superintendent of Schools in Concord from 1859 to 1865. In 1879, he established the Concord School of Philosophy, an early experiment in adult and continuing education.

Elizabeth Peabody gave much of her life to teaching and to improving educational methods. She taught school in a number of places, both on her own and with various members of her family, and she served as Alcott's assistant at the Temple School. More importantly, in terms of her lasting impact on education, she went on to establish kindergarten in the United States, beginning with her founding of the first American kindergarten in Boston in 1860. She also conducted conversational series (discussion groups) similar to those offered by Margaret Fuller.

Margaret Fuller was both a feminist and, in some of her efforts, an educator of women. A learned woman, she organized series of "conversations," for women. In the early 1840s, she held conversational classes at Elizabeth Peabody's West Street home and bookstore. Her major work *Woman in the Nineteenth Century* grew out of these classes. Like Bronson Alcott, she intended her conversations to stimulate the intuitive process more than to impart factual knowledge.

In addition to education, the Transcendentalists expressed their optimism in man's perfectibility in the antislavery movement. Most Transcendentalists were committed to abolition. Thoreau and (more hesitantly) Emerson were galvanizing speakers and writers on behalf of the movement. Theodore Parker spoke out against slavery from the pulpit and wrote on the subject. Bronson Alcott, Margaret Fuller, and Elizabeth Peabody were all involved in one way or another. Thoreau formed part of the Underground Railroad in Concord.

Other reform concerns that engaged the Transcendentalists included women's suffrage, Native American education and rights, and world peace. Some of these movements continued on into the late nineteenth century, and the enduring Elizabeth Peabody was involved with them until she died, in 1894.

The establishment of experimental living communities was an important expression of Transcendentalism. Bronson Alcott and Charles Lane set up Fruitlands at Harvard, Massachusetts. It lasted from June 1843 to January 1844. The Fruitlands regimen included a vegetarian diet and cold baths in the morning. Bronson Alcott's daughter, author Louisa May Alcott, who endured considerable privation with her family at Fruitlands, satirized the experiment in a piece titled "Transcendental Wild Oats."

Brook Farm at West Roxbury was larger and longer-lived than Fruitlands. It was established by George and Sophia Ripley in 1841 to promote a balance between intellectual exertion and manual labor. It continued until 1847, for part of its existence in accordance with the principles of Charles Fourier. Life at Brook Farm included entertainment and social life as well as back-breaking labor. Side-by-side with farming and other activities related to the necessities, there were dramatic productions, parties, singing, dancing, picnics, hikes, sledding, skating, reading and literature groups, and lectures.

Finally, although Thoreau's life at Walden Pond between 1845 and 1847 constituted a community of only one, his stay there was just as much an experiment in living and an attempt at applied idealism as were Brook Farm and Fruitlands. His *Walden, or, Life in the Woods*, based on his experience at the pond, was published in 1854. In the chapter "Where I Lived, and What I Lived For," Thoreau wrote:

> Men esteem truth remote, in the outskirts of the system, behind the farthest star. . . . In eternity there is indeed something true and sublime. But all these times and places and occasions are now and here. God himself culminates in the present moment. . . . And we are enabled to apprehend at all what is sublime and noble only by the perpetual instilling and drenching of the reality which surrounds us.

By living intimately with nature at Walden, Thoreau attained to the higher truths that so concerned all of the Transcendentalists.

Lasting Impact of the Movement

New England Transcendentalism as a movement really thrived only for about twenty-five years. The world was not completely reformed by the words and efforts of its proponents. But people today still read Emerson's *Nature* and Thoreau's *Walden*. The importance of these thinkers lies in the endurance of their major writings as American classics, worth reading in any period, in their influence upon later writers, American and foreign, and in the powerful inspiration that their reform efforts provided to later social movements, notably the impetus given to Mohandas Gandhi and to the American civil rights movement of the 1960s by Thoreau's principle of nonviolent resistance to oppressive civil government as expressed in *Civil Disobedience* (first published in 1849).

INTRODUCTION TO THE TIMES

Introduction

New England Transcendentalism flowered during a period in American history marked by expansion, change, a growing national self-awareness, and increasing political, social, and regional polarization. The 1830 United States Census recorded a population of 12,866,020. By the 1860 Census, the population had more than doubled, to 31,443,321. The years from 1830 to 1860 witnessed the exploration and annexation of much new territory, westward migration, dramatic improvements in transportation and communication, and development toward party politics as we recognize them today. The North became more urbanized and industrialized, whereas the South remained primarily agricultural, resulting in ultimately irreconcilable disagreement over the issue of slavery, as well as tension over the tariff question.

An idealistic reform impulse exposed and combatted social, political, and economic inequities, slavery foremost among them. The Native American was feared, displaced, romanticized, and made the object of reform efforts. There was a trend toward the democratization of educational and cultural opportunities, and an appetite for popular entertainment on a large scale.

It was the age of the Monroe Doctrine and of "manifest destiny," applied by advocates of territorial expansion to encourage acquisitive government actions. The composition of the population began to change in the 1840s and 1850s, as immigration into the United States increased in the wake of European political upheaval and the potato famine in Ireland, triggering reactionary response from some quarters.

Traditional New England Congregationalism was criticized, Unitarianism arose, and other new, distinctly American religions sprang up. While many Americans maintained a wary distance from, or blissful ignorance of, currents in foreign politics and culture, certain religious leaders and some intellectuals and writers were strongly influenced by foreign philosophy and literature, forging in Transcendentalism a radical expression of European idealism and Romanticism.

Historical Context

Some of the dominant historical themes in the first half of the nineteenth century were territorial exploration and expansion, growing tension around the issue of slavery (exacerbated by the annexation of new territory), and industrialization and technological development, including progress in transportation and communication. The New England Transcendentalists were keenly aware of these historical currents.

The country grew rapidly, sanctioned by the 1823 Monroe Doctrine, in which President James Monroe had declared North America no longer open to European acquisition and meddling, and by the concept of "manifest destiny," articulated in the 1840s, proclaiming America's mission to spread its culture and government across North America. The Louisiana Purchase of 1803 added most of the area between the Mississippi and the Rockies. Between 1804 and 1806, Lewis and Clark explored the Northwest from the Mississippi to the Pacific. In 1806, Zebulon Pike traveled through the Southwest, to New Mexico and Mexico City. During the 1820s, traders hauled goods over the Santa Fe Trail. The first American settlement in Texas, which was then under Mexican control, was established in 1821. Americans subsequently flocked to Texas until 1830, when Mexico passed more restrictive immigration laws. California and Oregon were explored in the 1820s. Jedediah Strong Smith led an expedition to Mexican-held California in 1826. Oregon Country, jointly controlled by the United States and Great Britain, was explored in the late 1820s, settled in the 1840s and 1850s. Gold drew thousands westward, to California (beginning in 1848), to Colorado and Nevada (beginning in 1859), to Idaho (beginning in 1860) and Montana (beginning in 1862).

John C. Frémont undertook a series of expeditions in the 1840s, to track the headwaters of the Des Moines River (1841), to explore the route to Oregon (1842 and 1843–1844), and to California, to survey the Rockies and the area around the Great Salt Lake (1845–1846). Under the leadership of Brigham Young, the beleaguered Mormons began their migration from Illinois in 1846, arriving at the Great Salt Lake in 1847.

In terms of their impact on the Transcendentalists, exploration and settlement were significant primarily in relation to slavery. As the possibility of statehood arose for a territory, the question of whether it would be a slave state or a free state became an issue that drew national attention and heated debate.

In 1819, Missouri requested admission to the Union as a slave state. The country at the time contained an equal number of slave and free states (twenty-two total—eleven free and eleven slave). Congress hammered out the Missouri Compromise of 1820 in order to preserve this balance and to prevent further rancor and division between slavery and antislavery interests. Under the Missouri Compromise, Missouri was admitted as a slave state, Maine was admitted as a free state, and slavery was prohibited in the rest of the Louisiana Purchase north of the southern boundary of Missouri. This arrangement satisfied neither the South, which resented any attempt by the federal government to control slavery, nor the North, which was angered by government complicity in expanding slave territory.

Texas, spurred on by defeat at the Alamo, won its freedom from Mexico in 1836. Its annexation to the United States in 1845 was opposed by antislavery forces because of the likelihood that it would become a slave state and because it also made war with Mexico, which had refused to recognize the independence of Texas, impossible to avoid. War was declared in 1846, further polarizing the nation. Southerners supported the war, Northerners opposed it. At the war's end in 1848, Mexico recognized Texas as part of the United States and surrendered additional territory (California, Nevada, and Utah, most of New Mexico and Arizona, parts of Colorado and Wyoming).

The addition of territory through war with Mexico inflamed slavery/antislavery tensions, resulting in the Compromise of 1850, which was an attempt to delay impending national crisis. By the Compromise, California was admitted as a free state, the territories of New Mexico and Utah would decide the slavery question for themselves upon admission to the Union, the boundary between Texas and New Mexico was established, and the slave trade was abolished in Washington, D.C. The Compromise of 1850 also included the Fugitive Slave Law, which required the return of runaway slaves to their owners. Many Northerners were furious over and unwilling to obey the Fugitive Slave Law.

Kansas was a hotbed of conflict following the Compromise of 1850. For a time, it had two governments, one that permitted and one that outlawed slavery. In this unsettled atmosphere, lives and property were lost. John Brown moved to Kansas in 1855. He became captain of a company formed to maintain Kansas as a free state, employing radically militant methods of achieving this end. (Brown led the ill-fated raid on the federal arsenal at Harper's Ferry, West Virginia, in 1859, for which he was executed.) In 1857, Kansas elected a free state legislature. It was not admitted to the Union until 1861.

The 1857 Supreme Court decision in the Dred Scott case further divided North and South. In deciding the slave Dred Scott's claim to freedom, the Supreme Court ruled that slaves could not sue because they were not citizens, and further pronounced that Congress could not prohibit slavery in territories, thereby declaring the Missouri Compromise of 1820 unconstitutional. Northerners were once again outraged. This long series of conflicts led to and was finally resolved by the Civil War (1861–1865).

Thoreau was able to view the exploits of the great explorers of the continent metaphorically, as parallel to the exploration by the individual of the world within himself. He wrote in the conclusion to *Walden*:

> What does Africa,—what does the West stand for? . . . Is it the source of the Nile, or the Niger, or the Mississippi, or a North-West Passage around this continent, that we would find? . . . Be rather the Mungo Park, the Lewis and Clark and Frobisher, of your own streams and oceans; explore your own higher latitudes. . . .

Though it might be considered metaphorically, however, through its consequences, expansion presented moral difficulties that the Transcendentalists could not ignore.

Most of the New England Transcendentalists—Thoreau and Emerson among them—supported the abolition of slavery. They were, for several reasons, predisposed to take up this cause. Dr. William Ellery Channing, the "father of Unitarianism" and a source of inspiration, wrote a treatise titled *Slavery* (1835) and frequently wrote and spoke in favor of abolition. Moreover, Boston was a center of antislavery activity. Radical abolitionist William Lloyd Garrison established the periodical *The Liberator* in Boston in 1831, and was a founder of the New England Anti-Slavery Society there in 1832.

But the Transcendentalists also felt some ambivalence about ardent abolitionists and others who sought to reform society through political and legal action. Transcendentalism stressed the reform of society through perfection of the individual from within, not through external social means. At times, both Emerson and Thoreau wrote disparagingly of reformers.

Despite their reservations, however, Emerson, Thoreau, Alcott, Theodore Parker, and others were important in the antislavery movement. Emerson delivered his first antislavery address in Concord in 1837, in response to the murder of abolitionist publisher Elijah Lovejoy in Alton, Illinois. Emerson delivered his passionate *An Address* . . .

on the Anniversary of the Emancipation of the Negroes in the British West Indies in 1844, in the Concord courthouse. During the 1840s and 1850s, he spoke out frequently against slavery, appearing with Garrison and other leaders of the movement. The Fugitive Slave Law enraged Emerson, and he advocated disobeying it.

In the 1840s, Alcott and Thoreau refused to pay the poll tax in Concord in protest against slavery. Thoreau was jailed briefly in July of 1846 for this refusal. In 1848, he delivered a lyceum lecture on the subject of civil disobedience. In 1849, his "Resistance to Civil Government"—later known as *Civil Disobedience*—first appeared in the one and only issue of Elizabeth Peabody's *Aesthetic Papers*. He urged obedience to higher laws than the temporal laws of civil government. He wrote, "This people must cease to hold slaves, and to make war on Mexico, though it cost them their existence as a people."

Several attempts to enforce the hated Fugitive Slave Law of 1850 were highly publicized and drew the attention of the Transcendentalists. In February of 1851, Shadrach Minkins, a runaway slave rescued from the courthouse in Boston, spent a night in Concord en route to safety in Canada via the Underground Railroad. In 1851, the case of Thomas Sims prompted Emerson to take a more radical stand regarding the necessity of opposing the institutionalization of slavery through the Fugitive Slave Law. On July 4, 1854, Thoreau delivered his powerful address "Slavery in Massachusetts" in response to the case of Anthony Burns. Bronson Alcott participated in an unsuccessful attempt to free Burns.

Emerson and Thoreau were among the many in Concord and Boston who saw in John Brown a man of principle, action, and disregard for personal safety rather than a fanatic. They both helped to create the image of Brown as saint and martyr. Thoreau lectured on Brown ("A Plea for Captain John Brown") as Brown's execution approached late in 1859.

Industrialization, technological progress, and tremendous advances in transportation and communication also touched the lives of the Transcendentalists. As large-scale, mechanized factories multiplied throughout New England, where textile manufacture thrived, Emerson, Thoreau, and their comrades could not help but observe the changes wrought by this trend. Because Transcendental philosophy espoused the spiritual and moral and denigrated the material, the Transcendentalists mistrusted technological progress and its effect on the workforce. Thoreau, for instance, wrote in the chapter of *Walden* titled "Economy":

As with our colleges, so with a hundred "modern improvements"; there is an illusion about them; there is not always
a positive advance. . . . Our inventions are wont to be
pretty toys, which distract our attention from serious
things. They are but improved means to an unimproved
end. . . . We are in great haste to construct a magnetic telegraph from Maine to Texas; but Maine and Texas, it may
be, have nothing important to communicate.

The simplicity of his life at Walden Pond from 1845 to 1847 was
Thoreau's proof that material progress was not necessary for a rich life.

Robert Fulton's steamboat the *Clermont* made a trial run from Albany
to New York in 1807. In 1838, transatlantic steamship service began.
Work on the Erie Canal began in 1817; the canal was opened in 1825.
Other canals followed quickly. Movement westward necessitated the
building of roads and bridges. The need for faster ships to accommodate
trade led to the building of the first clipper ship in Baltimore in 1832.
In the same year, the *horsecar* (the horse-drawn streetcar) was introduced
in New York. Beginning in 1828, the railroad revolutionized travel in
the United States. It spread rapidly and soon surpassed the canal in
importance. The Fitchburg Railroad opened in Emerson's and Thoreau's
Concord in 1844. The rate of railroad building was very rapid in the
1850s. The Pullman, or sleeper car, was introduced in 1859. Samuel F.B.
Morse developed the telegraph in 1835 and patented it in 1840. The
first successful transatlantic cable was laid in 1866.

Thoreau's mixed attitude toward progress is clearly illustrated in his
views on the railroad. In the "Economy" chapter of *Walden*, he wrote:

Men have an indistinct notion that if they keep up this
activity of joint stocks and spades long enough all will at
length ride somewhere, in next to no time, and for nothing; but though a crowd rushes to the depot, and the con-
ductor shouts "All aboard!" when the smoke is blown away
and the vapor condensed, it will be perceived that a few
are riding, but the rest are run over. . . .

On the other hand, he wrote lyrically of the railroad in the chapter titled
"Sounds":

. . . when I hear the iron horse make the hills echo with
his snort like thunder, shaking the earth with his feet, and
breathing fire and smoke from his nostrils, . . . it seems as
if the earth had got a race now worthy to inhabit it.

Thoreau was clearly moved by the raw power of mechanical invention.

Although Emerson had difficulty reconciling material progress with the Transcendental elevation of the individual, his successful lecture career would not have been possible without the railroad and the telegraph. For example, in 1871 Emerson crossed the country via railroad and lectured in California. Alcott, too, toured extensively as a lecturer from the 1850s until his stroke in 1882. Thoreau traveled by railroad and steamboat on his last and longest journey, to Minnesota in 1861. Despite the philosophical dilemma that technological advances raised for the Transcendentalists, they clearly displayed a certain degree of pragmatic acceptance of the fruits of progress.

Political Context

From 1828, when two-term Democratic president Andrew Jackson was first elected, to Republican Abraham Lincoln's election in 1860, an energetic and frequently rancorous brand of party politics formed part of the American scene.

Andrew Jackson was a military hero, known as an advocate for the interests of the common man, and a strong president. Determined to establish the sovereignty of the federal government over states' rights and the primary importance of the president within the governmental structure, Jackson used his veto power extensively and was known as "King Andrew" by his opponents. *Jacksonian democracy*—the political agenda expressed during his tenure in office and in Democratic politics up to the Civil War—included putting the Second Bank of the United States out of operation and attempting to return to a hard-money economy, opposing government-supported internal improvements, promoting minimal government, reforming bureaucracy through the introduction of rotation in office, and resisting government involvement in the growing controversy over slavery. Jackson's image as a champion of the people against the rich and corrupt made him tremendously popular. His appeal can be attributed in large part to widespread suspicion and resentment of the centralization of power and wealth in the hands of the elite, who had traditionally held both.

The democratizing impulse behind much of Jackson's program was counterbalanced by his enthusiasm for territorial expansion, his condemnation of abolition, and his culturally accepted disregard of Native American rights. The common man, whom he represented, was not sensitive to the plight of non-white inhabitants of the country. Those committed to abolition and social reform could not support Jackson in good conscience. Moreover, he had other opponents—for example, Southern aristocrats who bristled at his attitude toward states' rights.

In 1834, Jackson's political opposition formed the Whig Party. The Whigs were unable to settle upon a candidate for the 1836 presidential election, and Democrat Martin Van Buren was elected to the presidency. Whig candidate William Henry Harrison was elected in 1840, but he died soon after taking office and was succeeded by his vice president, John Tyler. Democrat James K. Polk took office in 1845, but two more Whig presidents followed—Zachary Taylor who took office in 1849, and Millard Fillmore who took office in 1850, upon Taylor's death. The Democratic/Whig campaign of 1840, featuring slogans, buttons, and mudslinging, was the first example of the type of election process that we know—and have come to expect—today.

The Whigs favored the Second Bank of the United States and protective tariffs, appealed to merchants and manufacturers, and supported reform (prison and educational reform, temperance, the abolition of capital punishment). For close to two decades, they were serious contenders in the competition for office against the Jacksonian Democrats. Henry Clay and Daniel Webster were major Whig leaders.

In 1852, the Whigs lost much of their support, and Democrat Franklin Pierce was elected president, followed by Democrat James Buchanan, elected in 1856. With the demise of the Whig Party, the anti-Catholic and anti-immigrant Know-Nothing, or American, Party arose, as did the modern Republican Party. The Republicans quickly became established as the party favored by the North and by antislavery proponents. Following a campaign devoted to the issue of slavery, Republican Abraham Lincoln was elected over Democrat Stephen A. Douglas in 1860.

For the New England Transcendentalists, interest in political life presented a philosophical difficulty quite apart from a specific platform or ideology. There was very little about contemporary party politics that nurtured or elevated the inner man. Politics was an outward, sometimes raucous process. Its contentious nature required the expression of aspects of human character not particularly compatible with moral and spiritual perfection. Moreover, in focusing on current politics, the individual was sidetracked from devoting attention to his own development.

The Transcendentalists understood that politics affected some of the issues about which they cared deeply, abolition foremost among them. At the same time, they felt a certain disdain for the process and the people involved in it. Ralph Waldo Emerson referred to Andrew Jackson a number of times in his journal. He wrote, for example, in a June 1840 journal entry, "The Democratic party in this country is more magnetic than the Whig. Andrew Jackson is an eminent example of it. . . . The lowest angel is better." Although certain Democratic ideas fit into the Transcendental viewpoint (that of minimal external government, for instance), political action as practiced by the Jacksonian Democrats did not have a place in the framework of Transcendental philosophy.

Moreover, when government policy and legislation—the end results of party politics—required the individual to accept an immoral situation, as in the case of the Fugitive Slave Law of 1850, the Transcendentalists did not hesitate to urge disobedience. _Civil Disobedience_ encapsulated not only Thoreau's thoughts but those of others in the Transcendental circle as well.

Emerson participated in the political process to the extent that his involvement forwarded the cause of abolition. Moreover, even though he did not care for the crudeness and hullabaloo of party politics and did not approve of making popular heroes out of politicians, Emerson was willing to recognize the worth and importance of a politician who conducted himself morally. Emerson voted for Abraham Lincoln. Although he remained for a time unsure of Lincoln's motivations and likely effectiveness, Lincoln won him over completely with the Emancipation Proclamation in 1863. From that point, Emerson, who devoted considerable thought to the subject of great men, respected Lincoln's greatness. He spoke on Lincoln at the service held in Concord on April 19, 1865, after Lincoln's assassination:

> This man grew according to the need. His mind mastered the problem of the day; and, as the problem grew, so did his comprehension of it. Rarely was man so fitted to the event. In the midst of fears and jealousies, and in the Babel of counsels and parties, this man wrought with all his might and all his honesty, laboring to find what the people wanted, and how to obtain that.

Lincoln was, in short, a politician above the political process. Even though the process was flawed, Emerson could appreciate an extraordinary individual who took part in it.

Social Context

The years from about 1820 until the Civil War, and the 1840s in particular, witnessed a heightened awareness of a range of social issues and gave rise to a number of active social reform movements. Emerson, in his 1841 lecture "Man the Reformer," assessed the climate of the times as follows

> In the history of the world the doctrine of Reform had never such scope as at the present hour. Lutherans, Hernhutters, Jesuits, Monks, Quakers, Knox, Wesley, Swedenborg, Bentham, in their accusations of society, all respected something,—church or state, literature or history, domestic usages, the market town, the dinner table, coined money. But now all these and all things else hear the trumpet and must rush to judgment,—Christianity, the laws, commerce, schools, the farm, the laboratory; and not a kingdom, town, statute, rite, calling, man, or woman, but is threatened by the new spirit.

There was not only an outpouring of concerned effort on behalf of society's unrepresented and underrepresented—Blacks, Native Americans, the labor force, women, children, the mentally ill—but also a trend toward the idealistic reshaping of society through communal living and through education and moral reform, including temperance.

The antislavery movement was the most visible reform movement of the period. Radical abolitionist William Lloyd Garrison edited and published *The Liberator* beginning in 1831 and established the New England Anti-Slavery Society in Boston in 1832. The American Anti-Slavery Society was established at Philadelphia in 1832. In 1840, Garrison took this national society over and radicalized it. In 1837, antislavery publisher Elijah Lovejoy died at the hands of rioters in Alton, Illinois. Lovejoy was quickly held up as a martyr to the cause, as John Brown (executed in 1859) would be later. The Underground Railroad, a covert operation managed by such leaders as Harriet Tubman and Levi Coffin and implemented by a network of thousands, conveyed slaves from the South northward to freedom. Harriet Beecher Stowe's *Uncle Tom's Cabin* was first published in 1852, generating much sympathy for the plight of slaves. Other books and articles depicting the human toll of slavery appeared. Wendell Phillips, a supporter of Garrison, delivered speeches and wrote articles for *The Liberator* and other antislavery organs. Frederick Douglass, born a slave, also lectured and wrote on the topic. Political events kept the issue before the public eye, as did news of slave uprisings and mutinies (the well-known mutiny on the slave ship *Amistad* took place in 1839) and fugitive slave cases.

Although government policy during the course of expansion westward was dedicated to uprooting Native Americans and to eradicating those among them who proved uncooperative, there was simultaneous interest in their cultures and languages and some outrage over their treatment. Henry Rowe Schoolcraft extensively researched Native history and culture. His six-volume work on the subject appeared between 1851 and 1857. From the 1820s, the Native American was depicted heroically and tragically in fiction. As treaties were signed and tribes relocated, some Americans spoke out. On April 23, 1838, for example, as the federal government prepared to employ soldiers to remove unwilling Cherokees from Georgia and Tennessee to Oklahoma, in accordance with the questionably negotiated 1835 Treaty of Echota, Ralph Waldo Emerson emotionally protested in a letter to President Martin Van Buren "the terrific injury which threatens the Cherokee tribe." Much later in the century, Elizabeth Palmer Peabody espoused the cause of Native American education.

Labor began to speak on its own behalf and to protest intolerable working conditions. Textile workers had unionized by 1820. Weavers (both male and female) went on strike in Pawtucket, Rhode Island, in 1824, over decreasing wages and increasing hours. In 1828, there was a strike of textile workers at a factory in Paterson, New Jersey, requiring the militia to quell violence. In 1842, the legality of labor unions and the right to strike was upheld by a Massachusetts Supreme Court decision. In the same year, legislation was signed in Massachusetts to limit the working hours of children under twelve. Similar laws followed elsewhere. In the 1840s, female mill workers in Lowell, Massachusetts, edited and wrote for their own magazine, the *Lowell Offering*. George Henry Evans founded the *Workingman's Advocate* and, in 1845, formed the National Reform Association for the benefit of labor. In 1860, Massachusetts shoemakers went on strike in response to the introduction of new machinery, which was being operated by children, thereby reducing the pay of skilled mature labor. (The shoemakers won a wage increase as a result of the strike

The women's rights movement also gained momentum in this climate of reform. In 1825, Frances Wright, a lecturer on such controversial topics as equal rights and birth control, moved from England to America. In 1828, Sarah Josepha Hale, advocate for women's education, became editor of the *Ladies' Magazine* in Boston. In 1837, she became editor of *Godey's Lady's Book* in Philadelphia. Transcendentalist and reformer Margaret Fuller tackled such issues as marriage, the employment of women, and prostitution in her controversial and influential *Woman in the Nineteenth Century*, which was published in 1845 and sold out within a week. In 1848, Lucretia Mott and Elizabeth Cady Stanton organized the first in a series of annual women's conventions in Seneca Falls, New York. Suffrage, property rights, and divorce were debated. Two years later, a national women's convention was held in Worcester, Massachusetts. Also in 1848, the Boston Female Medical School, the country's first medical school for women, opened. In the same year, New York State granted property rights to women commensurate to those for men. New, more radical suffrage periodicals arose. Amelia Bloomer's *Lily* appeared in 1849, *Una* in 1853.

The reform of society through the establishment of utopian communities was a phenomenon of the 1840s. Religiously based communities (the Ephrata Cloister in Pennsylvania, for example) had existed in America in the eighteenth century. The Harmony Society, a religious group, had come to America in 1804, under the direction of George Rapp, and established itself in Pennsylvania, then in Indiana. In 1824, the Harmony Society reestablished itself in Pennsylvania in a community called Economy. New Harmony, founded by Robert Owen in 1825 at the Harmonists' Indiana site, was the first secular utopian community in this country.

Brook Farm in West Roxbury, Massachusetts, and Fruitlands in Harvard, Massachusetts, were the two communities most closely associated with the Transcendentalists. Brook Farm was planned at Elizabeth Peabody's Foreign Library in Boston, where George and Sophia Ripley, Orestes Brownson, Theodore Parker, James Freeman Clarke, John Sullivan Dwight, and others gathered to talk about the reform of society. It was established by George Ripley in 1841 and continued until 1847. Residents lived a simple life, focused upon a balance between physical labor and individual self-culture. The community had a strong school and an active social life. Brook Farmers included the Ripleys, Nathaniel Hawthorne (who drew upon the experience in writing his *Blithedale Romance*, first published in 1852), George William Curtis, John Sullivan Dwight and his sister Marianne, Rebecca Codman, and Isaac Hecker. At its largest, in 1843, the Brook Farm community consisted of about one hundred people. Emerson and others of the Transcendentalists who chose not to join the community nevertheless supported the endeavor and were frequent visitors there. In his "Historic Notes of Life and Letters in New England," Emerson wrote of Brook Farm as a "noble and generous movement . . . an experiment in better living."

In 1844, the Brook Farm constitution was revised, and the Transcendental utopia became a Fourierist community. Charles Fourier (1772–1837) was a French socialist author and reformer whose "phalansteries" sprang up in America in the 1840s and 1850s. Fourier had developed a theory of labor freely chosen and enjoyed by communal members. The North American Phalanx in Red Bank, New Jersey, established in 1843 by Albert Brisbane (a disciple of Fourier), was the first Fourierist community in America. The periodical *The Harbinger* was published at Brook Farm after its conversion to Fourierism

The much smaller Fruitlands experiment, established by Bronson Alcott and Charles Lane in 1843, emphasized manual labor, vegetarianism, religious harmony, education, and the balanced development of the individual. However, the hardships endured by Mrs. Alcott and her children at Fruitlands caused tension between her husband and herself. Moreover, Lane's subordination of the individual to the community did not sit well with Bronson Alcott's Transcendentalism or with the needs of the Alcott family.

The only successful, industrial utopian community founded during this period was that established by John Humphrey Noyes at Oneida, New York, in 1848. The community at Oneida allowed a level of sexual freedom that many found shocking.

In their approach to utopian communities, as to all other reform movements, the Transcendentalists were clear and consistent in asserting that the individual was the key unit in the reform process. Even when they believed in the principles behind a movement, they could not support it unequivocally if it elevated the well-being of society at the expense of the development and perfection of the individual. In his "New England Reformers" (1844), Emerson declared:

> . . . union must be inward, and not one of covenants, and is to be reached by a reverse of the methods [men] use. The union is only perfect, when all the uniters are isolated. . . . Each man, if he attempts to join himself to others, is on all sides cramped and diminished of his proportion; and the stricter the union, the smaller and the more pitiful he is. But leave him alone, to recognize in

every hour and place the secret soul, he will go up and down doing the works of a true member, and, to the astonishment of all, the work will be done with concert, though no man spoke. . . . The union must be ideal in actual individualism.

This was the reason that Emerson and others did not join the experiment at Brook Farm.

For this reason, too, the Transcendentalists embraced educational reform as embodied in the efforts of Bronson Alcott and Elizabeth Palmer Peabody, who strove to develop the individual by encouraging intuitive understanding, but could not wholeheartedly take up the cause of common school reform as promoted by Horace Mann. A legislator and the secretary of the first Massachusetts Board of Education (formed in 1837), Mann addressed issues of curriculum, administration, teacher training, and pay. He also promoted a public educational system free of specific religious and political instruction, and the discontinuation of corporal punishment.

But Mann's vision of a system built upon an administrative structure did not satisfy the Transcendentalists' sense of education as a process built upon the individual. Moreover, the exclusion of religion from moral teaching seemed to some to diminish the importance of spirituality. Significantly, when Bronson Alcott offered to lecture at a normal school (that is, a teachers' training school), Mann turned him down. The Transcendentalists' belief that "the individual is the world" (as declared by Emerson in his "Historic Notes of Life and Letters in New England") did not mesh well with more pragmatic efforts at reform from within the system

Religious Context

New England Transcendentalism developed in part out of American Unitarianism, which was well established by 1825. It drew, in particular, upon the "liberal Christianity" of Dr. William Ellery Channing. Unitarianism spread from Massachusetts throughout New England, from church to church, primarily as dissatisfied members of Congregational parishes separated from conservative, Calvinistic parent churches. American Unitarianism had British and European antecedents traceable back to the Reformation.

Dr. Channing—described by Emerson in his "Historic Notes of Life and Letters in New England" as "one of those men who vindicate the power of the American race to produce greatness"—was the recognized leader of American Unitarianism. He proclaimed the major beliefs of the faith in 1819 in "Unitarian Christianity," a sermon delivered in Baltimore at the ordination of Jared Sparks. In 1820, Channing organized the Berry Street Conference, out of which the American Unitarian Association was established in 1825. In formulating his liberal Christianity, Channing looked to the Scriptures and to his own understanding, not to dogma handed down by preceding generations.

Strictly speaking, the term *Unitarian* refers to the belief that God is one being instead of the Trinity of Father, Son, and Holy Spirit. (The Congregational parishes from which Unitarian churches broke off in the nineteenth century were Trinitarian.) New England Unitarianism, however, represented more than a rejection of the doctrine of the Trinity. It encompassed a range of liberal ideas. The Unitarians believed in God's goodness and loving kindness, in man's likeness to and ability to comprehend God, and in the human capacity for spiritual, moral, and intellectual improvement. In his "Unitarian Christianity," Channing had declared, "The idea of God, sublime . . . as it is, is the idea of our own spiritual nature, purified and enlarged to infinity. In ourselves are the elements of the Divinity." Self-culture was the means of understanding God and of bringing the individual closer to God's perfection. This idea contrasted sharply with the Calvinistic concept of innate depravity. The Unitarians also denied the notion of predestination, accepting instead free will and personal responsibility. They believed simultaneously and inconsistently in the rationality of faith and in revelation as presented in the Bible, particularly in the New Testament miracles. They reconciled this inconsistency by asserting that rationality itself was a form of revelation.

The Unitarian point of view was promulgated through several periodicals: *The Christian Examiner* was established in 1813, *The Christian Register* in 1821, *The Western Messenger* (a periodical of Transcendental as well as Unitarian thought) in 1835.

Through the example of Dr. Channing, Unitarianism was associated with social reform. Channing spoke and wrote about the immorality of slavery, about the cause of peace, about temperance, labor issues, and public education. In this, as in his religious faith, he influenced the Transcendentalists of the following generation. He also devoted attention to literary subjects, foreshadowing the Transcendentalists in his sense of the urgency of creating a national literature.

Emerson and others among the Transcendentalists found much to admire in Channing's liberal Christianity. Channing's concept of "likeness to God" was incorporated into Transcendental philosophy as it evolved. But they could not accept Channing's sense of how to understand this likeness. Channing had declared in his "Unitarian Christianity" sermon:

> It [likeness to God] has its foundation in the original and essential capacities of the mind. In proportion as these are unfolded by right and vigorous exertion, it is extended and brightened. In proportion as these lie dormant, it is obscured. In proportion as they are perverted and overpowered by the appetites and passions, it is blotted out.

The notion here set forth owed much to the rationalism of Enlightenment philosopher John Locke. But the Transcendentalists responded to other influences besides rational Unitarianism, in particular to Kant's theory of the intuitive, mysterious, spontaneous nature of knowledge.

Other aspects of Unitarianism also failed to satisfy the needs of the Transcendentalists. As Emerson and others began careers in the ministry, it seemed to them that far too much of what was termed *religion* consisted solely of adherence to forms, doctrines, and literal interpretation of the Scriptures. Emerson decried the spiritual impoverishment of the "corpse-cold Unitarianism of Brattle Street and Harvard College." Minister at the Second Church in Boston, Emerson publicly rejected the practice of the Lord's Supper in 1832 and left his pastorate. Theodore Parker, in his 1841 "Discourse of the Transient and Permanent in Christianity" wrote, "It must be confessed, though with sorrow, that transient things form a great part of what is commonly taught as religion. An undue place has often been assigned to forms and doctrines, while too little stress has been laid on the divine life of the soul. . . ." Moreover, the New Testament miracles that the Unitarians had embraced as evidence of revelation became the subject of heated controversy. Emerson stated in his "Divinity School Address" (1838), "But the word Miracle, as pronounced by Christian churches, gives a false impression; it is Monster. It is not one with the blowing clover and the falling rain."

The Transcendental concept of truth was not based on the trappings of religion, which even relatively progressive Unitarian Christianity displayed. The Transcendentalists possessed a Platonic sense of the divine, independent of the changeable externals of religious practice. An individual's relationship with the kind of God the Transcendentalists envisioned could be achieved intuitively, without any connection to formal religion. This was a leveling notion, conferring authority upon the individual rather than upon those within the hierarchy of the church, elevating man from the position of passive recipient of divine truth as defined by the system and elucidated by the preacher. Channing's Unitarianism promoted liberal theology; Transcendentalism offered radical theology.

Philosophical Context

The philosophy of the eighteenth century Enlightenment in England and Europe was characterized by trust in reason, the elevation of the individual, the questioning and reform of religious, political, and social institutions, and more rigorous methods of scientific inquiry than had been practiced earlier. It emphasized progress, the improvement of society and of the individual, and tolerance. Enlightenment philosophers refused to accept tradition and authority on faith, thus paving the way for the later rise of Unitarianism in America and setting the stage for the subsequent Transcendental rebellion. But heirs though they were to this philosophical examination and evaluation of established beliefs and institutions, the New England Transcendentalists departed radically from their rationalist predecessors in their approach to the nature of knowledge and human understanding.

(English philosopher John Locke 1632–1704) was a major influence on the Enlightenment. Locke addressed many subjects, religion, politics, and society among them. In his *epistemology* (theory on the nature of knowledge), Locke had a significant impact on Transcendentalism, which arose partly in reaction to his philosophy. Locke asserted that ideas originated in the physical transmission of sensations to the *tabula rasa*—the blank slate—of the mind. In his *Essay Concerning Human Understanding* (1690), he declared that all ideas capable of conscious understanding were derived from experience in its interaction with human physiology.

For Locke, the human mind at birth was devoid of conscience, moral understanding, and intuition, all of which developed through experience. He rejected the notion that a sense of God and of moral law was innate. Locke equated the process by which religious and moral concepts were understood with the process by which mathematics and the sciences were understood. Religious perception was essentially a material, not an idealistic, process. It did not transcend the physical world. Locke's rationalism appealed to the American Unitarians as they struggled to throw off the negative view of human nature held by their Calvinistic forebears. As the Transcendentalists were defining religious understanding for themselves, however, they were repelled by Locke's materialism and eager to embrace a more idealistic model of the human mind, one that would permit an innate understanding of God and morality. During the "miracles controversy" of the 1830s and 1840s, Locke's theory guided Unitarian leaders in viewing the New Testament miracles as empirically understandable evidence of Christianity, an approach that the Transcendentalists could not accept.

The Transcendentalists found the ideas of German philosopher Immanuel Kant (1724–1804) more satisfying. In his theory of knowledge, Kant distinguished between the world of sense and that of understanding. He believed that sensory experience revealed things as they appeared, but understanding revealed them as they were. In his *Critique of Pure Reason* (1781) and his *Critique of Practical Reason* (1788), Kant asserted that there were aspects of knowledge—God, morality, freedom, and immortality, for example—that could not be understood by reason, but that were rather innate within man and understood intuitively. The human mind was not the tabula rasa that Locke had claimed it was. Man was a fundamentally moral and godly being. The understanding of such ideas was *transcendental*—it transcended sensation and reason. Although the modern reader may be unaccustomed to pondering such philosophical concepts, an understanding of the differences between sensationalism (materialism) and idealism (transcendence) was central to Transcendental philosophy. The Transcendentalists recognized their debt to Kant and understood the points on which Kant and Locke disagreed. Emerson, in his 1841 lecture "The Transcendentalist," provided the following summary:

> It is well known to most of my audience, that the Idealism of the present day acquired the name of Transcendental, from the use of that term by Immanuel Kant, of Königsberg, who replied to the skeptical philosophy of Locke, which insisted that there was nothing in the intellect which was not previously in the experience of the senses, by showing that there was a very important class of ideas, or imperative forms, which did not come by experience, but through which experience was acquired; that these were intuitions of the mind itself; and he

denominated them *Transcendental* forms. The extraordinary profoundness and precision of that man's thinking have given vogue to his nomenclature, in Europe and America, to that extent, that whatever belongs to the class of intuitive thought, is popularly called at the present day *Transcendental.*

All else that came under the heading "New England Transcendentalism" was predicated on the acceptance of Kant's view of the nature of knowledge.

The Transcendentalists read the writings of both Locke and Kant. Locke's work was part of their Unitarian heritage and the college curriculum of the era. As for Kant, some of the Transcendentalists—Frederic Henry Hedge and Theodore Parker, for example—were able to read his work in the original German. Others, including Emerson, read Kant in English translation. The ideas of Kant and other intuitive philosophers were also disseminated through the writings of British and French authors. In his emphasis on spirituality, intuition, and imagination, British poet-philosopher Samuel Taylor Coleridge was influenced by Kant and, in turn, influenced the Transcendentalists. The "Preliminary Essay" to James Marsh's 1829 edition of Coleridge's *Aids to Reflection* elaborated upon the difference between intuitive and sensational knowledge (from the modern point of view, somewhat confusingly termed Reason—but not in the Enlightenment meaning of reason—and Understanding, respectively). Scottish-born essayist and biographer Thomas Carlyle, highly regarded by the Transcendentalists, celebrated intuition over rationality and wrote about Goethe, Kant, Novalis, Richter, Schiller, and other German thinkers. French philosopher Victor Cousin both espoused idealistic philosophy and also interpreted Kant and other German philosophers for a general audience.

Cultural Context

Even before Emerson delivered his famous "American Scholar" address in 1837, American culture and the capacity of American thinkers to come to their own conclusions had been defended. Lawyer and congressman Charles J. Ingersoll had delivered his "Discourse Concerning the Influence of America on the Mind" before the American Philosophical Society in 1823. Dr. William Ellery Channing had, in his *Remarks on American Literature* (published in 1830), urged the creation of a "native literature" that would be something other and better than a "repetition of the old world." Simultaneously with the ascent of Jacksonian democracy, a vigorous popular culture thrived, based upon our national experience and identity. This culture existed side by side with more complex forms of expression—Transcendentalism, for example, and aesthetic Romanticism, in the work of such artists as Washington Allston and the Hudson River School—that drew openly on foreign thought and trends.

During the period between about 1825 and the Civil War, there was a proliferation of institutions designed to enrich the average person and to promote self-culture. The lyceum (an organization providing public lectures, concerts, and other entertainment) was established in America in 1826, and spread quickly. The social library (a partnership of individuals each contributing money toward the maintenance of a book collection which each had the right to use) multiplied to promote the "general diffusion of knowledge," as worded in the by-laws of one Massachusetts social library. The public library movement gained momentum mid-century, providing opportunities for reading to many who had not had easy access to book collections. Museums were established and exhibitions set up for the edification of the middle class. The Smithsonian Institution was founded in Washington, D.C., in 1846, through the bequest of James Smithson, who, at his death in 1829, left $500,000 to the United States for the "increase and diffusion of knowledge among men." The Crystal Palace Exhibition of the Industry of All Nations was held in New York City in 1853. Aesthetically conceived parks and public spaces were designed by landscape architects such as Frederick Law Olmsted, who undertook the design of New York's Central Park in 1857.

Mass entertainment of many kinds flourished. Circuses were popular. P.T. Barnum's freak show made its debut in 1837; his American Museum was opened in 1842. People in small towns as well as in cities enjoyed various types of musical performances and theatrical productions, including burlesques and *tableaux vivants* (posed stage presentations of static scenes by costumed participants). Blacks and Native Americans were portrayed on stage: The African Company (the first black acting group) began to present plays in New York in 1821; white actors began to play black roles in blackface; and numerous plays about Indians were written and portrayed in the years leading up to the Civil War. Journalists celebrated folk heroes like Davy Crockett. The availability of popular novels increased through advances in the technology of printing and bookmaking and in distribution and marketing. Prints like those of Currier and Ives circulated widely. Newspapers, magazines, and illustrated weeklies like *Frank Leslie's Illustrated* and *Harper's Weekly* had large readerships. As the country grew and as transportation and communication improved, a market existed for works that promoted the standardization of language and of a body of shared knowledge. Noah Webster's *American Dictionary of the English Language* was first published in 1828. The *Encyclopedia Americana* appeared between 1829 and 1833. McGuffey's *Eclectic Readers* began to appear in 1836. Baseball started to take its place as a national preoccupation. *Phrenology*— the study of the size and shape of the skull as a measure of character and intellect—drew popular attention in the United States in the 1820s and 1830s. Spiritualism drew similar attention in the 1850s.

Of all the manifestations of popular culture during this period, the New England Transcendentalists were most closely and actively associated with the lyceum. Emerson, Thoreau, Theodore Parker, Jones Very, Frederic Henry Hedge, James Freeman Clarke, and others among them were lyceum speakers. Emerson and Thoreau were speakers at the Concord Lyceum (formed in 1828). Emerson was its most frequent speaker, and Thoreau served as its secretary. The lyceum was a powerful medium for disseminating knowledge and ideas and was important in communicating Transcendental philosophy to parts of the country outside New England.

Preceded by the British mechanics' institutes, the first lyceum in America was established at Millbury, Massachusetts, by Josiah Holbrook, in 1826. The lyceum, a vehicle for adult education, grew out of the Enlightenment ideal of making knowledge available to all, not just to the privileged. (The constitutionally stated purpose of the Concord Lyceum, for example, was "improvement in knowledge, the advancement of Popular Education, and the diffusion of useful information throughout the community.") In addition to providing programs of lecture and debate, lyceums also promoted libraries and museums. The lyceum was not confined to New England. Once established, it spread rapidly westward as new regions were settled. Popular lecturers traveled long distances by railroad to speak. Lyceum lectures ran a broad gamut of subjects, literary, scientific, historical, social, and political, controversial as well as noncontroversial. Beyond the Transcendentalists, some well-known lyceum speakers included Louis Agassiz, Daniel Webster, Oliver Wendell Holmes, Nathaniel Hawthorne, William Lloyd Garrison, Wendell Phillips, Frederick Douglass, and Susan B. Anthony.

The lyceum movement was important to Emerson and Thoreau as writers, because some of what they first presented formally as lyceum lectures—many of Emerson's essays, for example, and Thoreau's essay "Walking"—was later revised for publication. Like the journals that these writers kept, an invitation to lecture provided an opportunity to record and develop thoughts that would later be refined.

Although the lyceum movement did not turn Everyman into a Transcendentalist, it allowed the New England Transcendentalists to connect with a far broader segment of the population than their writings alone reached. In his biography of his father, Edward Waldo Emerson related an anecdote about a woman (a working domestic) who regularly attended Emerson's lectures. When asked if she understood Emerson, the lady replied, "Not a word, but I like to go and see him stand up there and look as if he thought every one was as good as he was." Emerson clearly conveyed to his audiences a sense of the democratic impulse underlying Transcendentalism, expressed so clearly in his 1844 lecture "New England Reformers": "And as a man is equal to the Church and equal to the State, so he is equal to every other man."

Literary Context

The Romantic movement in Britain, Europe, and America provided the broad literary background for the rise of Transcendentalism. Romanticism permeated American literature between 1820 and the end of the Civil War in 1865. It was expressed not only in the writings of the Transcendentalists, but also by their literary contemporaries—James Fenimore Cooper, Edgar Allan Poe, Henry Wadsworth Longfellow, Nathaniel Hawthorne, Herman Melville, and Walt Whitman—who worked in a variety of genres. Romanticism informed the literature of the period and also gave direction to developments in art, architecture, and music. The landscape paintings of the Hudson River School, for example, and of Washington Allston (1779–1843)—whose work defined art for Margaret Fuller, Elizabeth Peabody, and others among the Transcendentalists—grew out of European Romanticism.

Romanticism (or "Romanticisms," as some literary scholars have preferred to term the multiplicity of expressions of the movement) emerged in England and Germany in the late eighteenth century. Influenced by the intuitive philosophy of Kant, Romantic writers looked at literature as an outpouring of the inner spirit, and saw imagination as the means of summoning this spirit. They reacted against classical formalism and symmetry, against rationalism, and against other restrictions on individual expression and imagination. Romantic writers celebrated the freedom of the individual, whom they placed at the center of life and art, and the expression of personal emotion. Perceiving physical objects as representative of spiritual, moral, and intellectual reality, Romantic writers relied heavily on symbolism and allegory. Romantic literature displayed a number of recurrent motifs: the theme of the individual in rebellion; the symbolic interpretation of the historic past; subjects from myth and folklore; the glorification of nature; faraway settings; sentimentalism; the nobility of the uncivilized man (the Native American, for example); admiration for the simple life; the elevation of the common man; a fascination with Gothic themes, with the supernatural and mysterious, with introspection, melancholy, and horror; and a humanitarian political and social outlook. The American experience provided much raw material suited to Romantic interpretation.

British Romantic authors William Wordsworth, Samuel Taylor Coleridge, and Thomas Carlyle greatly influenced the New England Transcendentalists. Poets Wordsworth (1770–1850) and Coleridge (1772–1834) together wrote *Lyrical Ballads*, the first edition of which was issued in 1798. In these poems, Wordsworth and Coleridge presented personal feeling, employed language that reflected the spoken rather than the stylized written word, and focused on both the supernatural and ordinary experience. In his *Biographia Literaria* (1817) and his *Aids to Reflection* (1825), Coleridge presented the Kantian distinction between knowledge gained through the senses ("Understanding") and that grasped intuitively ("Reason") and discussed German philosophy. Carlyle (1795–1881) impressed the Transcendentalists with his essays on German literature and philosophy, his translations from Goethe, his *Sartor Resartus* (1836), *The French Revolution* (1837), and *On Heroes and Hero-Worship* (1841). Some of the Transcendentalists had the opportunity to meet Wordsworth, Coleridge, and Carlyle. Emerson met all three of them on his first trip abroad (1832–1833). The Transcendentalists also read German and French Romantic authors, among them Goethe, Richter, Schlegel, Cousin, Chateaubriand, and Madame de Stäel.

American Romanticism was powerfully expressed with the anonymous publication of Emerson's *Nature* in 1836. This manifesto of Transcendentalism, based on earlier journal entries, sermons, and lectures, was soon followed by the important addresses "The American Scholar" (1837) and the "Divinity School Address" (1838). In "The American

Scholar," delivered before the Phi Beta Kappa Society at Harvard on August 31, 1837, and published in the same year, Emerson urged self-reliance, self-knowledge, and closeness to nature in the forging of an original American thought and literature. In the "Divinity School Address," delivered at Harvard on July 15, 1838, and first printed in the same year, he exhorted the pursuit of spiritual truth by the individual through intuition rather than through the passive acceptance of traditional religion. The publication of these three "scriptures" of Transcendentalism imparted energy and momentum to the efforts of the movement's proponents. The Transcendental Club was formed in 1836, the year in which *Nature* was published, providing the opportunity for Emerson, Alcott, Clarke, Parker, Fuller, Ripley, Brownson, Peabody, Thoreau, Very, Cranch, and others to explore their philosophical similarities and differences.

Romanticism in the form of Transcendentalism was communicated foremost through the writings of the faithful. Emerson, Thoreau, Fuller, and others published lengthy works of a range of types on a variety of subjects, each in its own way an expression of Romantic ideals. The Transcendentalists also conveyed their philosophy, concerns, and creativity through shorter pieces printed in the periodical publications that were important to the intellectual life of the mid-nineteenth century. *The Western Messenger*, published in Cincinnati and Louisville from 1835 to 1841, included pieces on Unitarianism, Transcendentalism, and German and Oriental literature. In 1838, Orestes Brownson began the *Boston Quarterly Review*. *The Dial*, the best-known organ of Transcendentalism, edited by Emerson and Margaret Fuller and published for a time by Elizabeth Palmer Peabody, was issued between 1840 and 1844. The Brook Farm publication *The Harbinger* commenced in 1845. Theodore Parker founded the *Massachusetts Quarterly Review* in 1847. The single issue of Elizabeth Peabody's *Aesthetic Papers* appeared in 1849. The *North American Review* began publication in 1854, *Atlantic Monthly* in 1857. Both were later bought by the Boston publishing firm of Ticknor and Fields. Neither publication was strictly a periodical of American Transcendentalism, but both included pieces by Emerson, Thoreau, and others. (Ticknor and Fields were major publishers, handling the work of such nineteenth century American authors as Emerson, Thoreau, Hawthorne, Holmes, Longfellow, and Lowell.)

The flowering of Transcendentalism was only one American expression of Romanticism—albeit the strongest one—in the period between 1820 and 1865. Moreover, the literary presentation of Romantic themes and ideas was not confined only to New England authors. Novelist James Fenimore Cooper (1789–1851) vividly wrote about the frontier experience, life at sea, America's past, the wilderness, and the individual's relation to society. His Leatherstocking Series was published between 1823 and 1841. A critic of Transcendentalism and an opponent of abolition and reform, Edgar Allan Poe (1809–1849) had nevertheless been influenced by Coleridge in his approach to literary criticism. His poetry conveyed intense emotion; his stories were full of mystery and horror. Popular poet Henry Wadsworth Longfellow (1807–1882) wrote personal sonnets, took history as subject matter (his narrative poem *Evangeline* was published in 1847), and drew upon Native American legend in his poem *The Song of Hiawatha* (1855). Although not a Transcendentalist, Nathaniel Hawthorne (1804–1864) spent a substantial portion of his life among Transcendentalists. Married to Sophia Peabody, sister of Elizabeth Palmer Peabody, he lived in Concord from 1842 to 1845, at the height of the Transcendental movement, and again later in life. He was also a resident of Brook Farm. His romances and stories, rich with symbolism and allegory, focused on the individual, explored morality, dealt with historical subjects, and examined the effect of the past upon the present. Herman Melville (1819–1891) wrote narratives drawing upon his personal experiences in exotic places and his knowledge of life at sea. His *Moby-Dick* (1851) was atmospheric, evocative, allegorical, symbolic, an exploration of good and evil—the embodiment of Romantic literature. Poet Walt Whitman (1819–1892) was deeply moved by Emerson's thought and writing. His *Leaves of Grass* (1855) extolled the individual in the person of the poet himself and celebrated personal expression, freedom, and the intuitive understanding of the world. Whitman went far beyond the Transcendental vision in assigning a place of importance to sensuality.

All of these voices of Romanticism, and other writers as well (Washington Irving, William Gilmore Simms, William Cullen Bryant, Nathaniel Parker Willis, and John Greenleaf Whittier among them), contributed to the development of that vigorous national thought and expression that Emerson had envisioned in 1837 in "The American Scholar." The Romantic impulse played a major role in the mid-nineteenth century blossoming of American literature and art that has been called the *American Renaissance.*

Timeline

1632	English philosopher John Locke born (died 1704)
1690	Locke's *Essay Concerning Human Understanding* published
1724	German philosopher Immanuel Kant born (died 1804)
1770	British Romantic poet William Wordsworth born (died 1850)
1772	British Romantic poet Samuel Taylor Coleridge born (died 1834)
	French socialist reformer Charles Fourier born (died 1837)
1779	Romantic artist Washington Allston born (died 1843)
1780	Minister William Ellery Channing born (died 1842)
1781	Kant's *Critique of Pure Reason* published
1783	Author Washington Irving born (died 1859)
1788	Kant's *Critique of Practical Reason* published
1789	Novelist James Fenimore Cooper born (died 1851)
1794	Poet William Cullen Bryant born (died 1878)
1795	British Romantic author Thomas Carlyle born (died 1881)
	Unitarian minister Convers Francis born (died 1863)
1798	*Lyrical Ballads* by Wordsworth and Coleridge published
1799	Amos Bronson Alcott born (died 1888)
1801	Reverend Joseph Stevens Buckminster traveled to Europe; returned home with books purchased abroad
1802	Unitarian minister and author William Henry Furness born (died 1896)
	Unitarian minister, editor, and Brook Farm founder George Ripley born (died 1880)
1803	Louisiana Purchase
	Ralph Waldo Emerson born (died 1882)
	Minister, editor, and essayist Orestes Brownson born (died 1876)
1804	Lewis and Clark began exploration of Northwest from the Mississippi River to the Pacific Ocean (continued until 1806)

1804 *(continued)*

Harmony Society came to America under direction of George Rapp; established first in Pennsylvania, then in Indiana

Author Nathaniel Hawthorne born (died 1864)

Transcendental activist and writer Elizabeth Palmer Peabody born (died 1894)

1805   Unitarian minister, author, editor, and professor Frederic Henry Hedge born (died 1890)

1806   Zebulon Pike traveled through Southwest, to New Mexico and Mexico City.

Author William Gilmore Simms born (died 1870)

Author Nathaniel Parker Willis born (died 1867)

1807   Robert Fulton's steamboat *Clermont* made trial run from Albany to New York.

Poet Henry Wadsworth Longfellow born (died 1882)

Poet John Greenleaf Whittier born (died 1892)

1809   Poet, critic, and writer of short stories Edgar Allan Poe born (died 1849)

1810   Unitarian minister and editor William Henry Channing born (died 1884)

Unitarian minister and abolitionist Theodore Parker born (died 1860

Feminist, author, lecturer, and editor (Sarah) Margaret Fuller born (died 1850)

Unitarian minister, author, and editor James Freeman Clarke born (died 1888)

1813   Madame de Staël's *De L'Allemagne* translated into English under title *Germany*

The Christian Examiner established

Poet and Harvard Greek tutor Jones Very born (died 1880)

Unitarian minister, editor, poet, and artist Christopher Pearse Cranch born (died 1892)

1814   Mill owner Francis Cabot Lowell introduced power loom into American textile industry at Boston Manufacturing Company, Waltham, Massachusetts

Edition of Madame de Staël's *De L'Allemagne* published in New York

1815   George Ticknor and Edward Everett went to Europe to study

1817   Work began on Erie Canal

Edward Everett first American to receive Ph.D. at University of Göttingen in Germany

Coleridge's *Biographia Literaria* published

Henry David Thoreau born (died 1862)

1819   Missouri requested admission to Union as slave state

William Ellery Channing delivered "Unitarian Christianity" sermon

Poet Walt Whitman born (died 1892)

Author Herman Melville born (died 1891)

1820   Missouri Compromise

William Ellery Channing organized Berry Street Conference

1821   First American settlement in Texas

The Christian Register established

1823   Monroe Doctrine

The Pioneers, the first of Cooper's Leatherstocking Series, published (series continued until 1841)

Charles Ingersoll delivered "Discourse Concerning the Influence of America on the Mind"

1824   Weavers in Pawtucket, Rhode Island, went on strike over decreasing wages and increasing hours

Harmony Society reestablished in Pennsylvania in the community named Economy

1825   Erie Canal opened

American Unitarian Association established

1825 *(continued)*

Equal rights lecturer Frances Wright moved from England to America

Robert Owen founded New Harmony (first secular utopian community in America) in Indiana

Coleridge's *Aids to Reflection* published

1826   Jedediah Strong Smith led expedition to Mexican-held California

First lyceum in America established at Millbury, Massachusetts

1828   Democrat Andrew Jackson first elected to presidency

Travel by railroad began

Strike of textile workers in Paterson, New Jersey, quelled by militia

Sarah Josepha Hale became editor of the *Ladies' Magazine*

Webster's *American Dictionary of the English Language* first published

Concord Lyceum formed

1829   Publication of *Encyclopedia Americana* began (continued until 1833)

James Marsh's edition of Coleridge's *Aids to Reflection*, including "Preliminary Essay" on German philosophy, published

1830   Mexico passed restrictive immigration laws

William Ellery Channing's *Remarks on American Literature* published

Charles Follen made professor of German literature at Harvard

1831   William Lloyd Garrison established *The Liberator* in Boston

Term *Underground Railroad* first used

1832   Democrat Andrew Jackson reelected to presidency

New England Anti-Slavery Society founded in Boston

American Anti-Slavery Society established in Philadelphia

First clipper ship built in Baltimore

Horsecar introduced in New York

Emerson rejected practice of Lord's Supper and left pastorate

Emerson's first trip abroad (returned 1833)

1834   Andrew Jackson's political opposition formed Whig Party

Emerson moved to Concord

Bronson Alcott established Temple School in Boston (continued until 1838)

James Walker's "The Philosophy of Man's Spiritual Nature in Regard to the Foundation of Faith" published in *The Christian Examiner*

1835   Treaty of Echota

Samuel F.B. Morse developed telegraph (patented 1840)

Dr. Channing's *Slavery* published

The Western Messenger established

Emerson bought home on Cambridge Turnpike in Concord

1836   Democrat Martin Van Buren elected to presidency

Texas declared its independence from Mexico; Alamo captured by Mexican leader Santa Anna; Texas won its independence at Battle of San Jacinto

Carlyle's *Sartor Resartus* published

McGuffey's *Eclectic Readers* began to appear

Emerson's *Nature* published

Transcendental Club formed

1837   Antislavery publisher Elijah Lovejoy killed by rioters in Alton, Illinois

First Massachusetts Board of Education formed

Emerson delivered "The American Scholar"

Emerson delivered first antislavery address in Concord

1837 *(continued)*

Carlyle's *The French Revolution* published

Hawthorne's *Twice-Told Tales* published

Sarah Josepha Hale became editor of *Godey's Lady's Book*

P.T. Barnum's freak show debuted

1838   Forcible removal of Cherokees from Georgia and Tennessee to Oklahoma

Transatlantic steamship service began

Emerson delivered "Divinity School Address"

Publication of George Ripley's 14-volume *Specimens of Foreign Standard Literature* began (continued until 1842)

Boston Quarterly Review established

1839   Slave mutiny on ship *Amistad*

Andrews Norton attacked Transcendentalism in *Discourse on the Latest Form of Infidelity*

1840   Democratic/Whig presidential campaign featured slogans, buttons, mudslinging

Whig William Henry Harrison elected to presidency

Publication of Transcendental periodical *The Dial* began (continued until 1844)

Elizabeth Palmer Peabody opened Foreign Library in Boston (where Margaret Fuller held "Conversations" and Brook Farm was planned)

1841   Vice President John Tyler succeeded President Harrison, who died shortly after taking office

John C. Frémont expedition to track headwaters of Des Moines River

Carlyle's *On Heroes and Hero-Worship* published

Emerson's *Essays* [First Series] published

Cooper's *The Deerslayer* (the final novel in his Leatherstocking Series, begun in 1823) published

Theodore Parker delivered "Discourse of the Transient and Permanent in Christianity" sermon (also called "South Boston Sermon")

George Ripley established Brook Farm (continued until 1847)

1842   Frémont expedition to explore route to Oregon

Massachusetts Supreme Court upheld legality of labor unions and right to strike

Massachusetts passed legislation to limit working hours of children

Lowell Offering began publication

Hawthorne moved to Old Manse in Concord (remained until 1845)

P.T. Barnum opened American Museum

1843   Second Frémont expedition to explore route to Oregon

North American Phalanx, first Fourierist community in America, established in Red Bank, New Jersey

Bronson Alcott and Charles Lane established Fruitlands

1844   Democrat James K. Polk elected to presidency

Constitution of Brook Farm revised; community became Fourierist

Emerson's *Essays: Second Series* published

Emerson delivered address in Concord on anniversary of e mancipation in British West Indies

Fitchburg Railroad opened in Concord

1845   Term *Manifest Destiny* first used in anonymous piece in July–August issue of *The United States Magazine and Democratic Review*, probably by John L. O'Sullivan

Texas annexed by United States

Frémont expedition to explore area around Great Salt Lake in Utah

George Henry Evans founded National Reform Association for benefit of labor

1845 *(continued)*

    Brook Farm periodical *The Harbinger* began publication

    Margaret Fuller's *Woman in the Nineteenth Century* published

    Thoreau built and moved into cabin at Walden Pond in Concord (remained until 1847)

1846   War with Mexico declared

    Mormon migration from Illinois to Utah began

    Smithsonian Institution founded in Washington, D.C.

    Hawthorne's *Mosses from an Old Manse* published

    Thoreau jailed for refusal to pay poll tax in protest against slavery

1847   *Massachusetts Quarterly Review* founded

    Emerson's first volume of poetry, *Poems*, published

    Longfellow's *Evangeline* published

1848   Whig Zachary Taylor elected to presidency

    Mexican War ended; Mexico surrendered much territory to United States

    Gold rush began

    Lucretia Mott and Elizabeth Cady Stanton organized first Seneca Falls women's convention

    New York State granted property rights for women commensurate to those for men

    Boston Female Medical School (first medical school for women in America) opened

    Industrial utopian community founded at Oneida, New York

1849   Amelia Bloomer's *The Lily* began

    Elizabeth Palmer Peabody published *Aesthetic Papers*, including Thoreau's "Resistance to Civil Government" (later known as *Civil Disobedience*)

    Thoreau's *A Week on the Concord and Merrimack Rivers* published

1850   Vice President Millard Fillmore succeeded President Taylor, who died in office

Compromise of 1850, including Fugitive Slave Law, passed

National women's convention held in Worcester, Massachusetts

Hawthorne's *The Scarlet Letter* published

Emerson's *Representative Men* published

Harper's Monthly Magazine began publication

1851   Henry Rowe Schoolcraft's six-volume work on Native American history and culture began publication (completed 1857)

Melville's *Moby-Dick* published

Hawthorne's *The House of the Seven Gables* and *The Snow-Image* published

Fugitive slave Shadrach Minkins spent night in Concord en route to Canada via Underground Railroad

Fugitive slave Thomas Sims was returned to master in Georgia

1852   Democrat Franklin Pierce elected to presidency

Harriet Beecher Stowe's *Uncle Tom's Cabin* published

Hawthorne's *Blithedale Romance* published

1853   Crystal Palace Exhibition held in New York City

Feminist periodical *Una* began publication

1854   Thoreau's *Walden* published

North American Review began publication (later bought by Ticknor and Fields)

Thoreau delivered "Slavery in Massachusetts" address in response to fugitive slave case of Anthony Burns

1855   John Brown moved to Kansas

Longfellow's *The Song of Hiawatha* published

Whitman's *Leaves of Grass* published

1856   Democrat James Buchanan elected to presidency

Emerson's *English Traits* published

1857	Dred Scott case
	Kansas elected free state legislature
	Frederick Law Olmsted designed New York's Central Park
	Atlantic Monthly began publication (later bought by Ticknor and Fields)
	Harper's Weekly began publication
1859	John Brown led raid on federal arsenal at Harper's Ferry, West Virginia
	Thoreau delivered "A Plea for Captain John Brown"
	Bronson Alcott became Superintendent of Schools in Concord (continued until 1865)
	Pullman (sleeper) car introduced
1860	Republican Abraham Lincoln elected to presidency
	Strike by Massachusetts shoemakers
	Elizabeth Palmer Peabody established first American kindergarten in Boston
	Hawthorne's *The Marble Faun* published
	Emerson's *The Conduct of Life* published
1861	Kansas admitted to Union
	Civil War began
1862	Henry David Thoreau died
1863	President Lincoln's Emancipation Proclamation
1865	Civil War ended
	President Lincoln assassinated
1866	First successful transatlantic cable laid
1867	Emerson's second volume of poems, *May-Day*, published
1870	Emerson's *Society and Solitude* published
1875	Emerson's *Letters and Social Aims* published
1879	Bronson Alcott established Concord School of Philosophy
1882	Ralph Waldo Emerson died

RALPH WALDO EMERSON

Life and Background of Emerson

Ralph Waldo Emerson—essayist, poet, lecturer, philosopher, Unitarian minister, and central figure among the American Transcendentalists—was born in Boston, Massachusetts, on May 25, 1803. He was the fourth of eight children born to the Reverend William Emerson (1769–1811), pastor of the First Church in Boston, and Ruth Haskins Emerson (1768–1853). Emerson's roots in both Concord and in the ministry were deep. On his father's side, his ancestry extended back to early colonial Massachusetts, to the Reverend Peter Bulkeley (1583–1659), a Puritan who had come from England and, in 1635, became a founder and the first minister of Concord. Bulkeley's granddaughter had married the Reverend Joseph Emerson, son of Thomas, a settler in coastal Ipswich, Massachusetts. Joseph's grandson Joseph, also a minister, was the father of William Emerson, Ralph Waldo's grandfather. William Emerson (1743–1776), minister of the First Parish in Concord, had gone to Fort Ticonderoga in New York to serve as chaplain of the Revolutionary army, became ill, and died before he could return to Concord. Ralph Waldo Emerson's maternal grandfather was successful Boston merchant John Haskins (1729–1814), a cooper and distiller.

William Emerson and Ruth Haskins were married on October 25, 1796. Their eight children were: Phebe Ripley (1798–1800); John Clarke (1799–1807); William (1801–1868); Ralph Waldo (1803–1882); Edward Bliss (1805–1834); Robert Bulkeley (1807–1859); Charles Chauncy (1808–1836); and Mary Caroline (1811–1814). William and Ruth Emerson paid careful attention to both the religious and the intellectual development of their children, and provided a stable early home life for them. William, a liberal minister with a taste for literary activity, encouraged scholarship as well as religious devotion in his sons. He was a sociable man, well-respected in the community. His public position brought frequent visitors to the Emerson home. Ruth Haskins was a pious woman who met the various demands placed upon her as the wife of a prominent man and as a mother. The Emersons lost their first child, Phebe Ripley, in 1800. Their second child, John Clarke, died in 1807 from tuberculosis—a constant, looming threat in the nineteenth century, and one that repeatedly touched Ralph Waldo Emerson's life. From childhood, Emerson was close to his brothers William, Edward Bliss, and Charles Chauncy. Robert Bulkeley (called Bulkeley) was mentally retarded. His condition and care concerned his brothers until his death, in 1859.

Ralph Waldo Emerson's world was radically altered in 1811, when his father died, leaving Mrs. Emerson to support and raise the young family on her own. Although she managed to care for and to educate her sons, financial insecurity quickly became a fact of life. The First Church granted her a stipend for a time, as well as the use of the parish house. Mary Moody Emerson (1774–1863), William Emerson's unmarried sister, stayed with the family for several months after her brother's death, and returned again later. A woman of strong religious devotion and intellect, conservative in some ways and liberal in others, opinionated, unafraid to express herself either face-to-face or in her letters, she was a powerful influence on Emerson and his brothers. Her correspondence with him in the 1820s helped to inform his Transcendentalism.

The Emerson brothers stayed in Concord from time to time during their childhood. The Reverend Ezra Ripley, who had married Phebe Bliss Emerson, the widow of Revolutionary minister William Emerson, was their step-grandfather. When in Concord, Ralph Waldo stayed at the Old Manse, Ripley's home, and formerly the home of their grandfather William Emerson. From November 1814 until the following spring, the entire Emerson family lived at the Manse. (Their temporary relocation was prompted by fear of a possible British attack on Boston during the War of 1812, and by high prices in the city.) Ezra Ripley shared his extensive knowledge of Concord history with the Emerson boys, and gave them a sense of their ancestors' importance in the town. In Concord, they had the opportunity to experience both small-town life and the pleasures of nature. Having returned to Boston in 1815, Mrs. Emerson took in boarders to keep her household financially afloat. The family moved frequently, but Ruth Emerson, encouraged by her sister-in-law Mary Moody Emerson, steadfastly applied herself to providing her sons with an education that reflected the standards, the values, and the aspirations of her late husband.

Emerson's education began in Boston, at dame school (a school for small children, in which the basics were taught by a woman in her own home). He then attended grammar school. In 1812, he entered the Boston Public Latin School, where his studies included Latin and Greek. He simultaneously attended a separate writing school. After the family's 1814–1815 stay in Concord, Emerson read extensively on his own in the spring of 1815 and returned to Boston Latin in the fall. He was a serious, though unremarkable, student.

Ralph Waldo Emerson entered Harvard College in 1817 as *president's freshman*, or *orderly*, a position that helped pay his way through college and that required him to serve as messenger for Harvard's president, John Kirkland. He also tutored and later served as a waiter in the junior commons, and during college vacations taught in Waltham, Massachusetts, in the college preparatory school kept by the Reverend Samuel Ripley (son of Ezra Ripley) and his learned wife Sarah Alden Bradford Ripley.

Emerson's Harvard curriculum included Latin, Greek, English, rhetoric, history, mathematics, and modern languages. Emerson read English philosopher John Locke as part of his formal studies. A middling student, he read widely on his own. Shakespeare, Montaigne, Swift, and Byron were among the authors he selected independently of his class work. His Harvard teachers included George Ticknor in modern languages, Edward Everett in Greek, and Edward Tyrrel Channing in English composition. (In 1815, Ticknor and Everett had traveled to Europe and studied at the University of Göttingen, where they were exposed to the German literature and thought that would become so important to the New England Transcendentalists.) Emerson was a member of Harvard's Pythologian Club (a literary society). He won a prize for an essay on Socrates and graduated from Harvard in 1821.

The first surviving journal volume kept by Emerson dates from his college years. (His manuscript journals are located in the Houghton Library of Harvard University.) He kept a journal until 1875, when declining health and diminished intellect made it impossible for him to continue. As with Thoreau's journal, Emerson's journal entries became the basis for his lectures, essays, and books. They were sufficiently developed that Emerson sometimes extracted passages just as they were for use in lecture or publication. He indicated his awareness of the value of his journals to his thought and writing in the first entry he made in the volume for 1837, in which he described his journal as his "savings' bank," to be drawn upon in future endeavors. Although maintained over a longer period of time than Thoreau's journal, Emerson's is not nearly as extensive as Thoreau's. Emerson was less inclined than Thoreau to regard journalizing as an end in itself.

After graduating from Harvard, Emerson taught in the Boston school for girls kept by his brother William in their mother's home. He felt himself ill suited to the work and did not enjoy it, but he continued because he needed to contribute toward the education of his younger brothers, Edward and Charles. In 1823, William left to study theology at Göttingen, leaving Waldo (the name that he had decided in college that he preferred) to keep school alone. Shortly before his twenty-first birthday, Emerson decided that he would devote himself to the ministry. His decision was not an unexamined one. He had already expressed doubts about formal religion and his personal fitness to preach it. Nevertheless, he entered the Harvard Divinity School in 1825. Almost immediately, poor health interrupted his studies and, along with the need to continue teaching in order to earn money, prevented him from taking a degree. In 1826, however, he was approbated to preach, and delivered his first sermon in Waltham.

Having decided against a career in the ministry, William Emerson had returned from Göttingen in 1825. In 1826, William and Edward (who, beset by health problems, had in 1825 also gone to Europe) began to study law—William as an apprentice in a New York law office, Edward in Daniel Webster's Boston office. Waldo's health again declined. Showing symptoms of tuberculosis, he traveled south in 1826, to Charleston, South Carolina, and St. Augustine, Florida, to regain his health. He worked on sermons and developed a friendship with Achille Murat, a nephew of Napoleon and an atheist. His health improved, he returned to Boston in 1827 and served as a supply preacher to parishes in Massachusetts and New Hampshire.

In 1827, while in Concord, New Hampshire, Emerson fell in love with Ellen Louisa Tucker, daughter of the late Beza Tucker, a successful Boston merchant. Ellen, considered beautiful, was an intelligent, confident girl, a writer of poetry, and the love of Emerson's life. She, like Emerson, was also tubercular. In March of 1829, Emerson became pastor of the Unitarian Second Church of Boston. He had been asked to serve as the colleague of the ailing Reverend Henry Ware, whom he soon succeeded. Emerson was generally well-liked by his congregation, which appreciated the weekly sermons that he delivered with directness and simplicity. The necessity of producing sermons on a regular schedule fostered discipline in writing, and the delivery of these sermons honed Emerson's skills in public speaking. But preaching also forced Emerson uncomfortably to consider how much church doctrine he truly accepted. At the same time, he became aware that he possessed a certain emotional aloofness that made it difficult for him to deal with some of the personal interactions required of a pastor. Nevertheless, at this point his prospects for a long career in the ministry were promising. In September of 1829, when Ellen's precarious health seemed stable, the two were married.

Emerson's pastoral salary and the likelihood of prosperity through Ellen's inheritance from her father gave Emerson a new, welcome financial security. He bought books for his personal library and enjoyed the benefits of urban life, including a subscription to the Boston Athenaeum and access to the Harvard College Library and the Boston Library Society. He read Aristotle, Plato, Montaigne, and British Romantic writers Coleridge and Carlyle, among other authors. Coleridge made a particularly deep impression on him. At the same time, Emerson's life expanded in other ways. He accepted roles in public life that never interested his future friend Henry David Thoreau. In 1829, Emerson was chaplain of the Massachusetts Senate, in 1830 and 1831 a member of the Boston School Committee. Later, when he moved to Concord, he would assume an important place in community life. Moreover, in 1863, he would serve on the West Point Board of Visitors, and from 1867 to 1879 as an overseer at Harvard.

In December of 1830, Emerson's brother Edward, also tubercular, sailed to Puerto Rico in search of a more healthful climate. Emerson's wife, Ellen Tucker Emerson, died on February 8, 1831, at the age of nineteen. Emerson was desolate, but quickly returned to his duties at the Second Church. After Ellen's death, he had an increasingly difficult time pushing back the doubts that he had long felt about orthodox Christianity. In the summer of 1832, Emerson wrote a letter to his church, recommending the observation of the Lord's Supper (the communion) as a remembrance rather than a sacrament, and asking to discontinue the use of bread and wine. The church rejected his proposal. On September 9, 1832, Emerson delivered a sermon in which he explained his position and resigned from his pastorate.

Still grieving for Ellen, shaken by Edward's condition, and exhausted by the soul-searching that had led to his resignation, Emerson sailed for Europe on December 25, 1832. He arrived at Malta, traveled through Italy, visited Paris, and headed for England and Scotland. The trip opened his eyes to the world and provided opportunities to meet people who stimulated and influenced him. He met English writer Walter Savage Landor in Florence, American sculptor Horatio Greenough in Rome, Romantic poets Samuel Taylor Coleridge and William Wordsworth in England, and Thomas Carlyle—with whom he developed a lasting friendship and correspondence—in Scotland. Emerson arrived back in the United States in October of 1833.

On his return, he served as a supply minister in various Unitarian parishes—a practice that he continued for years—and took up a new career as a lecturer, an occupation that engaged him for over four decades. The rise of the lyceum in America fortuitously coincided with

Emerson's need to find a new occupation. Lecturing allowed him to draw on skills that he had developed as a preacher, gave him scope to refine ideas on God, man, and nature that he had been pondering, and fostered expression of his literary aspirations. Moreover, it provided an income. He delivered his "Uses of Natural History" in Boston in November 1833, proclaiming, "The whole of Nature is a metaphor or image of the human mind." Shortly thereafter, he lectured "On the Relation of Man to the Globe." Years of reading, thinking, and journalizing were shaping a new understanding of man's place in the universe, which the lecture platform permitted him to develop more fully and to clothe in powerful, suggestive vocabulary and style. The influence of his reading—he was stimulated by the German philosophers, Goethe, Plato, the Neoplatonic writers, eastern sacred books, the English Romantics, the Swedish mystic Swedenborg, Montaigne, and others—converged and reacted with his Unitarian background and were distilled into his own particular brand of visionary idealism as he readied his thoughts for public presentation. He delivered lectures (which he read to his audiences) on a range of subjects—among them history, Italy, and great men (including Michelangelo, Martin Luther, and John Milton). He presented a lecture series titled "The Philosophy of History," "Human Culture," and "The Present Age." And he found success. Audiences were ready to hear what Emerson had to say.

Having established himself as a lecturer and looking forward to a literary career, Emerson settled in Concord, the home of his ancestors, a place that offered peace and access both to nature and to the advantages of Boston. In October of 1834, just two weeks after Edward's death in Puerto Rico, Emerson and his mother moved into the Old Manse as Ezra Ripley's boarders. While living at the Manse, Emerson worked at writing *Nature*, which upon publication in 1836 would unleash a period of intense expression of Transcendental thought, and reaction to it.

Emerson quickly became Concord's most prominent citizen, a man respected and beloved by his townsmen. Along with his Concord heritage, his characteristic humility and inclination to deal with others directly and kindly, no matter what their station in life, made residents of the town feel that he was truly one of them. He delivered his first public address in the town on September 12, 1835, the two hundredth anniversary of Concord's incorporation. (The manuscript of the address is now in the Concord Free Public Library.) In 1837, Emerson's poem "Concord Hymn," written at the request of the town, was sung at the dedication of a monument erected near the site of the North Bridge to commemorate the Concord Fight of April 19, 1775. Over the years, he served the town as a Sunday school teacher in the First Parish, through its lyceum, as a member of its School Committee and Library Committee, and through attendance at town meetings (a form of local democratic government that he appreciated). He also made Concord a destination for pilgrims who hoped to meet one of the most recognized men in America.

On September 14, 1835, two days after his civic debut at Concord's bicentennial celebration, Emerson married Lydia Jackson of Plymouth, Massachusetts, and brought her back to Concord to live in the home (called "Bush") that he had bought on the Cambridge Turnpike. He and Lidian (Emerson changed her name to prevent the final "a" from turning into "er" through local pronunciation) had a relatively stable, happy married life, although it lacked the intensity of Emerson's first marriage. Lidian was a spiritual and intellectual woman. Their relationship was based on mutual respect and upon shared love and concern for their children. The second Mrs. Emerson understood and accepted how deeply her husband had cared for his first wife, but at times she had difficulty coping with his emotional aloofness and with his absences from the household while on lecture tours and trips. The Emersons had four children: Waldo (1836–1842); Ellen Tucker (1839–1909; named for Emerson's first wife); Edith (1841–1929; later Mrs. William H. Forbes); and Edward Waldo (1844–1930).

The year 1836 was one of the most eventful in Emerson's life. His younger brother Charles, a lawyer, had become engaged in 1835 to Elizabeth Hoar, daughter of well-known Concord lawyer Samuel Hoar and sister of Ebenezer Rockwood Hoar, George Frisbie Hoar, and Edward Sherman Hoar. Intelligent, learned, and widely respected, Elizabeth Hoar was always welcome in the Emerson home. In May of 1836, Charles Emerson died of tuberculosis—a severe blow to his fiancée and to the Emersons. Emerson was restored in October, when Lidian gave birth to their first child, Waldo. In the same year, he met Transcendental thinkers Margaret Fuller and Bronson Alcott. Alcott, who later became a neighbor, was a friend until Emerson's death in 1882. In 1836, Emerson also wrote the preface to an American edition of Carlyle's *Sartor Resartus*. Moreover, Emerson's own *Nature* was published by James Munroe in September of the year. While hardly a popular success, *Nature* was taken seriously by those who, like the author himself, sought new insights to replace dogma, convention, and received wisdom. With the publication of *Nature*, both Emerson's reputation as a thinker and Transcendentalism as a movement gained momentum. Shortly after *Nature* appeared, a group gathered at George Ripley's home in Boston at the urging of Frederic Henry Hedge, "for the free discussion of theological & moral subjects." The first meeting of the informal "Transcendental Club" included Ripley, Hedge, Emerson, Alcott, Orestes Brownson, James Freeman Clarke, and Convers Francis. Later meetings included Theodore Parker, Margaret Fuller, Ellery Channing, Elizabeth Palmer Peabody, Thoreau, and others. The club met until 1840, providing opportunity for the exchange of ideas and leading to the establishment of *The Dial*.

The Dial, named by Bronson Alcott, was issued between July of 1840 and April of 1844. Margaret Fuller was its first editor; Emerson took over from Fuller in 1842. He was a major contributor of poems, essays, and reviews to the magazine throughout its four-year run. Although *The Dial* did not circulate widely, it was nevertheless important as a stimulus to and medium for Transcendental thought. Aside from Fuller and Emerson, contributors included Bronson Alcott, Lydia Maria Child, James Russell Lowell, Theodore Parker, Elizabeth Palmer Peabody, Henry David Thoreau, and Jones Very.

Nature was followed in quick succession by two other major expressions of Transcendentalism, Emerson's "American Scholar" address before the Phi Beta Kappa Society at Harvard (1837) and his "Divinity School Address" before the senior class of the Harvard Divinity School (1838). "The American Scholar," referred to by Oliver Wendell Holmes as "our intellectual Declaration of Independence," called for a new American thought based on intellectual self-reliance rather than the thought of the past. Published in 1837, it was well received. In "The "Divinity School Address," Emerson deplored the lack of vigor and meaning in established religion and urged men to form a more direct, individual understanding of God. "The Divinity School Address," also published the year it was delivered, was defended by those sympathetic to Transcendental thought and denounced by more conservative members of the Unitarian clergy and by biblical scholar and Harvard Divinity School professor Andrews Norton. (Norton's *Discourse on the Latest Form of Infidelity* was published in 1839.) As a result of "The Divinity School Address," Emerson was not welcome at Harvard for decades.

Emerson tried to remain above the controversy that "The Divinity School Address" generated. He continued lecturing and began to pull together his first collected edition of essays, which was published by

Munroe in Boston under the title *Essays* in March of 1841. It was also issued by James Fraser in London, with a preface by Thomas Carlyle, in the same year, a fact that indicates the degree of recognition that Emerson had achieved by this time. The volume met with mixed reviews on both sides of the Atlantic. It was described in the *New York Review* for April 1841 as "a godless book" that the reviewer was inclined to censure both for its theology and its philosophy, a book in that "the meditative and wise man may find ambrosial food, but which will prove poison to the simple and undiscerning." A reviewer for the English *Literary Gazette* for September 25, 1841, stated that *Essays* "out-Carlyles Carlyle himself, exaggerates all his peculiarities and faults, and possesses very slight glimpses of his excellences." Although the reviews were mixed, Emerson's work was acknowledged as significant. His *Essays: Second Series* was published by Munroe in October of 1844 and in London by John Chapman in November of that year. This volume reinforced Emerson's reputation both in America and abroad. For the remainder of his life, even after his creative spark had died, he enjoyed a position of preeminence among American thinkers and men of letters.

By the late 1830s, Emerson had befriended Henry David Thoreau, who had returned to Concord after graduating from Harvard in 1837. In 1841, the younger man joined the Emerson household as a handyman, in which capacity he took care of things that the well-known, much-demanded, and distinctly unhandy Emerson could not. In his biography of his father written for the Second Series of *Memoirs of Members of the Social Circle in Concord* (1888), Edward Waldo Emerson recalled Thoreau's stable presence, his usefulness about the house and garden, and his particular rapport with children. Whatever distance eventually came between Emerson and Thoreau, Thoreau's friendship was always valued by Mrs. Emerson and her children. Thoreau lived with the Emersons until 1843, and returned to look after things while Emerson made his second trip to Europe, in 1847 and 1848. In 1844, Emerson offered Thoreau the use of property he had purchased at Walden Pond, where Thoreau moved in 1845. In January of 1842, shortly after the death of Thoreau's brother John, the Emersons' first child Waldo died of scarlet fever. The Emersons were overwhelmed with grief. With time, Emerson was able to come to terms with his loss. He later wrote the poem "Threnody" in honor of Waldo.

In the 1830s, Concord was already sensitive to the issue of slavery, but Emerson's involvement in abolition grew slowly. Concord residents took an active part in the Middlesex County Anti-Slavery Society, established in 1834. The Ladies' Anti-Slavery Society of Concord was formed in 1837; Lidian Emerson belonged to it from the beginning. Other members of Emerson's family (his aunt Mary Moody Emerson and his brother Charles) also openly expressed antislavery sentiment in the 1830s. Emerson delivered his first antislavery address in Concord in 1837, in response to the murder of abolitionist publisher Elijah Lovejoy in Alton, Illinois. But his speech disappointed many. It focused not so much on the wrong of slavery as on the right of free speech. It took time for him to overcome equivocal feelings about abolition. He was committed to the ideas of the central importance and the dignity of the individual, but he had difficulty overcoming a sense that slaves had not displayed evidence of a potential for full development. Moreover, like Thoreau, Emerson believed that reform could be effected only through the individual, not through organized movements. Following the delivery of his 1837 speech, Emerson did not speak publicly on the subject again until 1844. He was moved to action only by the steady unfolding of events that, in their threat to the individual and to conscience, could no longer be ignored. Emerson supported the choice of abolitionist Wendell Phillips as speaker for the Concord Lyceum in the early 1840s, despite the objections of conservative community members. By 1844, the annexation of Texas was imminent and Emerson was disgusted with the failure of government and political leaders like Daniel Webster to stop the spread of slavery. He consequently delivered a speech on August 1, 1844, at a Concord celebration of the anniversary of emancipation in the British West Indies. This was much more powerful in its opposition to slavery than had been the 1837 speech, and it placed Emerson among effective public supporters of abolition. The passage of the Fugitive Slave Law in 1850 further fueled his antislavery activism. Throughout the 1850s, he spoke at abolition meetings around the country. He opposed the Kansas-Nebraska Bill, and supported radical abolitionist John Brown (whom he heard speak at the Concord Town Hall in February of 1857).

Emerson's renown as a lecturer drew him farther away from Concord each year. The railroad opened up the west in the 1840s and 1850s, and as it did, it expanded the lyceum circuit. Emerson had made his first train trip in England (between Manchester and Liverpool) in 1833. His career as a successful lecturer depended upon the railroad. The Fitchburg Railroad opened in Concord in 1844, making it faster and more convenient to get to Boston and, from there, to the rest of the country. Frequent travel and the discomforts of "life on the road" wore on him as he grew older.

In 1845, Emerson delivered a series of lectures on "Representative Men." *Representative Men: Seven Lectures* was published in Boston by Phillips, Sampson and in London by John Chapman in 1850. In December of 1846, *Poems*—his first volume of poetry—was published in Boston by Munroe and in London by Chapman (the title pages dated 1847). *May-Day and Other Pieces*, his second and final volume of poetry, appeared in 1867. Although his abilities as a poet have been variously assessed by contemporary and later commentators, Emerson, like Thoreau, attributed powerful possibilities of expression to poetry.

Emerson made his second trip abroad in 1847. Leaving Thoreau to look after his family, he sailed for Liverpool in October. Lecturing in Manchester, Liverpool, and London, he discovered that he had developed fame and a following in England since his first European trip (1832–1833). He saw Carlyle and Wordsworth again (Coleridge had died), spent time in the company of writers Harriet Martineau, Thomas De Quincey, Charles Dickens, William Makepeace Thackeray, James Anthony Froude, Thomas Babington Macaulay, and geologist Charles Lyell, and met many people active in literary and intellectual circles, politics, and other areas. He also visited Scotland and France. While at Edinburgh, Emerson sat for artist David Scott, who painted a well-known oil portrait (now in the Concord Free Public Library). In France, he visited Alexis de Tocqueville (French author of a book on American democracy) and English poet Arthur Hugh Clough. He returned home at the end of July 1848. In 1849, he lectured on England. His *English Traits* was published by Phillips, Sampson at Boston in 1856, in London by G. Routledge.

In 1852, the *Memoirs of Margaret Fuller Ossoli* was published. The book was written and edited by Emerson, William Henry Channing, and James Freeman Clarke. Fuller had gone to Italy, worked on a history of the Roman revolution of 1848–1849, and in 1850 boarded the ship *Elizabeth* to return to America with her Italian husband (the Marchese d'Ossoli) and their child. The ship was wrecked in a storm off Fire Island (New York). Thoreau searched for Fuller's body, in vain.

Along with Oliver Wendell Holmes, Henry Wadsworth Longfellow, Nathaniel Hawthorne, Louis Agassiz, and other prominent New England writers and thinkers, Emerson was a member of the Saturday Club, a literary and intellectual group that formed in 1854 and met monthly in Boston. In the late 1850s, he went with the Adirondack Club (an offshoot of the Saturday Club) to Follensby Pond and Big Tupper Lake in the Adirondacks, under the guidance of artist William

James Stillman. (Stillman's painting of members of the club—including Emerson—at the "Philosophers' Camp" is held by the Concord Free Public Library.)

Emerson's influence on the thought and literature of his time was expressed in Walt Whitman's comment that as he was writing his *Leaves of Grass*, "I was simmering, simmering, simmering; Emerson brought me to a boil." In 1855, Whitman sent Emerson a copy of his newly published book of poems. Emerson responded with a letter acknowledging Whitman's promise, and recommended *Leaves of Grass* to friends and correspondents.

Emerson presented lectures early in 1851 on "The Conduct of Life." His *Conduct of Life*—consisting of essays based on the lectures—was published in Boston by Ticknor and Fields in 1860, in London by Smith, Elder. The Civil War began in 1861, and occupied Emerson's thoughts as well as those of the rest of the nation. During the 1860s, he began to be aware of the decline of his powers, and keenly to feel the loss of many people close to him. His mother had died in 1853, his brother Bulkeley in 1859. Thoreau died in 1862, his aunt Mary Moody Emerson in 1863, Hawthorne in 1864, his brother William in 1868. On a happier note, his daughter Edith had married William H. Forbes in 1865 and made him a grandfather in 1866. He continued lecturing and writing through the 1860s and beyond, but he no longer possessed his earlier intellectual vigor.

Harvard finally forgave Emerson for his 1838 "Divinity School Address" and invited him back in 1866 to receive an honorary degree, in 1867 to deliver the Phi Beta Kappa oration, and in 1870 to present a course of lectures (the "Natural History of Intellect"). Exhausted by his intense schedule and declining strength, Emerson journeyed to California in 1871 at the invitation of John Murray Forbes, Edith's father-in-law. He traveled by train, did some lecturing, and met naturalist John Muir on the trip. During the 1870s, he published two more collections of essays—*Society and Solitude* in 1870, *Letters and Social Aims* in 1876. He also edited an anthology of poetry under the title *Parnassus* (1875). He required substantial assistance from his daughter Ellen and from his biographer and literary executor James Elliot Cabot in putting together *Parnassus* and *Letters and Social Aims*.

As Emerson lectured early in the decade, his audiences grew painfully aware of the failure of his memory. His health and stability were shaken in July of 1872, when his house burned. He and Lidian were forced to move temporarily into the Old Manse. Friends and neighbors joined forces to finance a final trip to Europe to restore his health. In October of 1872, with Ellen as companion, Emerson sailed for England. He visited London, Paris, Florence, Rome, and Egypt and returned again to England, where he saw Carlyle for the last time and met John Ruskin and Robert Browning; he returned home in May of 1873. Emerson was greeted by a welcoming crowd at the Concord Depot and escorted back home to "Bush," which had been restored during his absence.

In *Emerson in Concord* (written for publication in the *Memoirs of the Social Circle in Concord* and also published separately), Edward Waldo Emerson movingly described the waning of his father's powers:

> His last few years were quiet and happy. Nature gently drew the veil over his eyes; he went to his study and tried to work, accomplished less and less, but did not notice it. . . . As his critical sense became dulled, his standard of intellectual performance was less exacting, and this was most fortunate, for he gladly went to any public occasion where he could hear, and nothing would be expected of him.

Despite his progressive debilitation, Emerson held the respect of Concord until the end of his life. He died of pneumonia on April 27, 1882, one month before his seventy-ninth birthday. The church bell tolled seventy-nine times in his honor. People poured into Concord for Emerson's funeral on April 30. He was buried in Sleepy Hollow Cemetery, on Authors' Ridge. His death was widely mourned. James Elliot Cabot, his literary executor, and his son Edward Waldo Emerson edited his writings after his death.

Emerson and Thoreau both expressed Transcendental idealism and optimism in their writings. But despite the radicalism of some of his ideas, in his life and in much of his work Emerson embraced society, civilization, and the heritage of the past far more than Thoreau was able to do. Emerson was a man of the world as well as a man of the mind and spirit. He was born to a certain social position and to certain expectations, and he sought to do his duty by them. It grieved him to reject the traditions of the religion in which he had been raised and to sever his ties with the Second Church in Boston. He followed his intellect and his conscience, but not without awareness of the tension between life and philosophy. The unity of Thoreau's life and his art was far greater than that of Emerson's. Ironically, Emerson's less perfect synthesis, his more worldly pragmatism, allowed him to achieve greater recognition and respect during his lifetime than did Thoreau and, consequently, more immediately to advance the idealism and individuality to which both of these major Transcendental thinkers were committed.

Introduction to Emerson's Writing

Nearly a century and a quarter after his death, Emerson remains one of the most widely read and frequently quoted of American authors. The newness of his ideas and the vigor of his style captured the attention of his lecture audiences and contemporary readers, and continue to move readers today. Emerson expressed the idealistic philosophy underlying his writings with conviction. The degree to which he himself was moved by his thoughts on God, man, and nature enabled him to strike emotional chords and to inspire understanding in the reader.

Style & Language

Emerson's influence as a prose writer derives in part from his incisive observation and his vivid expression. Although he dealt with abstruse concepts, his writing nevertheless possesses clarity, directness, and careful progression from one idea to the next. Difficult concepts are elucidated through analogy and metaphor. Moreover, individual perceptions and ideas progress toward broad generalizations that sweep the reader along. Emerson's phraseology and construction frequently and engagingly suggest the spoken rather than the written word. This impression is reinforced by his propensity for adapting existing words into his own unique creations and for employing quotable maxims. His rhetorical style builds up to peaks of language and emotion. Indeed, Emerson's appeal as a writer—his ability to affect his audience—owes much to his experience as a preacher and public speaker and to the fact that many of his essays were delivered as lectures before they were revised for publication.

Emerson's poetry presents, symbolically and in compressed form, the same major themes found in his addresses and prose writings. The rise and fall of emotional intensity in the poetry parallel the crescendos and cadences of the essays. There are considerable stylistic differences among the poems. Critics have varied widely in assessing the technical success and overall merit of Emerson's poems.

Emerson's thought was informed by a variety of influences, among them New England Calvinism and Unitarianism, the writings of Plato, the Neoplatonists, Coleridge, Carlyle, Wordsworth, Montaigne, and Swedenborg, and eastern sacred texts like the Bhagavad Gita. But his interpretation and synthesis of his antecedents and contemporaries were his own. More than any other thinker and writer of his period, Emerson defined in his work what we think of as American Transcendentalism.

Theme

At the end of his life, Emerson looked back on the rise of New England Transcendentalism in the essay "Historic Notes on Life and Letters in Massachusetts," later published under the title "Historic Notes of Life and Letters in New England." He wrote of this vital period: "The idea, roughly written in revolutions and national movements, in the mind of the philosopher had far more precision; the individual is the world." Although disinclined to take credit for his own influence, he himself did much to advance the central position of mankind and of the individual in relation to God, nature, and human institutions. From before the 1836 publication of *Nature* (his first, most comprehensive exposition of the principles of Transcendental philosophy), every lecture that he gave and every piece that he wrote elevated the importance and dignity of man as an expression of God, as a part of the unity of God, man, and nature in the Oversoul. The assumptions underlying *Nature* invalidated the subordination of the individual in more traditional religious, social, and political frameworks. In Chapter VII of *Nature* ("Spirit"), Emerson wrote:

> . . . that spirit, that is, the Supreme Being, does not build up nature around us, but puts it forth through us, as the life of the tree puts forth new branches and leaves through the pores of the old. As a plant upon the earth, so a man rests upon the bosom of God; he is nourished by unfailing fountains, and draws, at his need, inexhaustible power. Who can set bounds to the possibilities of man? . . . man has access to the entire mind of the Creator, is himself the creator in the finite.

This outlook was radically humanistic, and challenged the distant sovereignty of God that formed part of New England's Calvinistic heritage.

Emerson not only uplifted mankind to oneness with, rather than subservience to, God. He also suggested a distinctly democratic view of each man as equal in worth and capacity to all other men. Human hierarchies, distinctions between the great and the humble, were irrelevant in measuring the value of the individual. Emerson wrote in Chapter VIII of *Nature* ("Prospects"):

> All that Adam had, all that Cæsar could, you have and can
> do. Adam called his house, heaven and earth; Cæsar called
> his house, Rome; you perhaps call yours, a cobler's trade;
> a hundred acres of ploughed land; or a scholar's garret. Yet
> line for line and point for point, your dominion is as great
> as theirs, though without fine names. Build, therefore,
> your own world.

This affirmative vision of equality among men, all possessing divinity in some degree, appeals to us today as powerfully as it did to Emerson's contemporaries. Emerson asserted a kind of democracy far more basic than any political or social system can promote. Moreover, he strengthened the individual's claim to significance and respect by philosophically framing extraordinary expressions of human ability within the context of humanity as a whole. Emerson perceived the particular man who had achieved distinction in some way as a demonstration of the possibilities of all men. He proclaimed in "The American Scholar":

> The main enterprise of the world for splendor, for extent,
> is the upbuilding of a man. Here are the materials strown
> along the ground. The private life of one man shall be a
> more illustrious monarchy,—more formidable to its
> enemy, more sweet and serene in its influence to its friend,
> than any kingdom in history. For a man, rightly viewed,
> comprehendeth the particular natures of all men. Each
> philosopher, each bard, each actor, has only done for me,
> as by a delegate, what one day I can do for myself.

Emerson was fascinated by the attributes—both positive and negative—of a variety of exceptional individuals. He delivered lectures and published essays (contained within his *Representative Men*) on Plato, Swedenborg, Montaigne, Shakespeare, Napoleon, and Goethe. But he focused on these men not so much to highlight their particular excellences as to suggest the potentialities and aspirations of humanity as a whole. He wrote in "Uses of Great Men" (the first piece in *Representative Men*):

> As to what we call the masses, and common men;—there
> are no common men. All men are at last of a size; and true
> art is only possible, on the conviction that every talent has
> its apotheosis somewhere. Fair play, and an open field, and
> freshest laurels to all who have won them! But heaven
> reserves an equal scope for every creature. Each is uneasy

until he has produced his private ray unto the concave sphere, and beheld his talent also in its last nobility and exaltation.

Emerson saw the external limitations imposed by civilization, society, institutions, and materialism as greater impediments to individual self-realization than the differences of gifts among men.

Theme

Emerson's exaltation of the individual was based upon his view of the integral connection between God, man, and nature. Man is capable of much—imagination, insight, morality, and more—but all of his aptitudes derive from his intimate relationship with a larger, higher entity than himself. Emerson expressed the essential oneness of man with the divine in his essay "The Over-Soul":

> We know that all spiritual being is in man. . . . [A]s there is no screen or ceiling between our heads and the infinite heavens, so there is no bar or wall in the soul, where man, the effect, ceases, and God, the cause, begins. The walls are taken away. We lie open on one side to the deeps of spiritual nature, to the attributes of God.

The divine is accessible because God communicates directly to man. Moreover, the influence of the divine on each individual grants the unlimited possibility of higher development, "the infinite enlargement of the heart with a power of growth." The individual may approach ever closer to the perfection of God: "Ineffable is the union of man and God in every act of the soul. The simplest person, who in his integrity worships God, becomes God; yet forever and ever the influx of this better and universal self is new and unsearchable." Self-improvement—moral and spiritual elevation toward the divine—is unbounded, growth an open-ended process.

Nature, which, as Emerson wrote in "Idealism" (Chapter VII of *Nature*), "is made to conspire with spirit to emancipate us," forms a third part of the equation between the divine, the human, and the material. It is a key element in man's realization of his relationship with God: "The world proceeds from the same spirit as the body of man. It is a remoter and inferior incarnation of God, a projection of God in the unconscious." Man's understanding of the importance and meaning of nature is essential to his achieving the insight into God that is available to all. The failure to recognize nature results in distance from God: "As we degenerate, the contrast between us and our house is more evident.

We are as much strangers in nature, as we are aliens from God." The channels of interaction between man, God, and nature must remain unobstructed for the universal to express itself in the particular mind and existence of the individual.

Theme

Emerson explained the means by which the individual understands his place in the encompassing as oracular and revelatory. He wrote in "The Over-Soul":

> And this deep power in which we exist, and whose beat-itude is all accessible to us, is not only self-sufficing and perfect in every hour, but the act of seeing and the thing seen, the seer and the spectacle, the subject and the object, are one. We see the world piece by piece, as the sun, the moon, the animal, the tree; but the whole, of which these are the shining parts, is the soul. Only by the vision of that Wisdom can the horoscope of the ages be read, and by falling back on our better thoughts, by yielding to the spirit of prophecy which is innate in every man, we can know what it saith.

The broad scope of the universe and man's position in it are fathomable not by the logic of the human intellect, but by the divine spark of intu-ition. In his glorification of intuitive "reason" (a usage adopted from the English Romantic poets) over more rational, experiential "understand-ing," Emerson was influenced by Kant and by the interpretation of German idealistic philosophy offered by the English Romantics, particularly Coleridge.

Emerson saw that there was no way to explain intuition in terms of ordinary mental processes. "We know truth when we see it . . . as we know when we are awake that we are awake," he wrote in "The Over-Soul." If mysteriously inexplicable, however, intuition is exhilarating

> We distinguish the announcements of the soul, its mani-festations of its own nature, by the term *Revelation*. These are always attended by the emotion of the sublime. For this communication is an influx of the Divine mind into our mind. . . . Every distinct apprehension of this central commandment agitates men with awe and delight. . . . By the necessity of our constitution, a certain enthusiasm attends the individual's consciousness of that divine pres-ence. The character and duration of this enthusiasm varies

with the state of the individual, from an extasy and trance and prophetic inspiration . . . to the faintest glow of virtuous emotion. . . .

Indeed, Emerson added, intuitive insight and religious revelation are similar to insanity, another intense expression of a force beyond the control of the individual.

Theme

To remain receptive to the intuitive process, a man must trust in himself. In "Self-Reliance," Emerson wrote of the need for each man to think for himself, to trust in his own ability to understand, evaluate, and act. He warned his audiences and his readers not to give up their freedom as individuals to constricting beliefs and customs, to common values, to established institutions:

> But now we are a mob. Man does not stand in awe of man, nor is his genius admonished to stay at home, to put itself in communication with the internal ocean, but it goes abroad to beg a cup of water of the urns of other men. We must go alone. I like the silent church before the service begins, better than any preaching. . . . Why should we assume the faults of our friend, or wife, or father, or child, because they sit around our hearth, or are said to have the same blood? All men have my blood, and I have all men's. Not for that will I adopt their petulance or folly. . . . But your isolation must not be mechanical, but spiritual, that is, must be elevation.

The intellectually, morally, and spiritually independent individual maintains his ability to come to a direct understanding of the world around him and of his place in it and in the universe.

Emerson argued against reliance on the thought of the past in "The American Scholar," and against conformity to established religion in the "Divinity School Address." Unquestioning acceptance and compliance close off spontaneous communication with the divine and limit the fulfillment of human potential. Self-reliance is equivalent to trust in the divine. Emerson wrote in "Self-Reliance":

> The magnetism which all original action exerts is explained when we inquire the reason of self-trust. . . . What is the aboriginal Self on which a universal reliance may be grounded? What is the nature and power of that science-baffling star, without parallax, without calculable

elements, which shoots a ray of beauty even into trivial and impure actions, if the least mark of independence appear? The inquiry leads us to that source, at once the essence of genius, of virtue, and of life, which we call Spontaneity or Instinct. We denote this primary wisdom as Intuition. . . . In that deep force, the last fact behind which analysis cannot go, all things find their common origin.

Thus, self-reliance permits intuition, which allows the individual to grasp the divinity that enfolds the human and natural realms. Conformity is passive, while openness to intuition is part of an active, dynamic process. Reliance on tradition fixes values and understanding, preventing growth. Intuition, on the other hand, a force of intense flux, results in the ever-higher perfection of man toward godliness.

Theme

Idealist though he was, Emerson was keenly aware of the difficulty of reconciling the material and the spiritual. He attempted to bridge the gap between the two with the theory of correspondence, which he understood in large part through the thought and work of mystical Swedish theologian Emanuel Swedenborg, and through that of Sampson Reed, Swedenborg's American disciple. Emerson developed the idea of correspondence in *Nature*. He perceived the physical world as a manifestation of spirit—of the creator's mind—and therefore as symbolic of the divine, and saw a one-for-one correspondence between natural laws and spiritual laws. In its symbolism, he wrote, nature is designed to afford man comprehension of God. Human expressions and constructs such as language, architecture, and even morality are based upon and reflect the forms and laws of nature, and consequently also provide evidence of and insight into God.

The principle of correspondence allowed Emerson to frame external reality within the context of divine absolutes and, at the same time, to harness the material world to man's striving to spiritualize and to make himself a more perfect reflection of God. Emerson wrote of correspondence in "Language," Chapter IV of *Nature*:

This relation between the mind and matter is not fancied by some poet, but stands in the will of God, and so is free to be known by all men. . . . There seems to be a necessity in spirit to manifest itself in material forms; and day and night, river and storm, beast and bird, acid and alkali, preëxist in necessary Ideas in the mind of God, and are what they are by the virtue of preceding affections, in the world of spirit. . . . The visible creation is the terminus or the circumference of the invisible world.

Toward the end of understanding correspondence and of perceiving the divine through it, Emerson advocated a "life in harmony with nature, the love of truth and of virtue." Gradually, he wrote, the relationship between the material world and the ideal in the mind of God will be understood. Through intuition, which works on the human mind as it observes nature, "the world shall be to us an open book, and every form significant of its hidden life and final cause."

Emerson and Thoreau both regarded poetry as a form of literature peculiarly suited to express Transcendental insight into the divine. Emerson also presented poetry as a kind of demonstration of correspondence, a simultaneous manifestation of the properties of physical form and ethereal spirit. He wrote in his essay "The Poet":

For it is not metres, but a metre-making argument, that makes a poem,—a thought so passionate and alive, that, like the spirit of a plant or an animal, it has an architecture of its own, and adorns nature with a new thing. The thought and the form are equal in the order of time, but in the order of genesis the thought is prior to the form.

Ultimately, then, the spiritual origin of the poem precedes the poem as "thing," as an object possessing physical form as well as idea. And through the beauty of its form, something of the underlying spiritual impetus behind the poem is revealed.

Emerson not only explored the relationship between the material and the spiritual in his writings, but also directly addressed the discrepancy between philosophy and our experience of life, notably in the essay "Experience." While he rejected narrow and limiting approaches and institutions, he was tolerant of humanity and of social forms. On a basic level, he accepted the world he lived in as it was, and sought to reconcile it with the higher spiritual reality that he perceived beyond.

In *Nature*, "The American Scholar," "The Divinity School Address," and a few other key early pieces, Emerson expressed most of the major ideas that he explored throughout the rest of his work. In the course of his career, he examined a broad range of subjects—poets and poetry, education, history, society, art, politics, reform, and the lives of particular individuals among them—within the Transcendental framework that he set forth early in his career as a lecturer and a man of letters.

Selective Chronology of Emerson's Writings

1820   Emerson began to keep regular journals

1822   "Thoughts on the Religion of the Middle Ages" published in *The Christian Disciple and Theological Review*

1835   *A Historical Discourse, Delivered Before the Citizens of Concord, 12th September, 1835. On the Second Centennial Anniversary of the Incorporation of the Town* published (Concord: G.F. Bemis)

1836   *Nature* published (Boston: James Munroe)

1837   *An Oration, Delivered Before the Phi Beta Kappa Society, at Cambridge, August 31, 1837,* ["Phi Beta Kappa Address," or "American Scholar"] published (Boston: James Munroe)

        "Michael Angelo" published in *North American Review*

1838   *An Address Delivered Before the Senior Class in Divinity College, Cambridge, Sunday Evening, 15 July, 1838,* ["Divinity School Address"] published (Boston: James Munroe)

        An Oration, Delivered Before the Literary Societies of Dartmouth College, July 24, 1838, published (Boston: Charles C. Little and James Brown)

        Pieces (review, letter, and essay) published in *The Christian Examiner*, the Washington *Daily National Intelligencer*, and the *North American Review*

1839   Pieces (including poems "Each and All" and "The Rhodora") published in *The Western Messenger*

1840   Pieces (essays, poems, review) published in *The Dial*

1841   *Essays* [First Series] published (Boston: James Munroe; also in London)

        The Method of Nature. An Oration, Delivered Before the Society of the Adelphi, in Waterville College, in Maine, August 11, 1841, published (Boston: Samuel G. Simpkins)

        Pieces published in *The Dial*

1842   Emerson began to edit *The Dial* (served as editor until 1844)

          Pieces published in *The Dial*

1843   Pieces published in *The Dial,* review in *The United States Magazine and Democratic Review*

          First British edition of "Phi Beta Kappa Address" published

1844   *Essays: Second Series* published (Boston: James Munroe)

          An Address Delivered in the Court-House in Concord, Massachusetts, on 1st August, 1844, on the Anniversary of the Emancipation of the Negroes in the British West Indies published (Boston: James Munroe)

          Pieces published in *The Dial*

          Multiple titles published in London (including *Orations, Lectures, and Addresses*; *The Young American. A Lecture*; and *Essays: Second Series*)

1847   *Poems* published in Boston (James Munroe) and London (both editions published December 1846; title pages dated 1847)

1848   Pieces published in *Massachusetts Quarterly Review*

1849   *Nature; Addresses, and Lectures* published (Boston and Cambridge: James Munroe); later published under title *Miscellanies; Embracing Nature, Addresses, and Lectures*

          Essay "War" published in Elizabeth Peabody's *Aesthetic Papers*; pieces published in *Massachusetts Quarterly Review*

1850   *Representative Men* published in Boston (Phillips, Sampson) and in London

1852   *Memoirs of Margaret Fuller Ossoli* (written and edited by Emerson, William Henry Channing, and James Freeman Clarke) published (Boston: Phillips, Sampson)

1855   Letter to Walt Whitman published in *New York Daily Tribune*, also separately

1856   *English Traits* published in Boston (Phillips, Sampson) and London

1857   Pieces (primarily poems) published in *Atlantic Monthly*

1858   Pieces (poems, essays) published in *Atlantic Monthly*

1860   *The Conduct of Life* published in Boston (Ticknor and Fields) and London

Many pieces published in the Cincinnati *Dial* (a publication distinct from the Boston *Dial*)

1862   Pieces published in *Atlantic Monthly* (including "Thoreau" in August)

"Henry D. Thoreau" (distinct from piece in *Atlantic*) published in *Boston Daily Advertiser*

1866   *The Complete Works of Ralph Waldo Emerson* published in two volumes in London (a third volume added in 1883)

1867   *May-Day and Other Pieces* published in Boston (Ticknor and Fields) and London

1868   First German edition of *Nature* (*Die Natur*) published

1870   *Society and Solitude* published in Boston (Fields, Osgood) and London

The Prose Works of Ralph Waldo Emerson published in Boston (Fields, Osgood) in two volumes; a third volume added in 1879 (Houghton, Osgood)

1875   *Parnassus* (anthology edited by Emerson) published (Boston: James R. Osgood)

Letters and Social Aims published in Boston (James R. Osgood) and London (English title page dated 1876)

1876   Little Classic Edition of Emerson's writings began publication (completed 1893); a total of twelve volumes published

1883   *The Correspondence of Thomas Carlyle and Ralph Waldo Emerson, 1834–1872* published in two volumes in Boston (James R. Osgood) and London

"Historic Notes on Life and Letters in Massachusetts" (later titled "Historic Notes of Life and Letters in New England") published in *Atlantic Monthly*

Two editions of Emerson's works published (in one volume in New York, in six volumes in London)

1883 *(continued)*

Houghton, Mifflin began publication of Riverside Edition of Emerson's writings (completed 1893); a total of twelve volumes published

1892 "The Emerson-Thoreau Correspondence," edited by F. B. Sanborn, published in *Atlantic Monthly*

1903 Houghton, Mifflin began publication of Centenary Edition of Emerson's writings (completed 1904); a total of twelve volumes published

1909 *Journals of Ralph Waldo Emerson,* edited by Edward Waldo Emerson and Waldo Emerson Forbes, published (Boston: Houghton, Mifflin) in ten volumes

1938 *Young Emerson Speaks: Unpublished Discourses on Many Subjects,* edited by Arthur Cushman McGiffert, Jr., published (Boston: Houghton, Mifflin)

1939 *The Letters of Ralph Waldo Emerson,* edited by Ralph L. Rusk, published (New York: Columbia University Press). Most letters earlier printed—Emerson's correspondence with Carlyle, John Sterling, Samuel Gray Ward, Herman Grimm, William Henry Furness, Arthur Hugh Clough—not included

1959 *The Early Lectures of Ralph Waldo Emerson* began publication (Cambridge: Harvard University Press); completed 1972. A total of three volumes published

1960 *The Journals and Miscellaneous Notebooks of Ralph Waldo Emerson* began publication (Cambridge: The Belknap Press of Harvard University Press); completed 1982. A total of sixteen volumes published

1964 *The Correspondence of Emerson and Carlyle,* edited by Joseph Slater, published (New York and London: Columbia University Press)

1971 *The Collected Works of Ralph Waldo Emerson* began publication (Cambridge: The Belknap Press of Harvard University Press)

Emerson's Reputation and Influence

Both during his lifetime and since his death, Emerson's reputation and influence have been enormous. Unlike his contemporary and friend Thoreau, Emerson was acknowledged during his own time as a major thinker and author and as the central proponent of Transcendental philosophy. Because Emerson's efforts straddled a number of disciplines—among them literature, philosophy, theology, psychology, education, and social commentary—critics and scholars have been anything but unified in assessing the nature of his most important contributions to American thought and letters. Emerson's writings are so encompassing that they have permitted a wide variety of approaches to their study and understanding. To a large degree, particular reviewers and scholars have expressed the concerns of their own major areas of interest in examining Emerson's work. But if Emerson's importance has been widely recognized, few commentators have accepted all aspects of his work as valid, and some—even those who admit his tremendous appeal—have denied that he was a great writer of prose or poetry. Nevertheless, the vast body of literature about Emerson attests to his influence.

The first monographic treatment of Emerson, George Searle Phillips' *Emerson, His Life and Writings* ("by January Searle") was published in London in 1855, more than twenty-five years before its subject's death. The first biography of Emerson, George Willis Cooke's *Ralph Waldo Emerson*, appeared in 1881. Cooke also prepared the first separate bibliography of Emerson's writings (*A Bibliography of Ralph Waldo Emerson*, published in 1908). Reviews of Emerson's writings, articles about him, bibliographies of his work and of secondary sources, biographies, specialized discussions of aspects of his thought, and critical articles and books number in the thousands. Moreover, Emerson is considered in every history of American literature and overall treatment of New England Transcendentalism. It is consequently difficult to discuss Emerson's reputation and influence briefly, except in the most general terms.

Throughout his life, Emerson's thought and work generated mixed reactions—sometimes entirely positive or negative, but more often a combination of the two. Many found aspects of his approach radical and unsettling, even when they were moved by his optimism about man's place in the universe. This dichotomy is found in writings by those of Emerson's contemporaries inclined to defend Transcendentalism as well as by those who had no particular sympathy with it. When *Nature* appeared in 1836, for example, Orestes Brownson (Unitarian preacher, editor, reviewer, and writer for *The Christian Examiner* and the *Boston Quarterly Review*) wrote about it in the September 10, 1836, issue of the *Boston Reformer*. He opened the piece, "This is a singular book. It is the creation of a mind that lives and moves in the Beautiful, and has the power of assimilating to itself whatever it sees, hears, or touches. We cannot analyze it; whoever would form an idea of it must read it." He proclaimed the book "the forerunner of a new class of books, the harbinger of a new literature as much superior to whatever has been, as our political institutions are superior to those of the Old World." Having defined *Nature* as "aesthetical rather than philosophical," Brownson went on to question the logical soundness of Emerson's denial of the existence of nature as a reality independent of spirit and the human mind: "He all but worships what his senses seem to present him, and yet is not certain that all that which his senses place out of him, is not after all the mere subjective laws of his own being, existing only to the eye, not of a necessary, but of an irresistible Faith."

The more conservative Francis Bowen, a critic of Transcendentalism, likewise admitted the power of *Nature*, but expressed a number of reservations. In a lengthy review ("Transcendentalism," written for the January 1837 issue of *The Christian Examiner*), Bowen stated, "We find beautiful writing and sound philosophy in this little work; but the effect is injured by occasional vagueness of expression, and by a vein of mysticism, that pervades the writer's whole course of thought." He continued:

> The highest praise that can be accorded to it, is, that it is a *suggestive* book, for no one can read it without tasking his faculties to the utmost, and relapsing into fits of severe meditation. But the effect of perusal is often painful, the thoughts excited are frequently bewildering, and the results to which they lead us, uncertain and obscure. The reader feels as in a disturbed dream, in which shows of surpassing beauty are around him, and he is conversant with disembodied spirits, yet all the time he is harassed by an uneasy sort of consciousness, that the whole combination of phenomena is fantastic and unreal.

Bowen charged Emerson with offending good taste, and pointed out that there was nothing original in his ideas. He characterized Transcendentalism as "a revival of the Old Platonic school," and criticized the "self-complacency" of Romantic writer Samuel Taylor Coleridge and his "English adherents," who were major influences on Emerson and the Transcendentalists.

Samuel Osgood, writing for *The Western Messenger* (January 1837), pointed to the peculiar power of *Nature* to stir the philosophically unsympathetic as well as devotees of Transcendentalism:

> The work is a remarkable one, and it certainly will be called remarkable by those, who consider it "mere moonshine" as well as those, who look upon it with reverence, as the effusion of a prophet-like mind. Whatever may be thought of the merits, or of the extravagances of the book, no one, we are sure, can read it, without feeling himself more wide awake to the beauty and meaning of Creation.

But the generally enthusiastic Osgood could not overlook what he perceived as Emerson's lack of conclusive logic in argument. And Elizabeth Palmer Peabody, herself in many ways the consummate Transcendentalist, in a favorable review of *Nature* for *The United States Magazine and Democratic Review* (February 1838), urged Emerson to write another book to clarify the philosophy that the reader could only understand "by glimpses" in *Nature*, and to expand upon certain of his religious ideas.

To a greater or lesser degree, the reviews of *Nature* set the tone for the contemporary critical reaction to much of Emerson's later work. Commentators responded to his rhetorical prose and to his philosophical idealism with a sense of exhilaration, which was offset by reservations about the soundness of his philosophy and of his religious views, the derivation of his ideas from German and English writers, his logic, his mysticism, his perceived vagueness, and sometimes the aesthetics of his poetry and his prose. Two of the most commonly appreciated aspects of Emerson's work were his ability to inspire others, to serve as a springboard from which others might attain heights of thought and expression, and his optimism. Respected American critic James Russell Lowell (who in his 1848 satirical poem *A Fable for Critics* had poked fun at Emerson as an idealistic/pragmatic "mystagogue") vigorously underscored Emerson's inspirational quality in his 1871 *My Study Windows*: "We look upon him as one of the few men of genius whom our age has produced, and there needs no better proof of it than his masculine faculty of fecundating other minds. Search for eloquence in his books and you will perchance miss it, but meanwhile you will find that it has kindled your thoughts." British poet and literary and social critic Matthew Arnold, who lectured on Emerson in Boston in 1883 and published his lecture in his *Discourses on America* (1885), denied that Emerson was a great poet, a great man of letters, or a great philosophical writer, but found him insightful, perceptive of truth, and admirable in his inspirational optimism. Arnold wrote: "the secret of his effect . . . is in his temper. It is in the hopeful, serene, beautiful temper. . . . [F]or never had man such a sense of the inexhaustibleness of nature, and such hope."

The serious attention paid to Emerson by English as well as American critics was a remarkable feature of his early critical reception. In fact, British commentators were at first more generally positive than American reviewers in their assessments. A piece by British poet and literary and political writer Richard Monckton Milnes in the *London and Westminster Review* (March 1840) was particularly influential. Although Milnes pointed out Emerson's debt to European philosophy and his similarity to Carlyle, he also focused on the value of his work in fostering intellectual sympathy between England and America. His reactions were mixed, but the fact that so prominent a critic had taken the time to prepare a lengthy review had an effect on the overall British response to Emerson. Emerson's subsequent work was eagerly read and reviewed in Britain.

"The Divinity School Address" (1838) was regarded by some as a pronounced threat to established religion. It drew a more polarized response than did Emerson's other offerings. Andrews Norton, a biblical scholar and professor at the Harvard Divinity School, was reactionary and vitriolic in his evaluation of it. Norton wrote a review for the *Boston Daily Advertiser* (August 27, 1838). In "The New School in Literature and Religion," he attacked Emerson's insult to religion, his inability to reason logically, his poor taste (evidenced by his oracular tone and lack of humility), his vagueness of expression and distortion of ideas, his relation to "German barbarians" and to Carlyle. Norton's hostile criticism set off a volley of responses (James Freeman Clarke noted in a review in *The Western Messenger*, "We perceive that our friends in Boston, and its vicinity, have been a good deal roused and excited by an address. . . ."), and effected Emerson's long banishment from Harvard. Theophilus Parsons (writing under the pseudonym "S.X.") took Norton to task for his harshness and incivility. Finding considerable fault with Emerson's theology, Parsons explained that he responded to Norton "not because I am unwilling to have the faults of this 'New School' exposed and dealt with, but because I would have them dealt with as to do good, not harm." George Ripley—minister, editor, and (later) founder of Brook Farm—took on Norton in print in part because of the latter's response to "The Divinity School Address." Positive commentators praised Emerson's noble vision of humanity and of human possibility. Clarke's defense in *The Western Messenger* evoked the image of Emerson as an upright man. Clarke wrote of Emerson as "a man of pure and noble mind, of original genius and independent thought," and referred to Emerson as the center of a coterie: "[H]e has been surrounded by a band of enthusiastic admirers, whom the genius, life, and manliness of his thoughts attracted, and his beautiful delivery as a public speaker charmed."

Clarke's reference to Emerson as a public speaker suggests one major factor that contributed to the favorable reception of Emerson's work during his lifetime. Emerson's contemporaries were able to experience firsthand the man's persuasiveness as a lecturer and his detached benevolence. He enjoyed a positive popular following, even among those who had little sustained interest in serious philosophical and religious issues, in large part because his personal presence exuded a kind of disinterested goodness and a humility that appealed to others on a basic level. Although these qualities may have had negligible effect on commentators who had no opportunity to see him in person, they influenced the opinion of those who knew him as a speaker. In his *Partial Portraits* (1888), novelist Henry James remarked on Emerson the lecturer:

> He was in an admirable position for showing, what he constantly endeavored to show, that the prize was within. Anyone who in New England at that time could do that was sure of success, of listeners and sympathy: most of all, of course, when it was a question of doing it with such a divine persuasiveness. Moreover, the way in which Emerson did it added to the charm—by word of mouth, face to face, with a rare, irresistible voice and a beautiful mild, modest authority. If Mr. Arnold [Matthew Arnold] is struck with the limited degree in which he was a man of letters, I suppose it is because he is more struck with his having been, as it were, a man of lectures.

In New England, where Emerson became established as a kind of regional saint (particularly later in his career, when the substance of his earlier expressions no longer generated controversy), he inspired not only respect but also a feeling akin to pride of ownership.

Emerson's death in 1882 generated a flurry of printed paeans attesting to his greatness. Then, beginning with Matthew Arnold's 1883 lecture, critics began to consider the man's major contributions more objectively. As during his life, posthumous opinions varied about what kind of thinker he was and about his effectiveness as a writer.

Walt Whitman, whose *Leaves of Grass* echoed Emerson, wrote about him, as did (from various points of view) Henry James, William James, John Dewey, D. H. Lawrence, George Santayana, and many others who achieved recognition and influence through their own work. A range of important twentieth-century American scholars—Perry Miller, F. O. Matthiessen, and Lewis Mumford among them—examined Emerson's work and assessed his significance. Religious thinkers and historians have analyzed his role in the development of Unitarianism. Today, a number of scholars are at work on critical, intellectual, biographical, and bibliographical studies of Emerson, as well as on authoritative editions of his writings. In 1955, the newly formed Emerson Society began publication of the *Emerson Society Quarterly*, which became *ESQ: A Journal of the American Renaissance*. Although the intensity of British regard for Emerson—strong in the nineteenth century—has waned, American interest in him continues to grow.

Emerson's writings have been readily available to readers since their first publication in the nineteenth century. Collected editions were published in the author's lifetime. Edward Waldo Emerson edited the long-standard Centenary Edition of his father's writings (published 1903–1904). Modern scholars have prepared editions of Emerson's early sermons, his lectures, and his journals. A new edition of his works, *The Collected Works of Ralph Waldo Emerson*, began publication in 1971. A variety of popular twentieth-century collections (for example: the Modern Library Edition of *The Selected Writings of Ralph Waldo Emerson*, edited by Brooks Atkinson; Mark Van Doren's *The Portable Emerson*; William H. Gilman's *Selected Writings of Ralph Waldo Emerson*; and the Library of America volumes) have kept Emerson's thought accessible to a broad audience.

Today, Emerson is widely taught at the college level, in courses on American literature, Romanticism, and other topics as well. His writings provide a ready source of inspiration for public speakers, who frequently introduce or illuminate some point by reading an appropriate quotation from Emerson. His thought has seeped so far into popular culture that passages from his writings—and sometimes passages mistakenly attributed to him—are found in greeting cards. His home in Concord is visited by pilgrims from all over the world. Although there may not be consensus about the exact nature of Emerson's significance, his primary position is unquestioned.

Nature

As he returned from Europe in 1833, Emerson had already begun to think about the book that would eventually be published under the title *Nature*. In writing *Nature*, Emerson drew upon material from his journals, sermons, and lectures. The lengthy essay was first published in Boston by James Munroe and Company in September of 1836. A new edition (also published by Munroe, with Emerson paying the printing costs, his usual arrangement with Munroe) appeared in December of 1849. This second edition was printed from the plates of the collection *Nature; Addresses, and Lectures*, published by Munroe in September 1849. (The second edition of this collection was published in Boston in 1856 by Phillips, Sampson, under the title *Miscellanies; Embracing Nature, Addresses, and Lectures*.) *Nature* was published in London in 1844 in *Nature, An Essay. And Lectures on the Times*, by H. G. Clarke and Co. A German edition was issued in 1868. It was included in 1876 in the first volume (*Miscellanies*) of the Little Classic Edition of Emerson's writings, in 1883 in the first volume (*Nature, Addresses, and Lectures*) of the Riverside Edition, in 1903 in the first volume (*Nature, Addresses, and Lectures*) of the Centenary Edition, and in 1971 in the first volume (*Nature, Addresses, and Lectures*) of the *Collected Works* published by the Belknap Press of Harvard University Press. *Nature* has been printed in numerous collections of Emerson's writings since its first publication, among them the 1940 Modern Library *The Complete Essays and Other Writings of Ralph Waldo Emerson* (edited by Brooks Atkinson), the 1965 Signet Classic *Selected Writings of Ralph Waldo Emerson* (edited by William H. Gilman), and the 1983 Library of America *Essays & Lectures* (selected and annotated by Joel Porte).

Synopsis

Emerson prefaced the prose text of the 1836 first edition of *Nature* with a passage from the Neoplatonic philosopher Plotinus. The 1849 second edition included instead a poem by Emerson himself. Both present themes that are developed in the essay. The passage from Plotinus suggests the primacy of spirit and of human understanding over nature. Emerson's poem emphasizes the unity of all manifestations of nature, nature's symbolism, and the perpetual development of all of nature's forms toward the highest expression as embodied in man.

Nature is divided into an introduction and eight chapters. In the Introduction, Emerson laments the current tendency to accept the knowledge and traditions of the past instead of experiencing God and nature directly, in the present. He asserts that all our questions about the order of the universe—about the relationships between God, man, and nature—may be answered by our experience of life and by the world around us. Each individual is a manifestation of creation and as such holds the key to unlocking the mysteries of the universe. Nature, too, is both an expression of the divine and a means of understanding it. The goal of science is to provide a theory of nature, but man has not yet attained a truth broad enough to comprehend all of nature's forms and phenomena. Emerson identifies nature and spirit as the components of the universe. He defines nature (the "NOT ME") as everything separate from the inner individual—nature, art, other men, our own bodies. In common usage, nature refers to the material world unchanged by man. Art is nature in combination with the will of man. Emerson explains that he will use the word "nature" in both its common and its philosophical meanings in the essay.

At the beginning of Chapter I, Emerson describes true solitude as going out into nature and leaving behind all preoccupying activities as well as society. When a man gazes at the stars, he becomes aware of his own separateness from the material world. The stars were made to allow him to perceive the "perpetual presence of the sublime." Visible every night, they demonstrate that God is ever-present. They never lose their power to move us. We retain our original sense of wonder even when viewing familiar aspects of nature anew. Emerson discusses the poetical approach to nature—the perception of the encompassing whole made up of many individual components. Our delight in the landscape, which is made up of many particular forms, provides an example of this integrated vision.

Unlike children, most adults have lost the ability to see the world in this way. In order to experience awe in the presence of nature, we need to approach it with a balance between our inner and our outer senses. Nature so approached is a part of man, and even when bleak and stormy is capable of elevating his mood. All aspects of nature correspond to some state of mind. Nature offers perpetual youth and joy, and counteracts whatever misfortune befalls an individual. The visionary man may lose himself in it, may become a receptive "transparent eyeball" through which the "Universal Being" transmits itself into his consciousness and makes him sense his oneness with God. In nature, which is also a part of God, man finds qualities parallel to his own. There is a special relationship, a sympathy, between man and nature. But by itself, nature does not provide the pleasure that comes of perceiving this relationship. Such satisfaction is a product of a particular harmony between man's inner processes and the outer world. The way we react to nature depends upon our state of mind in approaching it.

In the next four chapters—"Commodity," "Beauty," "Language," and "Discipline"—Emerson discusses the ways in which man employs nature ultimately to achieve insight into the workings of the universe. In Chapter II, "Commodity," he treats the most basic uses of nature— for heat, food, water, shelter, and transportation. Although he ranks these as low uses, and states that they are the only applications that most men have for nature, they are perfect and appropriate in their own way. Moreover, man harnesses nature through the practical arts, thereby enhancing its usefulness through his own wit. Emerson quickly finishes with nature as a commodity, stating that "A man is fed, not that he may be fed, but that he may work," and turns to higher uses.

In Chapter III, "Beauty," Emerson examines nature's satisfaction of a nobler human requirement, the desire for beauty. The perception of nature's beauty lies partly in the structure of the eye itself, and in the laws of light. The two together offer a unified vision of many separate objects as a pleasing whole—"a well-colored and shaded globe," a landscape "round and symmetrical." Every object in nature has its own beauty, which is magnified when perspective allows comprehensive vision of the whole.

Emerson presents three properties of natural beauty. First, nature restores and gives simple pleasure to a man. It reinvigorates the over-worked, and imparts a sense of well-being and of communion with the universe. Nature pleases even in its harsher moments. The same landscape viewed in different weather and seasons is seen as if for the first time. But we cannot capture natural beauty if we too actively and consciously seek it. We must rather submit ourselves to it, allowing it to react to us spontaneously, as we go about our lives.

Secondly, nature works together with the spiritual element in man to enhance the nobility of virtuous and heroic human actions. There is a particular affinity between the processes of nature and the capabilities of man. Nature provides a suitably large and impressive background against which man's higher actions are dramatically outlined.

Thirdly, Emerson points out the capacity of natural beauty to stimulate the human intellect, which uses nature to grasp the divine order of the universe. Because action follows upon reflection, nature's beauty is visualized in the mind, and expressed through creative action. The love of beauty constitutes taste; its creative expression, art. A work of art—"the result or expression of nature, in miniature"—demonstrates man's particular powers. Man apprehends wholeness in the multiplicity of natural forms and conveys these forms in their totality. The poet, painter, sculptor, musician, and architect are all inspired by natural beauty and offer a unified vision in their work. Art thus represents nature as distilled by man. Unlike the uses of nature described in "Commodity," the role of nature in satisfying man's desire for beauty is an end in itself. Beauty, like truth and goodness, is an expression of God. But natural beauty is an ultimate only inasmuch as it works as a catalyst upon the inner processes of man.

In Chapter IV, "Language," Emerson explores nature's service to man as a vehicle for thought. He first states that words represent particular facts in nature, which exists in part to give us language to express ourselves. He suggests that all words, even those conveying intellectual and moral meaning, can be etymologically traced back to roots originally attached to material objects or their qualities. (Although this theory would not be supported by the modern study of linguistics, Emerson was not alone among his contemporaries in subscribing to it.) Over time, we have lost a sense of the particular connection of the first language to the natural world, but children and primitive people retain it to some extent. Not only are words symbolic, Emerson continues, but the natural objects that they represent are symbolic of particular spiritual states. Human intellectual processes are, of necessity, expressed through language, which in its primal form was integrally connected to nature. Emerson asserts that there is universal understanding of the relationship between natural imagery and human thought. An all-encompassing universal soul underlies individual life. "Reason" (intuitive understanding) affords access to the universal soul through the natural symbols of spirit provided by language. In language, God is, in a very real sense, accessible to all men. In his unique capacity to perceive the connectedness of everything in the universe, man enjoys a central position. Man cannot be understood without nature, nor nature without man. In its origin, language was pure poetry, and clearly conveyed the relationship between material symbol and spiritual meaning. Emerson states that the same symbols form the original elements of all languages. And the moving power of idiomatic language and of the strong speech of simple men reminds us of the first dependence of language upon nature. Modern man's ability to express himself effectively requires simplicity, love of truth, and desire to communicate efficiently. But because we have lost the sense of its origins, language has been corrupted. The man who speaks with passion or in images—like the poet or orator who maintains a vital connection with nature—expresses the workings of God.

Literary Device

Finally, Emerson develops the idea that the whole of nature—not just its particulate verbal expressions—symbolizes spiritual reality and offers insight into the universal. He writes of all nature as a metaphor for the human mind, and asserts that there is a one-to-one correspondence between moral and material laws. All men have access to understanding this correspondence and, consequently, to comprehending the laws of the universe. Emerson employs the image of the circle—much-used in *Nature*—in stating that the visible world is the "terminus or circumference of the invisible world." Visible nature innately possesses a moral and spiritual aspect. Man may grasp the underlying meaning of the physical world by living harmoniously with nature, and by loving truth and virtue. Emerson concludes "Language" by stating that we understand the full meaning of nature by degrees.

Nature as a discipline—a means of arriving at comprehension—forms the subject of Chapter V, "Discipline." All of nature serves to educate man through both the rational, logical "Understanding" and the intuitive, mystical "Reason." Through the more rational understanding, we constantly learn lessons about the similarities and differences between objects, about reality and unreality, about order, arrangement, progression, and combination. The ultimate result of such lessons is common sense. Emerson offers property and debt as materially based examples that teach necessary lessons through the understanding, and space and time as demonstrations of particularity and individuality, through which "we may know that things are not huddled and lumped, but sundered and individual." Each object has its own particular use, and through the understanding we know that it cannot be converted to other uses to which it is not fitted. The wise man recognizes the innate properties of objects and men, and the differences, gradations, and similarities among the manifold natural expressions. The practical arts and sciences make use of this wisdom. But as man progressively grasps the basic physical laws, he comes closer to understanding the laws of creation, and limiting concepts such as space and time lose their significance in his vision of the larger picture. Emerson emphasizes the place of human will—the expression of human power—in harnessing nature. Nature is made to serve man. We take what is useful from it in forming a sense of the universe, giving greater or lesser weight to particular aspects to suit our purposes, even framing nature according to our own image of it. Emerson goes on to discuss how intuitive reason provides insight into the ethical and spiritual meanings behind nature. "All things are moral," he proclaims, and therefore every aspect of nature conveys "the laws of right and wrong."

Literary Device

Nature thus forms the proper basis for religion and ethics. Moreover, the uses of particular facets of nature as described in "Commodity" do not exhaust the lessons these aspects can teach; men may progress to perception of their higher meaning as well. Emerson depicts moral law as lying at the center of the circle of nature and radiating to the circumference. He asserts that man is particularly susceptible to the moral meaning of nature, and returns to the unity of all of nature's particulars. Each object is a microcosm of the universe. Through analogies and resemblances between various expressions of nature, we perceive "its source in Universal Spirit." Moreover, we apprehend universal order through thought—through our grasp of the relationship between particular universal truths, which are related to all other universal truths. Emerson builds upon his circle imagery to suggest the all-encompassing quality of universal truth and the way it may be approached through all of its particulars. Unity is even more apparent in action than in thought, which is expressed only imperfectly through language. Action, on the other hand, as "the perfection and publication of thought," expresses thought more directly. Because words and conscious actions are uniquely human attributes, Emerson holds humanity up as the pinnacle of nature, "incomparably the richest informations of the power and order that lie at the heart of things." Each human example is a point of access into the universal spirit. As an expression of nature, humanity, too, has its educational use in the progression toward understanding higher truth.

At the beginning of Chapter VI, "Idealism," Emerson questions whether nature actually exists, whether God may have created it only as a perception in the human mind. Having stated that the response to this question makes no difference in the usefulness of nature as an aid to human comprehension of the universal, Emerson concludes that the answer is ultimately unknowable. Whether real or not, he perceives nature as an ideal. Even if nature is not real, natural and universal laws nevertheless apply. However, the common man's faith in the permanence of natural laws is threatened by any hint that nature may not be real. The senses and rational understanding contribute to the instinctive human tendency to regard nature as a reality. Men tend to view things as ultimates, not to look for a higher reality beyond them. But intuitive reason works against the unquestioned acceptance of concrete reality as the ultimate reality. Intuition counteracts sensory knowledge, and highlights our intellectual and spiritual separateness from nature. As the intuition is increasingly awakened, we begin to perceive nature differently, to see the whole, the "causes and spirits," instead of individual forms.

Emerson explores idealism at length. He first points out that a change in perspective is caused by changes in environment or mechanical alterations (such as viewing a familiar landscape from a moving railroad car), which heighten the sense of the difference between man and nature, the observer and the observed. Altered perspective imparts a feeling that there is something constant within man, even though the world around him changes, sometimes due to his own action upon it. Emerson then discusses the way in which the poet communicates his own power over nature. The poet sees nature as fluid and malleable, as raw material to shape to his own expressive purposes. Inspired by intuition and imagination, he enhances and reduces facets of nature according to his creative dictates. He provides an ideal interpretation of nature that is more real than concrete nature, as it exists independent of human agency. The poet, in short, asserts "the predominance of the soul" over matter. Emerson looks to philosophy, science, religion, and ethics for support of the subordination of matter to spirit. He does not uniformly approve of the position assigned to nature by each of these disciplines, but nevertheless finds that they all express an idealistic approach to one degree or another. He points out that although the poet aims toward beauty and the philosopher toward truth, both subject the order and relations within nature to human thought in order to find higher absolutes, laws, and spiritual realities. Scientists, too, may elevate the spiritual over the material in going beyond the accumulation of particulars to a single, encompassing, enlightening formula. And although they distrust nature, traditional religion and ethics also promote the spiritual and moral over the physical. In "Idealism," Emerson again takes up the capacity of all men to grasp the ideal and universal. Intellectual inquiry casts doubt upon the independent existence of matter and focuses upon the absolute and ideal as a higher reality. It encourages approaching nature as "an appendix to the soul" and a means of access to God. Although these complex ideas are expressed by specialists in "intellectual science," they are nevertheless available to all. And when any man reaches some understanding of divinity, he becomes more divine and renews himself physically as well as spiritually. Knowledge of the ideal and absolute brings confidence in our existence, and confers a kind of immortality, which transcends the limitations of space and time.

Emerson points out that in the quest for the ideal, it does not serve man to take a demeaning view of nature. He suggests nature's subservience merely to define its true position in relation to man, as a tool for spiritual education and perfection (as discussed in "Discipline"), and to distinguish the real (that is, the ideal) from the unreal (the concretely apparent). He concludes the chapter by advocating the ideal theory of nature over more popular materialism because it offers exactly the kind of view of the world that the human mind craves and intuitively wants to adopt. It subordinates matter to mind, places the world in the context of God, and allows man to synthesize a mass of details into a whole.

Emerson deals with nature's spiritual qualities and purpose in Chapter VII, "Spirit." He states that a true theory of nature and man must allow progressive, dynamic comprehension. In its fidelity to its divine origin and its constant illumination of spirit and of the absolute, nature allows satisfaction of this condition. Emerson writes of the difficulty of visualizing and expressing the divine spirit. The noblest use of nature is to help us by representing God, by serving as the medium "through which the universal spirit speaks to the individual, and strives to lead the individual back to it." Emerson then addresses three questions: What is matter?; Where does it come from?; and What is its purpose?

The first question—What is matter?—is answered by idealism, which holds that matter is a phenomenon (in Kantian philosophy, something that appears to the mind independently of its existence outside the mind) rather than a substance. This theory both underscores the difference between the incontrovertible evidence of human existence in the intellect and the questionable existence of nature as a distinct reality outside the mind, and at the same time allows us to explain nature in terms other than purely physical. But it is not enough to say that nature does not have independent existence. The divine spirit and human perception must also form part of the equation. Emerson adds that the very importance of the action of the human mind on nature distances us from the natural world and leaves us unable to explain our sympathy with it. He then turns to the questions of where matter comes from, and to what end. He refers to the "universal essence," an all-encompassing creative life force, which God expresses in nature as it is passed through and invigorates man. Man's capabilities are unlimited in proportion to his openness to nature's revelatory and transforming properties. Nature affords access to the very mind of God and thus renders man "the creator in the finite." The world is thus explained as proceeding from the divine, just as man does. Emerson describes it as "a remoter and inferior incarnation of God, a projection of God in the unconscious." Nature possesses a serenity and order that man appreciates. His closeness to God is related to his appreciation of and sympathy with nature. Emerson closes the chapter by referring to the difficulty of reconciling the practical uses of nature, as outlined in "Commodity," with its higher spiritual meaning.

In "Prospects," the eighth and final chapter of *Nature*, Emerson promotes intuitive reason as the means of gaining insight into the order and laws of the universe. Empirical science hinders true perception by focusing too much on particulars and too little on the broader picture. "Untaught sallies of the spirit" advance the learned naturalist farther than does precise analysis of detail. A guess or a dream may be more productive than a fact or a scientific experiment. The scientist fails to see the unifying principles behind the bewildering abundance of natural expressions, to address the ultimately spiritual purpose of this rich diversity, to recognize man's position as "head and heart" of the natural world. Emerson points out that men now only apply rational understanding to nature, which is consequently perceived materially. But we would do better to trust in intuitive reason, which allows revelation and insight. He cites examples of intuition working in man (Jesus Christ, Swedenborg, and the Shakers among them), which provide evidence of the power of intuition to transcend time and space. Emerson refers to the knowledge of God as *matutina cognitio*—morning knowledge. He identifies the imbalance created by man's loss of an earlier sense of the spiritual meaning and purpose of nature. By restoring spirituality to our approach to nature, we will attain that sense of universal unity currently lacking. If we reunite spirit with nature, and use all our faculties, we will see the miraculous in common things and will perceive higher law. Facts will be transformed into true poetry. While we ponder abstract questions intellectually, nature will provide other means of answering them. Emerson concludes *Nature* optimistically and affirmatively. He asserts that we will come to look at the world with new eyes. Nature imbued with spirit will be fluid and dynamic. The world exists for each man, the humble as well as the great. As we idealize and spiritualize, evil and squalor will disappear, beauty and nobility will reign. Man will enter the kingdom of his own dominion over nature with wonder.

Major Themes

Accessibility of Universal Understanding. *Nature* expresses Emerson's belief that each individual must develop a personal understanding of the universe. Emerson makes clear in the Introduction that men should break away from reliance on secondhand information, upon the wisdom of the past, upon inherited and institutionalized knowledge:

> Our age is retrospective. It builds the sepulchres of the fathers. It writes biographies, histories, and criticism. The foregoing generations beheld God and nature face to face; we, through their eyes. Why should not we also enjoy an original relation to the universe? Why should not we have a poetry and philosophy of insight and not of tradition, and a religion by revelation to us, and not the history of theirs?

According to Emerson, people in the past had an intimate and immediate relationship with God and nature, and arrived at their own understanding of the universe. All the basic elements that they required to do so exist at every moment in time. Emerson continues in the Introduction, "The sun shines to-day also. There is more wool and flax in the fields. There are new lands, new men, new thoughts. Let us demand our own works and laws and worship."

Emerson's rejection of received wisdom is reinforced by his repeated references throughout *Nature* to perception of familiar things, to seeing things anew. For Emerson (and for Thoreau as well), each moment provides an opportunity to learn from nature and to approach an understanding of universal order through it. The importance of the present moment, of spontaneous and dynamic interactions with the universe, of the possibilities of the here and now, render past observations and schemes irrelevant. Emerson focuses on the accessibility of the laws of the universe to every individual through a combination of nature and his own inner processes. In "Language," for example, he states that the relation between spirit and matter "is not fancied by some poet, but stands in the will of God, and so is free to be known by all men." In his discussion of "intellectual science" in "Idealism," he writes that "all men are capable of being raised by piety or by passion" into higher realms of thought. And at the end of the essay, in "Prospects," he exhorts, "Know then, that the world exists for you. For you is the phenomenon perfect." Each man is capable of using the natural world to achieve spiritual understanding. Just as men in the past explored universal relations for themselves, so may each of us, great and small, in the present: "All that Adam had, all that Caesar could, you have and can do."

In "Discipline," Emerson discusses the ways in which each man may understand nature and God—through rational, logical "Understanding" and through intuitive "Reason." Although the mystical, revelatory intuition leads to the highest spiritual truth, understanding, too, is useful in gaining a particular kind of knowledge. But whichever mental process illuminates a given object of attention at a given time, insight into universal order always takes place in the mind of the individual, through his own experience of nature and inner powers of receptiveness.

Theme

Unity of God, Man, and Nature. Throughout *Nature*, Emerson calls for a vision of the universe as an all-encompassing whole, embracing man and nature, matter and spirit, as interrelated expressions of God. This unity is referred to as the Oversoul elsewhere in Emerson's writings. The purpose of the new, direct understanding of nature that he advocates in the essay is, ultimately, the perception of the totality of the universal whole. At present, Emerson suggests, we have a fragmented view of the world. We cannot perceive our proper place in it because we have lost a sense of the unifying spiritual element that forms the common bond between the divine, the human, and the material. But if we approach nature properly, we may transcend our current focus on isolated parts and gain insight into the whole. Emerson does not offer a comprehensive scheme of the components and workings of God's creation. Instead, he recommends an approach by which we may each arrive at our own vision of totality.

Emerson asserts and reasserts the underlying unity of distinct, particulate expressions of the divine. In the Introduction, he emphasizes man's and nature's parallel positions as manifestations of the universal order, and consequently as means of understanding that order. He elaborates upon the origins in God of both man and nature in "Discipline," in which he discusses evidence of essential unity in the similarities between various natural objects and between the various laws that govern them:

> Each creature is only a modification of the other; the likeness in them is more than the difference, and their radical law is one and the same. Hence it is, that a rule of one art, or a law of one organization, holds true throughout nature. So intimate is this Unity, that, it is easily seen, it

lies under the undermost garment of nature, and betrays its source in universal Spirit.

Our striving to comprehend nature more spiritually will illuminate natural order and the relationships within it as manifestations of God. In "Idealism," Emerson stresses the advantages of the ideal theory of nature (the approach to nature as a projection by God onto the human mind rather than as a concrete reality). Idealism makes God an integral element in our understanding of nature, and provides a comprehensively inclusive view:

> Idealism sees the world in God. It beholds the whole circle of persons and things, of actions and events, of country and religion, not as painfully accumulated, atom after atom, act after act, in an aged creeping Past, but as one vast picture, which God paints on the instant eternity, for the contemplation of the soul.

Spiritualization, hastened by inspired insight, will heal the fragmentization that plagues us. Emerson writes in "Prospects": "The reason why the world lacks unity, and lies broken and in heaps, is because man is disunited with himself. He cannot be a naturalist, until he satisfies all the demands of the spirit." By drawing upon our latent spiritual capabilities and seeking evidence of God's order in nature, we will make sense of the universe.

Throughout *Nature*, Emerson uses analogy and imagery to advance the conceptof universal unity. In Chapter I, he suggests, through the analogy of the landscape, the transformation of particulate information into a whole. Regarded from a transcendent, "poetical" point of view, the many individual forms that comprise the landscape become less distinct and form an integrated totality. (In addition to the poet, the painter, the sculptor, the musician, and the architect are all particularly sensitive to perceiving wholes.)

Emerson also uses the imagery of the circle extensively to convey the all-encompassing, perfect self-containment of the universe. For example, in "Beauty," he describes the way in which the structure of the eye and the laws of light conspire to create perspective:

> By the mutual action of [the eye's] structure and of the laws of light, perspective is produced, which integrates every mass of objects, of what character soever, into a well colored and shaded globe, so that where the particular

objects are mean and unaffecting, the landscape which they compose, is round and symmetrical.

In discussing the similarities between natural objects and between natural laws in "Discipline," Emerson reiterates and expands the image, making it more complex and comprehensive:

> It is like a great circle on a sphere, comprising all possible circles; which, however, may be drawn, and comprise it, in like manner. Every such truth is the absolute Ens [that is, being or entity] seen from one side. But it has innumerable sides.

The circle is thus not only all-encompassing, but allows multiple approaches to the whole.

Emerson develops the idea of each particle of nature as a microcosm reflecting the whole, and as such a point of access to the universal. In "Discipline," he writes of "the Unity of Nature,—the Unity in Variety," and goes on to state:

> . . . a leaf, a drop, a crystal, a moment of time is related to the whole, and partakes of the perfection of the whole. Each particle is a microcosm, and faithfully renders the likeness of the world.

The idea of microcosm is important in Emerson's approach to nature, as it is in Thoreau's. Because the parts represent the whole in miniature, it is consequently not necessary to see all of the parts to understand the whole. Through an insight akin to revelation, man may understand the "big picture" from just one example in nature. We need not be slaves to detail to understand the meaning that detail conveys.

Theme

Reason and Understanding. From the beginning to the end of *Nature*, Emerson stresses the particular importance of the intuitive type of comprehension, which he calls "Reason," in the terminology of English Romantic poetry. Reason is required to penetrate the universal laws and the divine mind. At the beginning of the Introduction, he calls for "a poetry and philosophy of insight" and "a religion by revelation"—his first references to intuition in the essay. Kantian "Reason" is linked with spiritual truth, Lockean "Understanding" with the laws of nature. Because *Nature* is a kind of manual for spiritualization, Reason holds a higher place in it than Understanding. Although Understanding is essential for the perception of material laws and in its application promotes a progressively broader vision, it does not by itself lead man to God.

In "Beauty," "Language," and "Discipline," Emerson examines Reason's revelation to man of the larger picture behind the multiplicity of details in the material world. In "Beauty," he describes the stimulation of the human intellect by natural beauty. He offers artistic creativity as the extreme love of and response to natural beauty. Art is developed in the essay as an insightful synthesis of parts into a whole, as are such other expressions of human creativity as poetry and architecture. The intuitively inspired formation of this sense of wholeness is similar to the comprehension of universal law, the ultimate goal advocated in *Nature*. In "Language," he describes the symbolism of original language as based on natural fact, and the integral relationship between language, nature, and spirit. He identifies Reason as the faculty that provides apprehension of spirit through natural symbols, and connects spirit with the universal soul itself:

> Man is conscious of a universal soul within or behind his individual life. . . . This universal soul, he calls Reason: it is not mine or thine or his, but we are its; we are its property and men. And the blue sky in which the private earth is buried, the sky with its eternal calm, and full of everlasting orbs, is the type of Reason. That which, intellectually considered, we call Reason, considered in relation to nature, we call Spirit. Spirit is the Creator. Spirit hath life in itself. And man in all ages and countries, embodies it in his language. . . .

Reason, which imparts both vision into the absolute and also creative force as well, is thus presented more as God's reaching out into man than as an active capacity solely within man.

In "Prospects," Emerson implores his readers to trust in Reason as a means of approaching universal truth. He writes of *matutina cognitio*—morning knowledge—as the knowledge of God, as opposed to *vespertina cognitio*—evening knowledge, or the knowledge of man. (This concept of morning knowledge is echoed in Thoreau's writings in the heightened awareness that Thoreau presents in connection with the morning hours. It is a spiritual, enhanced, spontaneous insight into higher truth.) In "Prospects," Emerson puts forward examples of intuition at work—the "traditions of miracles," the life of Jesus, transforming action based on principle (such as the abolition of slavery), the "miracles of enthusiasm, as those . . . of Swedenborg, Hohenlohe, and the Shakers," "animal magnetism" (hypnosis), "prayer; eloquence; self-healing; and the wisdom of children." These examples make evident the "instantaneous in-streaming causing power" that constitutes Reason.

Emerson explores at length the difference between Understanding and Reason. Both serve to instruct man. However, Understanding is tied to matter and leads to common sense rather than to the broadest vision. Emerson grants that as man advances in his grasp of natural laws, he comes closer to understanding the laws of creation. But Reason is essential to transport man out of the material world into the spiritual. In "Idealism," Emerson asserts that intuition works against acceptance of concrete reality as ultimate reality, thereby promoting spiritualization.

In "Spirit," Emerson presents the notion of the mystical and intuitively understood "universal essence" (a potent, comprehensive life force) which, expressed in man through nature's agency, confers tremendous power:

> Who can set bounds to the possibilities of man? Once
> inhale the upper air, being admitted to behold the absolute
> natures of justice and truth, and we learn that man has
> access to the entire mind of the Creator, is himself the
> creator in the finite.

Reason provides perception of God's creation and a direct link with God, and reinforces the divine within man. It bestows on man an exalted status in the world. And man's identification with God, his elevation through vision, underlies Emerson's sense of nature as a tool for human development. Man is second only to God in the universal scheme. The material world exists for him.

Theme

Relationship of Man and Nature. Both man and nature are expressions of the divine, Emerson declares in *Nature*. Man, in his physical existence, is a part of the material world. But throughout the essay, Emerson refers to man's separateness from nature through his intellectual and spiritual capacities. Man and nature share a special relationship. Each is essential to understanding the other. However, Emerson makes clear that man enjoys the superior position. In his higher abilities, he represents an endpoint of evolution. Moreover, man has particular powers over nature. Nature was made to serve man's physical and, more significantly, intellectual and spiritual needs.

In the poem with which Emerson prefaced the 1849 second edition of *Nature*, man's place as a developmental pinnacle is conveyed in the lines, "And, striving to be man, the worm / Mounts through all the spires of form." In "Language," he emphasizes the centrality of man, conferred by the inner qualities of mind and spirit

> . . . man is an analogist, and studies relations in all objects. He is placed in the centre of beings, and a ray of relation passes from every other being to him. And neither can man be understood without these objects, nor these objects without man.

Man's ascendancy over nature is powerfully expressed in the final passage of the essay:

> The kingdom of man over nature, which cometh not with observation,—a dominion such as now is beyond his dream of God,—he shall enter without more wonder than the blind man feels who is gradually restored to perfect sight.

Indeed, although Transcendentalism is sometimes perceived as a simple celebration of nature, the relationship that Emerson and other Transcendentalists suggested was considerably more complex.

In Chapter I, Emerson describes nature's elevation of man's mood, and the particular sympathy with and joy in nature that man feels. But he adds that nature by itself is not capable of producing human reaction. It requires man's inner processes to become meaningful: "Yet it is certain that the power to produce this delight, does not reside in nature, but in man, or in a harmony of both." And in "Beauty," focusing on nature's existence to satisfy man's need for beauty, he states that nature is not in and of itself a final end:

> But beauty in nature is not ultimate. It is the herald of inward and eternal beauty, and is not alone a solid and satisfactory good. It must therefore stand as a part and not as yet the last or highest expression of the final cause of Nature.

Nature's meaning resides in its role as a medium of communication between God and man.

Emerson stresses throughout *Nature* that nature exists to serve man, and explains the ways in which it does so. In "Commodity," he enumerates the basic material uses of nature by man. He then goes on to point out the fact that man harnesses nature to enhance its material usefulness. In "Beauty," Emerson discusses the power of natural beauty to restore man when exhausted, to give him simple pleasure, to provide a suitable backdrop to his glorious deeds, and to stimulate his intellect, which may ultimately lead him to understand universal order. Man's artistic expression is inspired by the perception and translation in his mind of the beauty of nature.

In "Language," Emerson details language's uses as a vehicle of thought and, ultimately, through its symbolism and the symbolism of the things it stands for, as an aid to comprehension and articulation of spiritual as well as material truth. A person effectively expresses himself, Emerson notes, in proportion to the natural vigor of his language. Nature both exists for and intensifies man's capabilities.

In "Discipline," he introduces human will, which, working through the intellect, emphasizes aspects of nature that the mind requires and disregards those that the mind does not need. Thus man imposes himself on nature, makes it what he wants it to be. Emerson writes,

> Nature is thoroughly mediate. It is made to serve. It receives the dominion of man as meekly as the ass on which the Saviour rode. It offers all its kingdoms to man as the material which he may mould into what is useful.

Emerson develops this idea in "Idealism," in discussing the poet's elevation of soul over matter in "subordinating nature for the purpose of expression"—giving emphasis and drawing connections as suits the message he wishes to convey. Nature is thus "fluid," "ductile and flexible," changeable by man.

Theme

Matter and Spirit. Emerson asserts throughout *Nature* the primacy of spirit over matter. Nature's purpose is as a representation of the divine to promote human insight into the laws of the universe, and thus to bring man closer to God. Emerson writes of nature in "Spirit" as "the organ through which the universal spirit speaks to the individual, and strives to lead back the individual to it." He explores the relationship between matter and spirit extensively in "Language," in which he discusses the correspondence between material and moral laws, and in "Idealism," in which he presents the concept of nature as a projection by God on the human mind, as opposed to a concrete reality.

Emerson's discussion in "Language" is based on three premises: that words—even those used to describe intellectual or spiritual states—originated in nature, in an elemental interaction between mind and matter; that not only do words represent nature, but, because nature is an expression of the divine, the natural facts that words represent are symbolic of spiritual truth; and that the whole of nature—not just individual natural facts—symbolizes the whole of spiritual truth. Emerson writes,

> The world is emblematic. Parts of speech are metaphors
> because the whole of nature is a metaphor of the human
> mind. The laws of moral nature answer to those of mat-
> ter as face to face in a glass.

Because the laws of the material world correspond to higher laws in the
spiritual world, man may "by degrees" comprehend the universal
through his familiarity with its expression in nature. Emerson states that
the symbolism of matter renders "every form significant to its hidden
life and final cause." Moral law, as he suggests in "Discipline," "lies at
the centre of nature and radiates to the circumference." At the end of
"Language," Emerson works toward the ideal theory in presenting all
the particulars of nature as preexisting "in necessary Ideas in the mind
of God, and are what they are by preceding affections, in the world of
spirit." He writes that a fact is "the end or last issue of spirit. The visible creation is the terminus or the circumference of the invisible world."
Matter thus issues from and is secondary to spirit.

In "Idealism" and "Spirit," Emerson takes a philosophical leap in
asking whether nature exists separately, or whether it is only an image
created in man's mind by God. Although he says that the answer cannot be known, and that it makes no difference in man's use of nature,
he suggests that idealism is preferable to viewing nature as concrete reality because it constitutes "that view which is most desirable to the
mind." Emerson supports the ideal theory by pointing to the ways in
which poetry, philosophy, science, religion, and ethics subordinate matter to higher truth. But he also acknowledges that idealism is hard to
accept from the commonsensical point of view—the view of those who
trust in rationality over intuition. "The broker, the wheelwright, the
carpenter, the toll-man, are much displeased at the intimation," he
writes at the beginning of "Idealism." Correspondence provides a bridge
between matter and spirit. In denying the actual existence of matter,
idealism goes much farther.

In various ways in *Nature*, Emerson appears to suggest that the natural world does, in fact, exist separately from spirit. For instance, he carefully distinguishes between man's inner qualities and his physical
existence, between the "ME" and the "NOT ME," which includes one's
own body. His progressive argument is marred by this seeming contradiction, and by his hesitancy to state outright that nature is an ideal, even
while he discusses it as such. He only goes so far as to say that idealism
offers a satisfactory way of looking at nature. But he does not want to
sidetrack his reader by attempting to prove that which cannot be proven.

Emerson concludes the essay by asking his readers to open themselves to spiritual reality by trusting in intuitive reason. He writes,

> . . . there are far more excellent qualities in the student than preciseness and infallibility; . . . a guess is often more fruitful than an indisputable affirmation, and . . . a dream may let us deeper into the secret of nature than a hundred concerted experiments.

Through receptivity to intuition, we may rise above narrow common sense and transcend preoccupation with material fact per se.

"The Divinity School Address"

Emerson delivered "The Divinity School Address" at Harvard on July 15, 1838, by invitation. The address was first published in August 1838, by James Munroe, in an edition of 1,000 copies, which sold quickly. It first appeared in England as part of the collection *Orations, Lectures, and Addresses* (London: H.G. Clarke) in 1844, and was included in *Nature; Addresses, and Lectures* (later titled *Miscellanies; Embracing Nature, Addresses, and Lectures*), published in Boston by Munroe in 1849. It was included in 1876 in the first volume (*Miscellanies*) of the Little Classic Edition of Emerson's writings; in 1883 in the first volume (*Nature, Addresses, and Lectures*) of the Riverside Edition; in 1903 in the first volume (*Nature, Addresses, and Lectures*) of the Centenary Edition; and in 1971 in the first volume (*Nature, Addresses, and Lectures*) of the Harvard-published *Collected Works*. A Danish edition of the address appeared in 1856, the first separate English edition in 1903. The Unity Publishing Company issued it in 1884, and reprinted it many times. The American Unitarian Association published editions of it in 1907 and 1938. "The Divinity School Address" has been printed in numerous popular collections of Emerson's writings, among them the 1940 Modern Library *The Complete Essays and Other Writings of Ralph Waldo Emerson* (edited by Brooks Atkinson), the 1946 *The Portable Emerson* (edited by Mark Van Doren), the 1965 Signet Classic *Selected Writings of Ralph Waldo Emerson* (edited by William H. Gilman), and the 1983 Library of America *Essays & Lectures* (selected and annotated by Joel Porte).

Synopsis

Emerson draws upon the physical reality of the present moment in opening "The Divinity School Address." He describes the lushness of nature in high summer (the address was delivered in the middle of July) and acknowledges the perfect loveliness of the physical world. Man under the summer stars is like a young child, and the world is his toy. But Emerson quickly turns away from the material and takes up universal laws, which dwarf the significance of nature's beauty and prompt questions about the world and its order. He proceeds to answer these questions in the first part of the address by reiterating ideas developed at length in *Nature*, thus laying the groundwork for what he will say about the state of religion at the current time."

A beauty more "secret, sweet, and overpowering" than that of nature is apparent when man opens himself to "the sentiment of virtue." Man then sees the divine and universal that encompass his existence, and knows that his place in the larger picture assures him a limitless capacity for goodness. When man strives to apprehend the absolutes of right, truth, and virtue, he is in harmony with God's creation of the universe for that very purpose, and he pleases God. The "sentiment of virtue" is identified as "reverence and delight in the presence of certain divine laws," which are revealed through experience of the world and through life. Universal laws cannot be fully envisioned or articulated, but are evident in our character and actions. The "sentiment of virtue" is at the heart of religion.

Emerson holds up intuition as the means of perceiving the laws of the soul, which are timeless and absolute, not subject to current values and circumstances. Goodness and evil are instantly rewarded or punished in the enlargement or diminishment of the man who practices them—external reward and punishment are beside the point. Man *is* God to the degree that he is inwardly virtuous. In subordinating himself to the expression of the divine virtue that speaks through him, he knows himself and realizes his capabilities. As he does so, he acts in accordance with the workings of the universe, and his efforts to understand and exercise virtue are reinforced. Emerson asserts that the human soul, in its ability to elevate itself, has the power to determine whether it will go to heaven or hell—that is, there is nothing predetermined about the ultimate fate of the soul. All of this is true because of the unity of man and nature in the divine mind (the , although here, as in *Nature*, Emerson does not so refer to it). Because the divine is intrinsically perfect, Emerson suggests, goodness is real, while evil—the absence of goodness—is not an absolute quality in and of itself. Goodness is identified with life; evil, with death. In straying from goodness, a man progressively loses his connection with the divine, is diminished, and—from a universal point of view, if not physically—ceases to exist.

The religious sentiment brings joy and makes sense of the world for us, empowers and deifies us. Through the religious sentiment, a man understands that goodness is within him, that he and every other man enjoys a direct relationship with God through intuitive Reason, and that virtue cannot be attained by emulating other men. All of society's forms of worship—Oriental as well as western—were founded on an original direct understanding of God by man. Emerson emphasizes the importance of intuition to the individual in achieving the religious sentiment, stating that it cannot be received "at second hand," and stresses that the process takes place through inspiration or revelation rather than learning. If religion is not based on this intuitive individual connection with the divine, the church is meaningless, man's importance is reduced, and the inner drive to achieve the true religious sentiment is perverted into rejection of a direct relationship with God. "Miracles, prophecy, poetry, the ideal life, the holy life" then are present through religion only historically, in its ancient intuitive origin, but not as it currently exists. Emerson points to the established Christian church as an illustration of this decline of religion from what it was and should be."

Jesus, Emerson declares, "belonged to the true race of prophets." He saw and lived the inherent relationship between God and man, perceived the human soul as the outlet of the universal soul, and consequently accorded man his proper greatness. In his life, he demonstrated the agency of God through men. But the example of Jesus has been misused by the church, which quickly came to deny his humanity and to focus upon "the idioms of his language, and the figures of his rhetoric" instead. The church has offered false miracles in place of the miracles of human life that Jesus himself recognized, and it has replaced inner perception of truth and goodness with externally imposed commandments.

Emerson then explores two errors in the administration of Christianity as an institution. Firstly, rather than promoting the doctrine of the soul as it applies to all, Christianity raises Jesus up above other men. The soul "knows no persons," Emerson writes, but indiscriminately invites each man "to expand to the full circle of the universe." Jesus has been made into a kind of eastern monarch, his name associated with official, formal titles that obscure his original position as "friend of man." If we accept this view of Jesus and subordinate our own importance to his, we do not recognize our ability also to enter into the divine. The approach that takes God out of man weakens man; that which reveals God within strengthens man. If God is not within, then there is no reason for man's existence, and he will "decease forever." Jesus and the prophets—the "divine bards"—only serve to remind us that our intuitions of the divine do not emanate from us, but from God. Ordinary men tend to exaggerate the importance of a "great and rich soul" like Jesus, and not to see that they themselves can elevate by "coming again to themselves, or to God in themselves." Emerson points out that the current "vulgar tone of preaching" denigrates Jesus as much as it does the rest of mankind. It isolates Jesus and discounts the warmth and vigor that characterized his life and words.

Secondly, Emerson examines the failure of traditional Christianity to acknowledge as its source "Moral Nature, that Law of laws, whose revelations introduce greatness,—yea, God himself, into the open soul." Consequently, men think that revelation happened long ago, once and for all, "as if God were dead," instead of being always possible for every individual. This belief makes it difficult for the minister to preach with meaning and to offer inspiration. Because he is obliged to preach a religion that has been formalized and codified, he cannot preach the primacy of the soul. Because "the seer is a sayer," the minister's words do not satisfy his own inner (although sometimes unrecognized) need to impart vision of the "beauty of the soul" to others; nor do they satisfy the innate craving of the members of his congregation to realize their own personal connection to God.

Emerson deplores the death of faith and the lifelessness of the church, and he urges his audience of new preachers embarking upon pastoral careers to restore truth, the soul, and intuitive revelation to the church. The barrenness of inherited religion must be acknowledged, and ministers must accept their true and exalted function. The preacher's particular office is to express the applicability of the moral sentiment to the duties of life, to help his parishioners relate the ideal to experience. Emerson laments how infrequently the preacher helps man to see "that he is an infinite Soul; that the earth and heavens are passing into his mind; that he is drinking forever the soul of God," and points out that we ourselves, sitting in church on Sunday, come to a better understanding of God than the preacher offers. Religious formalism leaves us empty. The preacher who does not convey his own humanity and the truth that he has gleaned from life says nothing that we need to hear.

But people so want to enlarge their sense of the moral sentiment that they still go to church. The "good hearer" takes what he can from bad sermons by finding in them echoes of more inspiring words he has heard and thoughts he has had at other times. People put up with preaching that does not acknowledge the soul, because the stale doctrines preached were all once intuitively inspired and preserve some of the vigor imparted by their origins. The minister is on some level aware of the lack of truth and life in what he preaches, and he suspects that he falls short of fulfilling his duty. He cannot even invite men to the Lord's Supper in good conscience, because he is unable to bring warmth to this rite, the "hollow, dry, creaking formality" of which is "too plain."

Emerson states that there are ministers who bring life to public worship. The exceptions, he says, are found not so much in the examples of a few extraordinary preachers as in the rare sincere moments of all. But by and large, preaching is hindered by tradition, by lack of a sense of the essentials of true religion—the soul, and the absolutes toward which the soul strives. By ignoring man's moral nature, historical Christianity destroys the power of preaching, takes the joy out of religion, and invalidates the very reason for the ministry's existence. The results are devastating—"the soul of the community is sick and faithless," man despises himself, and fails to achieve the goodness of which he is capable. People are leaving the church in droves. The loss of worship is the worst of all possible calamities

Emerson then asks what can be done to redeem the church. He calls on the fledgling ministers in his audience to recognize and preach the importance of the soul, thereby restoring man to his place of importance, and to combat the notion that religion is static and must be accepted as received. He asks them not to fear the presentation of Jesus as a man, and he urges them to show what God is, not what God was to other men. Emerson says that true Christianity—a faith like Christ's in the boundless capabilities of man—has been lost through our tendency to trust in established schemes of religion rather than in the power of the individual soul. Only the soul can restore to man a sense of the divine within himself. He exhorts his hearers "to go alone; to refuse the good models, . . . and dare to love God without mediator or veil," and in so doing to inspire their congregations to break from conformity. If ministers "acquaint men at first hand with Deity," their flocks will respond with love and gratitude. Society does not encourage development of the "absolute ability and worth" of every person, but after we form a direct connection with God, "the all-knowing Spirit," we will not care about society's values, which preoccupy us only as much as we allow them to. We must be independent of the opinions of others and draw upon the resources within ourselves, regardless of consequences. Emerson does not recommend establishing new rites and forms, but rather breathing life back into those already in existence. If we are fully alive with soul, the forms of worship that we employ will become "plastic and new." Emerson pays homage to two traditions that Christianity has provided, the Sabbath and the institution of preaching. Both will become meaningful again if life and conscience are restored to religion.

Emerson closes "The Divinity School Address" by looking to the time when the spirit that inspired the prophets of old will move men in the present, and bring forth "the new Teacher" who can see the universe and its laws in totality, the world as "mirror of the soul," and who can show the correspondence of natural laws with spiritual laws and the ultimate oneness of all absolutes.

Major Themes

Theme

Man as Outlet to the Divine. Emerson bases all that he says to the graduating class of Harvard Divinity School upon the intimate relationship between man and God earlier put forth in *Nature*. At the beginning of the address, he introduces the unity of God, man, and nature that he elsewhere terms the Oversoul, and he refers to this unity throughout. He stresses that a true sense of religion, indeed the very soundness of the individual and of society, are impossible to achieve unless a man realizes his direct access to God and recognizes that religion and virtue are within, not imposed or understood from without. Man has no need for "mediator or veil" between himself and God. This immediate connection gives man his innate and unlimited capacity for development toward God's perfection. Man expresses his oneness with God through virtue in character and action. Emerson is very clear about man's inherent potential for good, and about how the state into which the church has fallen has obscured our perception of human perfectibility: "[Man] learns that his being is without bound; that, to the good, to the perfect, he is born, low as he now lies in evil and weakness. That which he venerates is still his own, though he has not realized it yet." "The Divinity School Address" is Emerson's response to what he sees as a widespread crisis of faith caused by man's disconnection from the source of his powers.

Scholars and critics have frequently commented upon the view of evil expressed in the address. Emerson declares that God is perfection, and that, through his connection to God, man is perfectible. Goodness, and the reward of goodness, are within man, who therefore does not require external structures to ensure his virtue. All of the world exudes a kind of sympathetic support of man's goodness, because it is in harmony with the laws of the universe. Likewise, when a man deviates from the virtue to which God and the universal laws predispose him, he is instantly aware of disharmony within himself and with the universe, and evil is consequently its own punishment. Emerson goes on to state that, unlike good, which is a positive, absolute quality, evil does not have independent existence. It is "merely privative, not absolute"— nothing more than the absence of goodness. This sense of the relationship between good and evil departs radically from that offered by traditional religion. It presents a consummately affirmative outlook on human nature and possibility. However, some critics have found it one of the less convincing aspects of Emerson's philosophy.

Emerson emphasizes that a direct connection with God is available to and exemplified in each and every person. This belief guides his discussion of the nature and importance of Jesus, whom he regards as a man, and as the highest demonstration of the expression of the divine spirit through the life and actions of a man. Jesus serves as a model and a source of inspiration for other men, but he did not achieve anything beyond the capabilities of humankind in general. The church has held Jesus up as different from and superior to other men, and has focused excessively on "the person of Jesus"—that is, on the particular qualities that distinguish Jesus from other men—rather than on his inherent similarity to the rest of mankind. Emerson insists upon the complete equality of every man in regard to the knowledge of God: "The soul knows no persons. It invites every man to expand to the full circle of the universe, and will have no preferences but those of spontaneous love." Emerson sees the deification of Jesus as a disservice to man in general and to Jesus as well. Men cannot forge an understanding of the God within by emulating others, even such a powerful exemplar as Jesus. And Jesus loses humanity, warmth, and his true excellence when approached as "a demigod, as the Orientals or the Greeks would describe Osiris or Apollo." Jesus himself—"the only soul in history who has appreciated the worth of a man"—understood better than anyone the divine nature of mankind.

Theme

Inherited versus Intuited Religion. Throughout "The Divinity School Address," Emerson contrasts inherited religion—the religion handed down to man by the past—with the connection that each man may form with God directly. Inherited or "second hand" religion is presented as lifeless, empty of vitality and meaning, and stifling to the highest capabilities of man. Personal religion—man's intuitive grasp of his relationship with God—is full of warmth, vitality, and significance, and is experienced in the here and now. The individual's religious understanding—his "insight of the perfection of the laws of the soul"—constitutes a grasp of universal absolutes that transcend time, space, and temporal circumstance. Intuitive insight into divine laws is also timeless, possible at any given moment, independent of specific cultural values and conditions.

Emerson associates the church and its inherited traditions with "stationariness," with "the assumption that the age of inspiration is past, that the Bible is closed." In its institutionalization, the church has developed a fixed body of beliefs, dogmas, scriptures, and rites, which it offers as religion. This "petrification" has made us forget that these traditions originated in the distant past through intuition working on the religious and creative faculties of man. Whatever power and meaning they retain are vestiges of their archaic inspiration through intuitive Reason. At the end of the address, Emerson looks forward to the time when "that supreme Beauty, which ravished the souls of those Eastern men, and chiefly of those Hebrews, and through their lips spoke oracles to all time, shall speak in the West also." Spirit is eternal, but its revelation to man occurs over and over again, in each new generation and within each man. The religious sentiment about which Emerson writes flows continuously into man from God, is fluid and dynamic, and cannot be contained or transmitted in fixed form any more than the goodness of man can be compressed into particular examples of humanity.

Emerson carefully does not recommend that the individual apply his own intuitive apprehension of God to overthrowing the existing traditions of the church and to replacing them with new ones. He states, "I confess, all attempts to project and establish a Cultus with new rites and forms, seem to me vain. Faith makes us, and not we it, and faith makes its own forms." In religion as in other areas, Emerson is suspicious of external reform. He trusts in the reform of the individual as a means of reforming the institution of the church: "Rather let the breath of new life be breathed by you through the forms already existing. For, if once you are alive, you shall find they shall become plastic and new.

The remedy to their deformity is, first, soul, and second, soul, and evermore, soul." Rite and ritual are thus incidental and secondary. When the individual allows the spark of intuition to bring his own religious sense to life, the forms through which he expresses it will be enlivened as well. The prevalent failure of faith will be remedied only through each man's understanding of his own personal connection with God.

Theme

The Function of the Preacher. Emerson aims in "The Divinity School Address" to inspire his audience of new preachers to meet the currently unsatisfied spiritual needs of their future congregations. The codification of religion into fixed forms and beliefs has made their fulfillment of this responsibility difficult. Emerson declares, ". . . the Moral Nature, that Law of laws whose revelations introduce greatness,—yea, God himself, into the open soul, is not explored as the fountain of the established teaching in society." Men and their religious leaders no longer understand that revelation is always possible and also essential to their spirituality. They regard it as an isolated phenomenon that occurred in the past. It is the preacher's function to restore soul to his parishioners by encouraging intuitive spirituality and promoting an immediate relationship with God. Emerson emphasizes that only the minister who has experienced intuitive perception of God can preach it:

> The spirit only can teach. Not any profane man, not any sensual, not any liar, not any slave can teach, but only he can give, who has; he only can create, who is. The man on whom the soul descends, through whom the soul speaks, alone can teach.

Emerson laments the fact that the minister is frequently not such a man. In its failure to address all-encompassing soul as the first, central, necessary element of religion, the church has made worship joyless. If the minister likewise does not address the importance of spirit as the direct link between man and God, he not only neglects his true obligations, but is inwardly aware of his failure, and his congregation is profoundly dissatisfied. "Whenever the pulpit is usurped by a formalist," Emerson proclaims, "then is the worshipper defrauded and disconsolate." Conversely, when the minister is himself "a newborn bard of the Holy Ghost," he is able to reject conformity and to "acquaint men at first hand with Deity."

If a good preacher possesses divinely inspired spirit and values it above form, he must also have the ability to convey his own humanity to his flock. Emerson provides the specific example of a preacher so uninspired and uninspiring that he almost made his hearers (Emerson among them) wish to avoid church. (Emerson no doubt here indirectly refers to the Reverend Barzillai Frost, assistant minister and later minister of the First Parish in Concord.) In contrast with the raging snowstorm outside the church, this preacher lacked reality. He did not communicate that he, too, like the members of his congregation, was a man, that he had lived and experienced what they had lived and experienced. His sermon gave not a hint that "he had ever lived at all. Not a line did he draw out of real history." Emerson uses this example to underscore the key function of the preacher—bringing his parishioners to the realization of spirit. He asserts, "The true preacher can be known by this, that he deals out to the people his life,—life passed through the fire of thought." In so doing, the preacher offers his parishioners living proof that individual spirituality can coexist with and even thrive amidst the realities of experience. The minister's spirit and humanity together will infuse the dry rites of the church with relevance and meaning.

"Experience"

Emerson's essay "Experience" was first published without having been delivered as a lecture. It appeared in 1844 in his *Essays: Second Series* (published in Boston by James Munroe in October of 1844 and in London by John Chapman in November of 1844). *Essays: Second Series*, including "Experience," was issued in 1876 as the third volume of the Little Classic Edition of Emerson's writings, in 1886 as the third volume of the Riverside Edition, in 1906 as the third volume of the Centenary Edition, and in 1983 as the third volume of the *Collected Works* published by Harvard. The essay has been separately published, and also included in such collected editions as the 1940 Modern Library *The Complete Essays and Other Writings of Ralph Waldo Emerson* (edited by Brooks Atkinson), the 1965 Signet Classic *Selected Writings of Ralph Waldo Emerson* (edited by William H. Gilman), and the 1983 Library of America *Essays & Lectures* (selected and annotated by Joel Porte).

Synopsis

Emerson prefaces "Experience" with a poem describing the solemn procession of the "lords of life"—the forces that affect all men's experience of common life. God—the "inventor of the game"—is an unnamed presence in the poem. Man walks in confusion among the lords of life. He is comforted by nature, who assures him that the lords will "wear another face" tomorrow, and that his position is, in fact, one of ascendancy over them. In the essay, Emerson explores the action of these forces on the way we live and understand our lives.

The experience of life is confusing, Emerson writes at the beginning of the essay. Gaining perspective on life while we are engaged in living is difficult. This confusion affects our perception of our place in relation to nature, and of our powers. We are unable to see beyond our material existence and to utilize the creative vigor that nature has given us, and cannot distinguish between our productive and unproductive efforts. The distance created by time's passage sometimes reveals that what we thought were unoccupied hours were actually our most fruitful periods. Only in the long view do we understand the proper value of everyday occupations and actions. In taking the short view, we lose sight of the quality and significance of our lives in the present. Moreover, everyday details so preoccupy us that little time is left for more serious considerations. Emerson writes that "the pith of each man's genius contracts itself to a very few hours." As the history of literature contains only a few original ideas that have been worked and reworked, so the history of society reveals only a very few spontaneous human actions beyond "custom and gross sense." Although we attribute great importance to the calamities of life, they actually have no lasting meaning. Grief does not bring us any closer to the people we have lost, and it does not change who we are. Emerson refers specifically to his own grief at the death of his son Waldo in 1842. Grief cannot teach us anything, nor can it bring us closer to understanding the material world. Moreover, nature does not like to be observed and prevents us from focusing too clearly on objects that might offer insight through the material.

Emerson turns to the subject of perspective, and to the way temperament and mood—both parts of man's makeup—affect perspective. He writes of dream and illusion, and of how we see only what we are capable of seeing. Genius is useless if receptivity is limited by some temperamental trait that prevents "a focal distance within the actual horizon of human life." A man's talents cannot be effectively applied if he does not care sufficiently for higher truth to look for it, if he is overly sensitive, if he wants to reform but is not equal to the task. Mood even influences the ebb and flow of the religious sentiment, and temperament cannot be fully transcended by the moral sentiment. But "so-called sciences"—medicine and *phrenology* (the study of the size and shape of the skull to determine a man's character and abilities)—exaggerates temperamental limitations on human possibilities by suggesting that temperament is materially predetermined. Pseudoscience defines man by his physical traits and reduces inner qualities to the level of matter. Although temperament does color our perceptions and constrains our potential, the material approach to it discounts higher intuitive capabilities altogether and fails to recognize the direct, spontaneous transforming connection between God and the individual. Emerson summarily dismisses the approach.

Like temperament, man's need to move in succession from one object of focus to another—his disinclination to regard any one thing for too long—also influences his perception of experience and the world. Our innate love of absolutes draws us toward the permanent, but our human constitution requires "change of objects." After we have formed an impression of a book or a work of art, we want to move on, even though our lasting sense of that object may not be fully developed. We crave the larger, broader picture. Each book or work of art offers only partial insight into the whole. Individual men, too, only represent particular aspects of human nature and capability, and do not expand to illuminate traits or ideas beyond those they possess. Each man has a particular talent, and his tendency is to reinforce and capitalize upon that talent rather than to grow in other ways. This self-limitation necessitates our examining all of humankind to gain a sense of the whole. We must look at the weak as well as the admirable examples, because God underlies all of them. Each individual has his own educational value, as do all aspects of human experience in society—commerce, government, the church, marriage, and the various occupations. Power (used by Emerson to signify a kind of divinely imparted life force) speaks alternately through various examples of humanity but does not remain permanently in any one of them.

Emerson emphasizes that philosophical awareness of the shortcomings of human experience does not constitute life itself. Life must be lived, not considered. Thought and writings on social reform are not successfully translated into the ends toward which they aim. Constant criticism of various institutions and courses of action has led to widespread indifference. Emerson urges the reader to tend to his own life as it is. The balanced individual who accepts life will extract what can be enjoyed from it. A man may thrive anywhere, under the "oldest mouldiest conventions" as well as in "the newest world." Emerson advises living to the best of our abilities in the present moment, "accepting our actual companions and circumstances," approaching each day as "a sound and solid good," and making the best of what life brings, the bad as well as the good. If we expect nothing of life, we will be pleasantly surprised to receive anything at all. If we expect much, we will inevitably be disappointed. Life's gifts are not obtained by analysis, but in the process of living. We need to look after our own affairs regardless of what others think we should be doing. Emerson recommends "the temperate zone" between the ideal and the material. Life is composed of both power (life force) and form, which must be balanced if health and soundness are to be preserved. Every quality, even the good, is dangerous in excess.

Our lives would be easier, Emerson writes, if we could simply attend to our ordinary daily routines. But we are susceptible to intimations from a higher source, which shake the common, limited vision of reality. Measured and predictable though daily life is, God isolates us in the present moment and from one another so that we will live and respond spontaneously, will heed the call of intuition. Both nature and man operate "by pulses" and "by fits," and chance plays a key role. Human intention and design are not always factors in the way life plays out. The most attractive person is the one who exerts power incidentally, not directly. The thought of genius always contains the unpredictable. The moral sentiment is always new, always comes without direct sensory experience. Our experience of life, too, contains an element of divine inspiration, which won't bear analysis. Man's vital force derives from the eternal, and its results cannot be controlled or predicted.

Emerson describes intuition as the means of perceiving the underlying unity behind the multiple expressions of God. Insight into the harmonious divine source does not come sequentially, but rather in flashes, which bring joy as well as vision. Intuition opens up whole new worlds to us. Man's consciousness is a constant, unchanging element that serves as a "sliding scale" to rank all that is experienced according to its origin in the divine "First Cause" or in material nature. The spiritual and the material coexist as "life above life, in infinite degrees." The key question is not what a man does, but what source—the divine and spiritual, or the material and temporal—motivates him to do it. The spiritual life force is tremendously empowering. How we express the life force through what we think and do is less significant than "the universal impulse to believe"—our receptivity. Spirit is conveyed directly to man, without explanation, and likewise is expressed directly through man, in his character and actions. It allows us to influence others without words and even without physical proximity. Openness to spirit not only imparts personal force, but also allows the ever-greater understanding of "life and duty, of a doctrine of life which shall transcend any written record we have." This new doctrine must embrace both society's skepticism and its faith, and will reconcile its limiting as well as its affirmative characteristics.

Human subjectivity is an inescapable force that causes us to project ourselves onto what we perceive in life, of nature, even of God. There is an inequality between the subject perceiving and the object perceived. Deriving our strength and inspiration from God, we need what we perceive to validate and enhance our sense of our own importance in the divine scheme, and we focus on specific particulars that reinforce this sense. In our subjectivity, we go so far as to excuse ourselves for traits and actions that we condemn in others, thereby accepting the relative rather than the fixed and absolute. Emerson points to sin, which subjective intellect perceives only in relation to itself, although when viewed from the framework of traditional religion is an absolute quality. Because of our subjectivity, in order for the soul to attain "her due sphericity" (a completeness reflective of the larger whole), we must be exposed to the full range of particulars.

Self-reliance is essential to avoid distraction by the many particulars that life brings our way. We must not pay too much attention to custom and opinion, must live our own lives and think our own thoughts, must keep our focus on the eternal. Emerson admits that the eternal and the material are essentially irreconcilable. He attempts to answer the question of what the practical results of understanding the relationship between idealism and experience might be. The effects of our explorations of truth, he answers, are cumulative, incalculable within the span of a single human lifetime. Moreover, while people in general place too much emphasis on doing rather than knowing, he himself accepts the primary value of knowing. He recognizes that the world he lives in is not the world he thinks it is, and trusts that he will some day understand this discrepancy. But we cannot resolve it by attempting to translate the world of thought into reality, as is attempted by various reform movements. Emerson urges patience, avoidance of squandering precious time and attention on inconsequential details of living, and persistent, optimistic openness to the intuitive insight that will bring "the light of our life." Ultimately, genius will be transformed into practical power.

Major Themes

The Difficulty of Reconciling Philosophy and Life. The basic view of the relationship between God, man, and nature expressed in "Experience" is essentially that found in Emerson's earlier idealistic expressions of Transcendental philosophy. Emerson stresses that God is the source of man's unlimited strength and power, and that insight into the divine is the ultimate goal of living. Emphasizing the unity of the universe, he writes that "Underneath the inharmonious and trivial particulars, is a musical perfection; the Ideal journeying always with us, the heaven without rent or seam."

Emerson presents the divine "First Cause" as the inspiration behind all the nobler actions of man, as opposed to material influence. He vigorously dismisses materially based interpretations of human nature (like phrenology), which view character as the fixed result of physical traits, and disregard the influence of the divine spirit. Intuition affords vision of divine unity, imparting meaningful wholeness and coherence to the many separate expressions of God in the material world and in human life. It also inspires man's hitherto unrealized inner potential. He metaphorically alludes to the undiscovered capabilities within man as analogous to the unexplored American west: "I am ready to die out of nature, and be born again into this new yet unapproachable America I have found in the West." (Thoreau, too, developed the metaphor of "the West" in his work, notably in the essay "Walking.") Moreover, Emerson equates man's openness to spirit not only with his personal insight into the universal but with the ultimate transformation of society itself—"the transformation of genius into practical power."

However, as steadfastly as Emerson holds to his idealistic optimism, he recognizes in "Experience" that there is a discrepancy, a tension, between philosophical idealism and the experience of life. In the prefatory poem and throughout the essay, he acknowledges the thoughtful man's confusion as he confronts the forces that distort perception and prevent vision beyond the material into the divine, absolute, and permanent. He openly admits that philosophy is not life, that we cannot successfully alter the world we inhabit by imposing on it our sense of what it should be. Efforts to reform society don't achieve their desired results because, in the end, the gap between the ideal and the material cannot be so easily bridged. Grief at the loss of loved ones, one of the deepest human emotions, provides no insight into the relationship between the spiritual and the material, and leaves us empty and baffled.

Even nature herself, our ally and tool for comprehending the universal, does not readily allow us to make sense of her operations in human life.

But although idealism and human experience are difficult to reconcile satisfactorily, nowhere in the essay does Emerson suggest that one must be chosen over the other. They are coexistent elements, not mutually exclusive. They merge into one another by graded steps, "life above life, in infinite degrees." Emerson urges us to keep our sights on the ultimate purpose of our existence—to understand our place in the universe and our relationship to God and nature—but at the same time to live life as it is, not worrying too much about the discrepancy between the two. "Life is not dialectics," he writes. It must be lived on its own terms, not confused with the higher realm that exists side by side with it and that surpasses it in significance. Our experience of daily life will eventually contribute toward a broader sense of the universal.

Emerson asserts that the specific societal forms, personal relationships, and human conditions that constitute our experience are, in the long run and from the broad view, insignificant. We may thrive as spiritual beings as well under one set of conventions and circumstances as under another. He advocates avoidance of wasting precious energy on trying to alter the externals of life. We may find meaning in even the most trivial transactions and relationships:

> I settle myself ever firmer in the creed, that we should not postpone and refer and wish, but do broad justice where we are, by whomsoever we deal with, accepting our actual companions and circumstances, however humble or odious, as the mystic officials to whom the universe has delegated its whole pleasure for us.

Moreover, he recommends embracing life, not merely grimly accepting it. He distinguishes between two points of view that we might describe today as the difference between seeing the glass half-empty and seeing it half-full:

> I compared notes with one of my friends who expects everything of the universe, and is disappointed when anything is less than the best, and I found that I begin at the other extreme, expecting nothing, and am always full of thanks for moderate goods. I accept the clangor and jangle of contrary tendencies. I find my accounts in sots [drunkards] and bores also. . . . If we will take the good we find, asking no questions, we shall have heaping measures.

In attempting to analyze experience too closely, we fail to get from it what we can. Its lessons are learned "on the highway"—along the way, in the course of life, not through conscious intent to make sense of it. Emerson advises a tolerant, balanced approach, one that incorporates power (divinely granted and intuitively realized life force) and form (the particular external structures through which we express ourselves). We should aim toward the "middle region of our being," the "temperate zone," the "mid-world," the "equator of life, of thought, of spirit, of poetry,—a narrow belt." There we may both live life as we must and yet remain open to higher reality.

Theme

Perspective and Insight. Emerson explores the subject of perspective in detail throughout "Experience." We need somehow to find higher unity behind the mass of confusing detail that we encounter on a daily basis.

Literary Device

Emerson employs the image of the rapidly spinning, multicolored wheel to suggest that it takes the proper perspective on a great many particulars to provide a sense of the whole: "Of course, it needs the whole society, to give the symmetry we seek. The parti-colored wheel must revolve very fast to appear white." He discusses the various forces that hinder our maintaining a sufficiently large vision, that diminish our receptivity to intuitive insight into universal truth. While engaged in living, Emerson points out, it is difficult for us to gauge exactly where we stand, to make out the broader meaning and the true value of our thoughts and actions. Certain inherent human traits impede our ability to see beyond the material and temporal.

Mood and temperament, for example, may prevent even the most thoughtful and gifted from realizing the divine power that flows into them. Emerson writes of "young men who owe us a new world, so readily and lavishly they promise, but they never acquit the debt; they die young and dodge the account; or if they live, they lose themselves in the crowd." Because we see only what we are inclined to see, temperament affects insight. The undersensitive are insufficiently receptive to intuition, and the overly sensitive are too overwhelmed by it to properly assimilate the vision it offers.

Furthermore, the human mind is so constructed that men need to consider objects and ideas separately and in succession, rather than all at once. But the universal perspective that we inwardly require demands comprehensive vision. Thus, there is a certain tension between how we are made up and the ultimate insight toward which we are drawn. And if we cannot apply our minds to individual objects and ideas except in succession, neither do we express our characters through action, nor perceive the characters of other men, except particular trait by particular trait, focusing at any given time on one quality to the exclusion of the others that make up the full range of human characteristics. In the course of a single lifetime, the intellect by itself has difficulty processing enough particulate manifestations of God in us and in our lives to allow the deepest kind of comprehension. Moreover, because divine power expresses itself through individuals sporadically, not continuously, the machinery of the intellect—which regards things sequentially and consequently may miss the opportunity to perceive the divine when it makes itself apparent—is somewhat at odds with the way God acts upon us. We need to look at things over a period of time and to receive impressions of them all at once, and this is beyond the capacity of the intellect. Revelatory intuition is therefore essential to the process of insight.

Emerson focuses on the elements of chance and spontaneity in his discussion of man's recognition of the divine force working in our lives. Human design and intention have limited effect. Only intuition allows us to transcend constraining factors in the way we process experience. And God's agency on our lives as comprehended through intuition leads to unpredictable results:

> . . . I can see nothing at last, in success or failure, than more or less of vital force supplied from the Eternal. The results of life are uncalculated and uncalculable. The years teach much which the days never know. The persons who compose our company, converse, and come and go, and design and execute many things, and somewhat comes of it all, but an unlooked-for result. The individual is always mistaken. He designed many things, and drew in other persons as coadjutors, quarrelled with some or all, blundered much, and something is done; all are a little advanced, but the individual is always mistaken. It turns out somewhat new, and very unlike what he promised himself.

The unpredictable expression of the divine mind in human life is both paralleled by and understood through spontaneous intuition, which alone allows us to find unity and meaning in the particulars of our experience. Although the divine force behind human life is perceived sporadically, the absolutes that it expresses are permanent and unchangeable.

Toward the end of "Experience," Emerson explores subjectivity as an immutable condition affecting perspective, a given from which insight is, in the end, inseparable. He reminds us that "it is the eye which makes the horizon, and the rounding mind's eye which makes this or that man a type or representative of humanity. . . ." We can only see and evaluate things in relation to ourselves. We look for that which confirms the divinity within us, measuring one thing against another by what we need to see as well as by what we are capable of seeing. (Emerson thus develops a theme that he earlier expressed in *Nature*, particularly in his discussion of the way in which the poet picks and chooses subjectively among the objects of his consideration to create a unified whole in his work.) Man is the "receiver of Godhead," who feels "at every comparison . . . his being enhanced by the cryptic might," and requires what he perceives to reinforce his sense of his elevated position. Because subjectivity based on our intimate connection with God is part of the human constitution, intuition is all the more necessary to help us sort out the temporal from the absolute. We see everything—including moral issues—in relation to our own importance. Emerson contrasts our innate personal tendency to see morality in relative terms with the insistence of institutionalized religion on presenting it in absolute terms. Because the truly absolute emanates from a higher sphere, he thus indirectly underscores how unproductive it is to look for absolutes in the human scheme of things.

Emerson writes powerfully of revelatory insight into the permanent absolute that always lies beyond the temporal here and now:

> Do but observe the mode of our illumination. When I converse with a profound mind, or if at any time being alone I have good thoughts, I do not at once arrive at satisfactions, as when, being thirsty, I drink water, or go to the fire, being cold: no! but I am at first apprised of my vicinity to a new and excellent region of life. By persisting to read or to think, this region gives further sign of itself, as it were in flashes of light, in sudden discoveries of its profound beauty and repose, as if the clouds that covered it parted at intervals, and showed the approaching traveller the inland mountains. . . . But every insight from this realm of thought is felt as initial, and promises a sequel. I do not make it; I arrive there, and behold what was there already. . . . I clap my hands in infantine joy and amazement, before the first opening to me of this august

magnificence, old with the love and homage of innumerable ages, young with the life of life, the sunbright Mecca of the desert. And what a future it opens!

Intuition thus works upon us both immediately and cumulatively, providing deeper and deeper insight into the divine and absolute. It will allow us to form a "new picture of life and duty." This new vision will reconcile skepticism and faith, will permit us to incorporate the particulate and polarized aspects of experience into a unified vision and, ultimately, to translate that vision meaningfully into life. But we must be patient. Moreover, even while we live life, we must maintain the independent self-reliance of thought that leads us to understand that our characters, relations, and actions derive their true meaning from a higher source.

"Hamatreya"

The poem "Hamatreya" was based on a passage from the Vishnu Purana (one of the traditional Vedantic mythologies). Emerson copied the passage into his journal in 1845. "Hamatreya" first appeared in print in *Poems*, published by Chapman in London and by Munroe in Boston late in 1846 (the title pages dated 1847). The Boston edition of *Poems* was reprinted many times. (In 1865, Ticknor and Fields issued the title in their famous "Blue and Gold" format.) In 1876, the poem was included in the ninth volume (*Selected Poems*) of the Little Classic Edition of Emerson's writings, in 1884 in the ninth volume (*Poems*) of the Riverside Edition, and in 1904 in the ninth volume (*Poems*) of the Centenary Edition. It has been included in many collected editions of Emerson, among them the 1946 *The Portable Emerson* (edited by Mark Van Doren), the 1965 Signet Classic *Selected Writings of Ralph Waldo Emerson* (edited by William H. Gilman), and the 1994 Library of America *Collected Poems and Translations* (selected and annotated by Harold Bloom and Paul Kane)

Synopsis

Emerson drew on a passage in the Vishnu Purana in writing "Hamatreya." The origin of the poem's title is unclear, because there is no Hindu word or name "Hamatreya." Edward Waldo Emerson noted in his annotations to the poem in the Centenary Edition of his father's writings that "Hamatreya" appears to be an adaptation of "Maitreya," one of the characters in the Hindu text. In the original passage, Maitreya is engaged in a dialogue with the deity Vishnu (who was, to his devotees, the central deity, of whom all the other deities represented aspects). Vishnu tells Maitreya about the Hindu kings who mistakenly believed themselves possessors of the Earth. But the kings have disappeared, while the Earth endures. Vishnu recites the chant of the Earth, who laughs at and pities the egotistical kings and their blindness to their mortality. He tells Maitreya that the Earth's song will cause proud ambition to melt away.

Unlike many of Emerson's poems, "Hamatreya" is metrically varied and unconventional. The first section of the poem (in which Emerson describes the early settlers of Concord) is written primarily in blank verse (unrhymed iambic pentameter), from which Emerson varies in several lines. The second section (the Earth-Song) is metrically irregular and unidentifiable in terms of traditional meter and rhyme scheme. The final four lines (in which the first-person speaker comments on how he has been affected by the Earth-Song) is in an adaptation upon a more traditional verse form, the common meter (iambic heptameter).

Emerson opens "Hamatreya" with a list of some of the first settlers of Concord— "Minott, Lee, Willard, Hosmer, Meriam, Flint." (In the version of the poem printed in 1876 in *Selected Poems*, the first line was changed to begin with the name of the Concord founder who was Emerson's own ancestor and an alternate second name—Hunt— that prevented the repetition of sound that Lee would have created in juxtaposition with Bulkeley: "Bulkeley, Hunt, Willard, Hosmer, Meriam, Flint.") These names are followed closely (in the third line) by a list of the products of the land from which these solid men benefited. The founders took satisfaction in their ownership of the trees and hills, and believed that the land would belong to them and to their descendants forever. They imagined that they shared a special sympathy with the land. Emerson asks where they are now, and answers "Asleep beneath their grounds," suggesting a kinship with the earth quite different from that which the founders thought they possessed. He writes of the Earth laughing at her "boastful boys" (an image borrowed from the Vedantic original), who were so proud of owning what was not actually theirs, but who could not avoid death. Emerson enumerates the ways in which they altered their land. These men appreciated the stability of their property as they sailed back and forth across the ocean, never dreaming that the land that awaited their return would outlast their claims to it. They did not realize that death would transform each of them into "a lump of mould," turning them back into the land they owned.

The "Earth-Song" begins with the lines "Mine and yours; / Mine, not yours," which recall the words of the original passage in the Vishnu Purana—"The words 'I and mine' constitute ignorance." In her song, the Earth points out that she herself endures, whereas men do not. She mocks the legal deeds by which the property of the first settlers was supposedly conveyed to their heirs, and she sings that the inheritors of the land are, like their progenitors, also gone, as are the lawyers and the laws through which ownership was effected. Every one of the men who controlled the land is gone, even though all of them wanted to stay. The Earth underscores her hold over the men who firmly believed that they held her.

In the third section of "Hamatreya," a four-line stanza (quatrain), the speaker of the poem states that the Earth-Song took away his bravery and avarice, "Like lust in the chill of the grave," thus ending the poem on a note of sober awareness

Major Themes

"Hamatreya" presents a number of contrasts, each one of which highlights the central, paradoxical turning of the tables on the value traditionally placed by men upon land ownership. In the poem, Emerson opposes materialism and a more spiritual mysticism, reality and illusion, transience and permanence, separateness and unity, and human and universal concepts of history.

Theme

Material versus Spiritual. The settlers of Concord who form the subject of the first section of the poem are developed entirely as material men, defined (and defining themselves) solely in terms of their ownership, use, and alteration of the land. Emerson omits to tell the reader anything of them as emotional men, as religious men, or intellectual men, choosing instead to focus on their material orientation. (Significantly, in the 1876 revised version of the poem, in which Peter Bulkeley—Emerson's ancestor and the first minister and a founder of Concord—is placed at the beginning of the list of settlers, there is no hint of the fact that Bulkeley came from England for religious purposes.)

Style & Language

The purely physical nature of the founders' appreciation of their land is emphasized in the listings of their concrete and specific crops and commodities ("Hay, corn, roots, hemp, flax, apples, wool, and wood") and of the resources they exploited ("We must have clay, lime, gravel, granite-ledge, / And misty lowland, where to go for peat"). Even their enjoyment of their land is expressed in terms of owning features of the landscape, through the use of the possessive "my": "How sweet the west wind sounds in my own trees! / How graceful climb those shadows on my hill!" The Earth-Song, by contrast, conveys a more mystical, encompassing, spiritually suggestive vision of the permanence of nature as it exists independently of the claims and actions of these men

Theme

Reality versus Illusion. The founders of Concord imagine that their pride in property constitutes a special sympathy with the land: "I fancy these pure waters and the flags [wild irises] / Know me, as does my dog: we sympathize; / And, I affirm, my actions smack of the soil." Ironically, there is more truth than they know in this connection of themselves with the physical world over which they believe they exert control. In the end, death negates the importance they ascribe to material ownership, and serves as a warning to the first-person speaker at the end of the poem. The settlers' misguided belief that they can live on by holding tight to concrete reality proves illusory. Their eventual loss of particulate self into the land is reality. Despite the fact that they think that they can achieve permanence through ownership, their existence and impact are transient. Those who espouse a material approach to the world face an unexpected finality

Literary Device

In "Hamatreya," Emerson overturns a basic assumption not only of the founders of Concord but of his own contemporaries and of the current time as well: the belief that property ownership is a positive goal and a lasting benefit. Emerson owned land in Concord and elsewhere, including the property at Walden Pond where Thoreau lived from 1845 to 1847. Despite his philosophical idealism, Emerson was subject to the same human values that affected the early landowners of Concord. His recognition of his own susceptibility to illusion is indicated in the four-line stanza at the end of the poem, in which the first-person speaker says, "My avarice cooled." The poem is effectively paradoxical, not because the founders of Concord were particularly deluded, but because their delusion is a common trait, promoted by our culture. The paradox results from the contrast between a prevalent value and the less recognized but, from Emerson's point of view, more valid philosophical approach to man's position in the world.

The wrong-headed materialism of Concord's founders is counteracted by the Earth-Song. The personified Earth points out that the men who thought they owned her are gone, whereas the stars, the sea, the shores, and the land, "Shaggy with wood," continue on. Earth responds to those who said of the land "'Tis mine, my children's, and my name's" by mocking their efforts to ensure the permanence of their ownership through lawyers and deeds:

> The lawyer's deed
> Ran sure,
> In tail,
> To them, and to their heirs
> Who shall succeed,
> Without fail,
> Forevermore.

In the end, the Earth emphasizes, the land owns men, not vice versa: "They called me theirs, / Who so controlled me; / Yet every one / Wished to stay, and is gone. / How am I theirs, / If they cannot hold me, / But I hold them?"

Transience versus Permanence. Human existence is unalterably finite. An attitude that encourages any one man or any one generation of men to believe that human influence can be extended over time through material means is egotistical as well as misguided. A true understanding of the universe and of what is permanent can only come about when egotism is subdued and subordination to a higher, more encompassing power accepted. The first-person speaker at the end of the poem arrives at an understanding of this through the Earth-Song

Separateness versus Unity. In the first section of "Hamatreya," Emerson suggests the tendency of Concord's first settlers to see things in their separateness rather than as part of a unified whole.

The lists of their names in the first line of the poem, of the products of their land in the third line, and of Concord's natural resources near the end of the first section all contribute to the impression that these men viewed the world in particulars rather than in totality. The Earth, on the other hand, sings a broader vision, one that transcends time and specificity of place. The egotism of the founders is connected to the

Check Out Receipt

Savage Branch
410-313-0760
http://hclibrary.org

Tuesday, March 8, 2022 8:30:28 PM
n3116

Item: 31267503987701
Title: Thoreau, Emerson, and Transcendenta
lism (Cliffs Notes).
Call no.: BOOKLET CLIFFS NOTES
Due: 03/29/2022

Total items: 1

Self-pickup of holds now available.
Check out your own items using a
SelfCheck or HCLS CheckItout app.
New hours are M Th 10am - 9pm,
F Sa 10am 5pm,
Sun 1pm 5pm (as of Sep 12).

importance they attach to their own particulate existence and their own particulate parcels of land. They are forced to arrive at oneness on the most basic level, the level of physical unity with the earth through death and decay. The speaker in the last stanza reaches the point at which he is ready to recognize a more elemental underlying unity.

Theme

Human History versus Universal History. In "Hamatreya," Emerson affirms a broader, more spiritual outlook on history than that which emphasizes the individual achievements of particular men. He takes the long view, rather than the sequentially focused view. This outlook is consistent with that expressed in his essay "History" (published in his first series of *Essays*), in which he writes of the universal mind behind all history in all ages as comprehensible only through history in its entirety, and of each event throughout time as the "application of [the first man's] manifold spirit to the manifold world."

However, in putting the founders of Concord in proper historical perspective in "Hamatreya," Emerson exposes but does not scorn the men of whose fallacy he writes in the first section of the poem. Their efforts, after all, resulted in the development of the town he deeply loved. Moreover, philosophically at odds with their materialism though he was, Emerson admired and respected their steadfastness. In his 1835 discourse at the bicentennial celebration of Concord's incorporation, Emerson had helped to celebrate the accomplishments of these same men. Their efforts formed his personal heritage. In the poem, he presents the speaker's arrival at a stance conducive to true philosophical insight, but, at the same time, he reveals some degree of identification with the founders, even while making their error known. Because Emerson felt a connection to these men, the poem tacitly conveys a sense of how difficult it is to reconcile human experience with the universal and the spiritual, a theme also developed in the essay "Experience" and elsewhere in Emerson's writings.

HENRY DAVID THOREAU

Life and Background of Thoreau

Although an author's biography is always to some degree relevant to the study of his or her writings, a remarkable unity existed between Henry David Thoreau's life and his work. Thoreau's deliberately lived life and his writings were dual expressions of the same underlying principles and aspirations.

One of the major authors of American Transcendentalism, lecturer, naturalist, student of Native American artifacts and life, land surveyor, pencil-maker, active opponent of slavery, social critic, and almost lifelong resident of Concord, Massachusetts, Thoreau was born David Henry Thoreau on July 12, 1817, in his grandmother's house on Virginia Road in Concord, which is close to Boston and Cambridge. In 1635 it was the first inland settlement in Massachusetts. The scene of the first armed resistance of the American Revolution on April 19, 1775, Concord was, in 1817, a vigorous place, home to the courts of Middlesex County, a beehive of artisan activity, trade, and politics as well as a farming community. Thoreau was baptized in the First Parish—the church in which as an adult he would decline membership—on October 12, 1817.

His father, John Thoreau (1787–1859), storekeeper and pencil-maker, was of French Protestant descent. Jean (John) Thoreau (1754–1801), Henry's grandfather, born on the Isle of Jersey, came to America in 1773 and became a successful merchant in Boston. He married Jane Burns in 1781. In 1799, he bought part of what is now the Colonial Inn building in Concord and moved his large family there in 1800.

Henry's mother, Cynthia Dunbar Thoreau (1787–1872), was born in Keene, New Hampshire. On her mother's side, she descended from the Loyalist Jones family of Weston, Massachusetts. Her mother, Mary Jones, married the Reverend Asa Dunbar in 1772, was widowed, and married Captain Jonas Minott—who owned the farm where Thoreau was later born—in 1798.

Cynthia Dunbar and John Thoreau were married on May 11, 1812. They had four children: Helen (1812–1849); John (1815–1842); Henry (1817–1862); and Sophia (1819–1876). John Thoreau suffered business difficulties and found it necessary to move his young family several times, from Concord to Chelmsford, Massachusetts (in 1818), from Chelmsford back to Concord briefly (in 1821), then to Boston (in 1821), and finally back to Concord permanently (in 1823). After returning to Concord, John Thoreau rented a succession of houses before he could afford to build a home of his own (on Texas Street, now Belknap Street) in 1844. In 1849, John Thoreau bought and renovated a larger home on Main Street (the "Yellow House"), into which the family moved in 1850 and where Henry died in 1862.

Despite their early financial hardships, the Thoreau family shared a vital and sustaining home life that meant much to all of them—Henry included—as long as they lived. John and Cynthia Thoreau differed significantly from one another in temperament. John was quiet, obliging, patient, fond of reading and music (he played the flute, and passed along this love to Henry), observant, and a storehouse of information about those who populated the community around him. Cynthia, an intelligent woman, was far more outgoing, voluble, unafraid to speak her mind even at the risk of offending. Widely acknowledged as a good homemaker, she was generous in inviting those in need into her home for meals. She played an active part in the Concord Female Charitable Society (a volunteer social service organization) and participated in the abolition movement through membership in the Ladies' Anti-Slavery Society of Concord and involvement in the Underground Railroad. She took in boarders to supplement the family income. The Thoreau children were influenced not only by their parents but also by members of the extended family. Mrs. Thoreau's brother Charles Dunbar, along with Mrs. Thoreau, helped instill in the children a love of outdoor expeditions and an appreciation of the fact that they did not have to go far from home to enjoy nature. The children's aunts Louisa Dunbar and Maria, Jane, Sarah, and Elizabeth Thoreau also influenced the children (Sarah and Elizabeth lived and ran a boarding house in the Concord home that their father had bought in 1799).

Thoreau was educated in Concord at Miss Phoebe Wheeler's school, in the public school on what is now Monument Square, and under the tutelage of Phineas Allen at the Concord Academy. His schoolmates at the Academy, which he attended from 1828 until 1833, included Ebenezer Rockwood Hoar, who went on to become Attorney General of the United States in the cabinet of President Ulysses S. Grant; Rockwood's brother George Frisbie Hoar, later a United States senator; John Shepard Keyes, lawyer, United States marshal, judge, and Massachusetts senator; and William Whiting, Solicitor General for the War Department during the Civil War. Classmate Charles Stearns Wheeler was a special friend of Thoreau and later his college roommate.

Thoreau was a member of the Concord Academic Debating Society while in school. In general, however, he preferred wandering in the open air to indoor activities.

In 1833, Thoreau entered Harvard College. Far from well-off, the Thoreaus made a concerted effort to raise money for the tuition. Henry's sister Helen and brother John contributed some of what they earned as teachers, and his aunts contributed as well. Thoreau held a scholarship that also helped. In 1835, he took a temporary leave from his classes to teach school in Canton, Massachusetts, under the supervision of Orestes Brownson, with whom he studied German during his absence from Harvard. Thoreau performed creditably at Harvard, although he was not ranked near the top of his class. He read avidly in his spare time. His professors included Edward Tyrrell Channing, under whom he applied the basics of English composition in writing essays; Cornelius Felton, who taught Greek; and Francis Bowen, who taught philosophy. In addition to English, Greek, and philosophy, Thoreau studied Latin, mathematics, history, astronomy, theology, Italian, French, German, and Spanish. He was a member of the Institute of 1770, a Harvard lecture, debate and literary society.

Thoreau graduated from Harvard in 1837 and returned to Concord. Without explanation, he reversed the order of his first and middle names, signing himself "Henry David" instead of "David Henry" for the rest of his life. He taught public school for a short time (two weeks) in 1837. His disinclination to use physical punishment did not sit well with the Concord School Committee. Disgusted, Thoreau arbitrarily applied the rod to six students and promptly resigned. Unable to find another teaching job, he devoted himself to his father's pencil-making business.

In October of 1837, Thoreau began to keep a journal in which he made regular entries, recording his daily experiences, thoughts, observations of nature and of life, and reactions to reading. His journals, which he kept until 1861, became the source of much of his published writing. In a real sense, they form his *magnum opus*. Moreover, on April 11, 1838, Thoreau delivered his first lecture before the Concord Lyceum (the lecture "Society," based on journal entries that he had made in March of 1838). The lecture platform provided Thoreau with another means of expressing his developing thoughts prior to their reworking for publication. In Thoreau's writing, as in Emerson's, there is frequently a close relationship between journal, lecture, and published word.

In 1838, still unable to find work as a teacher, Thoreau opened a private school, running it first in his family's house, then in the Concord Academy building, which he rented when the Academy lost its schoolmaster. Thoreau took over the existing name as well as the building. The school was open to boarding and day students, the boarding students staying in the Thoreau family home. As the enrollment increased, Thoreau added his brother John to the teaching staff of one. Most of the pupils were from Concord and the immediate vicinity. A few, like Edmund Sewall of Scituate, Massachusetts, came from farther away. The curriculum included English, Latin, Greek, French, mathematics, physics, and natural history. The students engaged in hands-on learning, made frequent field trips, and focused considerable attention on nature. The Thoreau brothers shunned physical punishment. Successful though the school was, John's declining health forced its closing in 1841.

In 1839, while teaching school together, Henry and John Thoreau made a boat trip down the Concord River and up the Merrimack as far as Hooksett, New Hampshire, from there continuing by land to Concord and Plymouth, New Hampshire. This journey later provided the raw material for Thoreau's first published work, *A Week on the Concord and Merrimack Rivers* (published in 1849). Also during the period when they were teaching colleagues, Henry and John fell in love with the same girl, Ellen Sewall of Scituate, older sister of their pupil Edmund Sewall. Both proposed marriage—John in July of 1840, Henry later that year. Neither won Ellen's hand. Ellen later married the Reverend Joseph Osgood. None of John and Cynthia Thoreau's four children ever married. Although he did not marry, Henry valued the friendship and mutual respect of several women—Lidian Emerson (the wife of Ralph Waldo Emerson), Lucy Jackson Brown (Mrs. Emerson's sister), and Mary Moody Emerson (Emerson's strong-minded, forthright, and eccentric aunt).

Having closed his Concord Academy, Thoreau accepted an invitation to move into the Emerson household as a live-in handyman. He stayed with the Emersons from 1841 to 1843. Emerson, fourteen years older than Thoreau, had moved to Concord in 1834, while Thoreau was a student at Harvard. After Thoreau's graduation from Harvard and his return to Concord in 1837, a close bond had developed between the two. Because Emerson was older, published, and already a leader among Transcendental thinkers, he filled the roles of teacher and patron as well as friend to Thoreau. As time went on, the master/pupil aspect of the relationship became less appropriate and less satisfactory. But in the early 1840s, it suited both men.

Under Emerson's influence, Thoreau increasingly turned his thoughts to writing. While living in the Emerson home, he enjoyed the benefits of Emerson's encouragement, support, and advice. He also benefited from access to Emerson's library, which included important works of Oriental literature of great interest to Thoreau, books not readily available elsewhere. Members of the Transcendental Club came to Concord to converse with Emerson, and Thoreau was welcome among them. Thoreau contributed to *The Dial* during this period, and edited the April 1843 issue for Emerson, who became editor of the periodical after Margaret Fuller's resignation in 1842. Thoreau and Emerson also shared the common bond of grief from January of 1842, when Thoreau's brother John died of lockjaw and Emerson's first child Waldo died of scarlet fever.

Thoreau would again live in the Emerson household from 1847 to 1848, while Emerson was in Europe. By 1850, however, the friendship was strained. Despite their respect for one another, Emerson's sense of Thoreau's promise and Thoreau's idealization of Emerson did not quite fit the reality of how each conducted his life. Thoreau did not vigorously pursue the visible success as a writer of which Emerson thought him capable. Emerson increasingly became a man of the world and traveled in literary and social circles that Thoreau disdained. When Thoreau died in 1862, Emerson delivered the eulogy at the First Parish in Concord; it was later expanded for publication in the August 1862 issue of *Atlantic Monthly*. The piece, titled "Thoreau," clearly conveys Emerson's disappointment in what Thoreau had achieved.

In 1843, through Emerson's influence, Thoreau left Concord to tutor the children of Emerson's brother William on Staten Island, New York. He delighted in observing the local plant life, so different from that of his native town; he enjoyed the ocean; he visited New York City; he read and was able to take books out of the New York Society Library; he met Horace Greeley, founder of the *New York Tribune*, who helped him to publish some of his work in magazines. But Thoreau was unable to sell as many of his pieces as he had hoped he might. Moreover, he did not feel much intellectual kinship with the William Emersons, and he missed Concord. By the end of 1843, Thoreau was ready to return to the landscape and the community that formed such a large part of his identity.

Thoreau once again applied himself to the family pencil-making business, so improving the product that it was widely acknowledged as superior. (He remained involved with the pencil business to one degree or another until the end of his life, taking it over with his sister Sophia after their father's death in 1859.) Thoreau also renewed his association with the Concord Lyceum, both as lecturer and as curator for the 1843–1844 season. Although he also lectured outside Concord, Thoreau was never one of those popular lecturers who were solidly booked and who spoke to packed halls on the lyceum circuit.

Thoreau's friends and associates ranged from philosophers and authors to local farmers, whose ingenuity and simplicity he admired, to the outcast Irish who came to town to build the Fitchburg Railroad in the early 1840s. Concord at the time was home not only to Emerson, but also to Bronson Alcott; the poet (William) Ellery Channing (nephew and namesake of the liberal minister who had been so important in establishing American Unitarianism); and Nathaniel Hawthorne (who lived in the Old Manse from 1842 to 1845, while it was vacant following the death of Ezra Ripley). This community of thinkers and writers was extended by the many visitors—Margaret Fuller, Elizabeth Peabody, and Theodore Parker, for example—who visited Emerson. As his journals indicate, Thoreau enjoyed the company of farmers George Minott and Edmund Hosmer and of Edward Sherman Hoar—brother of Ebenezer Rockwood, George Frisbie, and Elizabeth Hoar (a learned woman, the fiancée of Emerson's brother Charles, who died in 1836, and an intimate of the Emerson family). Thoreau and Edward Hoar accidentally set fire to the woods near Concord's Fairhaven Bay in April of 1844, an event described in detail in Thoreau's journal.

Late in 1844, Emerson purchased land around Walden Pond. Thoreau had for some time been drawn to the idea of living with nature, away from town life. While in college, his friend Charles Stearns Wheeler had built a cabin on Sandy Pond in Lincoln (next to Concord). Thoreau himself had tried unsuccessfully to obtain permission to build a cabin on Sandy Pond. Emerson's purchase of land at Walden provided Thoreau with the opportunity he craved to live simply in nature and to devote himself to writing. He wanted to work the story of his 1839 journey with his brother John on the Concord and Merrimack Rivers into a book.

In March of 1845, Thoreau began cutting pines at Walden for lumber to build his cabin. The cabin was sufficiently finished to live in by July 4 of that year, when he moved in, although the chimney had not yet been built nor the shingling and plastering completed. Between the time he moved in and his departure from Walden on September 6, 1847, Thoreau lived self-sufficiently, as he wrote in the first paragraph of *Walden* "earning my living by the labor of my hands only." He fished and grew beans, potatoes, corn, peas, and turnips, selling what he did not need for his own use. He focused on the essentials only and spent the time that was not necessary for obtaining them on what was most important to him—observing the world around him and writing. Thoreau looked for the higher laws behind the facts of his existence. He did not, contrary to popular misconception in his own time and ours, live the life of a hermit or misanthrope. He visited family and friends in town often, and they returned the gesture. The experiment at Walden did what Thoreau had hoped and intended it would. He left Walden with the completed manuscript of *A Week on the Concord and Merrimack Rivers* and with much material that would eventually form his *Walden* as well.

In 1845, as Thoreau was preparing to build his cabin at the pond, he became involved in a local controversy that resulted in his taking a public stand on the side of abolition. There was opposition within the Concord Lyceum to inviting abolitionist Wendell Phillips to speak, ending in an abrupt change of Lyceum management and in the extension of the invitation to Phillips. (Phillips had earlier spoken before the Concord Lyceum, to the discomfort of some of the more conservative members of the community.) Thoreau consequently wrote a letter to William Lloyd Garrison's *The Liberator*, defending Phillips' right to speak. The letter was published in the March 28, 1845, issue. Thoreau's stance was in keeping with his family's ardent abolitionism. His mother and sisters, active in the Concord Ladies' Anti-Slavery Society and the Middlesex County Anti-Slavery Society, applauded his outspokenness.

In July of 1845, while living at Walden, Thoreau was arrested and jailed for nonpayment of the poll tax, which he had refused to pay since 1842 in protest against government complicity in slavery. Although Thoreau's debt was paid by an anonymous benefactor, and he therefore spent only one night behind bars, the event was significant because it led directly to the preparation of one of his most influential writings. In 1848, Thoreau first lectured before the Concord Lyceum on "The Rights and Duties of the Individual in Relation to Government." In 1849, he submitted "Resistance to Civil Government" to Elizabeth Palmer Peabody for publication in the May 1849 issue—as it turned out, the sole issue—of her *Aesthetic Papers*. The piece was later published under the title *Civil Disobedience*.

A Week on the Concord and Merrimack Rivers also appeared in May of 1849, under the imprint of Boston publisher James Munroe. Thoreau had had difficulty in arranging for the book's publication, and had finally had one thousand copies published at his own expense. Most of those copies remained unsold and eventually came back to him.

In the fall of 1847, Thoreau again took up residence in the Emerson home, where he remained until July of 1848, when he moved back into his parents' home and took odd jobs to earn money. In the late 1840s, he became proficient and sought-after as a land and property surveyor, a line of work that allowed him to spend time outdoors. He worked not only for private property owners, but also for the Town of Concord, assisting in laying out roads and walking the bounds in his capacity as "Civil Engineer." Most of his surveying was done in Concord and towns nearby, but occasionally he traveled farther afield, as when he surveyed Eagleswood in Perth Amboy, New Jersey, for Marcus Spring, in November of 1856. Thoreau's precision and accuracy as a surveyor were highly valued.

In the period after he returned from Walden, Thoreau reveled in tramping about the woods and fields of Concord, sometimes with the Emerson children and other young companions, and explored in his journal what Concord meant to him. He wrote repeatedly of the place as a sufficient microcosm of the world, at least as hospitable to individual development and self-realization as any larger, older, or more cosmopolitan place. In his journal entry for March 11, 1856, for example, he wrote:

> If these fields and streams and woods, the phenomena of nature here, and the simple occupations of the inhabitants should cease to interest and inspire me, no culture or wealth would atone for the loss. . . . At best, Paris could only be a school in which to learn to live here, a stepping stone to Concord, a school in which to fit for this university. I wish so to live ever as to derive my satisfactions and inspirations from the commonest events . . . so that what my senses hourly perceive . . . may inspire me, and I may dream of no heaven but that which lies about me. . . .

As deeply as Thoreau loved Concord, there was undeniably a certain philosophical detachment in his appreciation of it. The search for transcendent truth outweighed the attractions of specific locality for him. The simplification of and deliberate approach to life had been the crucial aspects of his experiment at Walden. Others, he knew, could find meaning in Waldens of their own, without ever setting foot in Concord.

During the late 1840s and the 1850s, Thoreau made a number of excursions beyond Concord—to Maine (first visited by Thoreau in 1846, while he lived at Walden) in 1853 and 1857; to Cape Cod in 1849, 1850, 1855, and 1857; to Quebec in 1850; to Mount Monadnock in southern New Hampshire (which he visited repeatedly over the years) in 1852 and 1858; and to the White Mountains (to which he first journeyed in 1839 with his brother John) in 1858. In July of 1850, Thoreau made a somber trip to Fire Island, off New York, to search for the body of Margaret Fuller, who had died in a shipwreck on her return to America with her Italian husband and their young child. Thoreau sometimes took companions when he traveled, among them Ellery Channing and Edward Sherman Hoar. His journeys provided the raw material for several posthumously published books—*The Maine Woods* (1864), *Cape Cod* (1865), and *A Yankee in Canada* (1866).

Thoreau's trips to Maine afforded him the chance to observe Native Americans. Since boyhood, Thoreau had been fascinated by Indians. There were Indians in Concord even in the 1850s, but their culture had long since lost its integrity. In Maine, Indians were still to a degree able to live "free and unconstrained in Nature." Thoreau used Indian guides on his Maine trips in order to learn what he could of their wisdom and their ways. He wrote about Joe Polis, his guide in 1857, in *The Maine Woods*. In Concord, Thoreau was a collector of arrowheads and other artifacts, highly skilled at finding them in places where others never suspected they might lay. He also kept volumes of research notes on the Indians, intending but ultimately unable to write a book on the subject.

For seven years after Thoreau's return from Walden Pond in 1847, he worked and reworked his material about his sojourn there, extensively and repeatedly revising what he had produced. The book was published in August of 1854 by the Boston company of Ticknor and Fields, publishers of a number of major authors of the American Renaissance. *Walden* was more widely and better reviewed than *A Week on the Concord and Merrimack Rivers* had been, and it sold well.

Thoreau found fellowship with others after the cooling of his relationship with Emerson. Ellery Channing—who accompanied him on walks around Concord—was chief among them. With the publication of his *Thoreau, the Poet-Naturalist* in 1873, Channing later became the first biographer of Thoreau. In 1848, Harrison Gray Otis Blake of Worcester, Massachusetts, began a correspondence with Thoreau. Thoreau sometimes visited Blake in Worcester, and the two hiked in Concord and elsewhere. Blake inherited Thoreau's manuscripts (except for his surveys, which went to the Concord Free Public Library) from Sophia Thoreau, who died in 1876. He subsequently edited journal material for the volumes *Early Spring in Massachusetts* (1881), *Summer* (1884), *Winter* (1888), and *Autumn* (1892). Theophilus Brown was another Worcester friend. Thoreau visited Daniel Ricketson in New Bedford, and corresponded with Calvin Greene of Rochester, Michigan. He met Englishman Thomas Cholmondeley in Concord in 1854. On his return to England, Cholmondeley corresponded with Thoreau and sent him a rich and much appreciated collection of Oriental books.

After the passage of the Fugitive Slave Law in 1850, Thoreau and certain other residents of Concord took an active part in the Underground Railroad. In the 1850s, Thoreau's mother concealed slaves on their way to freedom in her home. Thoreau escorted fugitives to the West Fitchburg railroad station, where they made connections for Canada. The prominent fugitive slave cases of Shadrach Minkins (who spent one night in February of 1851 at the house of the Mr. and Mrs. Francis Bigelow), Thomas Sims (1851), and Anthony Burns (1854) angered Thoreau. His speech "Slavery in Massachusetts," delivered at an abolition meeting in Framingham, Massachusetts, on July 4, 1854, was prepared in reaction to the return of the fugitive slave Burns to his Virginian master.

Thoreau admired radical abolitionist John Brown, in 1855 captain of a Kansas militia company determined to keep Kansas a free state, in 1859 leader of a raid on the federal arsenal at Harper's Ferry, West Virginia. Frank Sanborn of Concord was one of Brown's key supporters. In 1857, Brown visited Concord, lunched at Mrs. Thoreau's, and spoke publicly later in the day. He returned to Concord and spoke again in 1859. Following the raid at Harper's Ferry, Thoreau delivered "A Plea for Captain John Brown" in Concord, Boston, and Worcester. After Brown's execution, his "The Last Days of John Brown" was read at Brown's memorial service on July 4, 1860, in North Elba, New York. Thoreau also helped Francis Jackson Merriam, one of Brown's raiders at Harper's Ferry, escape to Canada.

Thoreau continued to make entries in his journal until November of 1861, six months before his death. He had always devoted considerable attention in his journals to recording his observations of the natural world. But the character of these observations changed over time. By the 1850s, Thoreau was aware that he had become more scientific, more attentive to detail and data. He took a measure with him on his walks, bought a spyglass, and systematically recorded the blooming dates of flowers and statistics of all kinds. Having supplied naturalist Louis Agassiz with animal specimens in his Walden days, Thoreau occasionally struggled with the urge to kill something in order to study it. He reminded himself in his journals that his ultimate purpose in immersing himself in nature—the search for broader meaning—would be subverted by too scientific an approach

Late in 1860, Thoreau caught a cold, which turned to bronchitis and aggravated the tuberculosis that had shadowed him since his college days. In an effort to regain his health, he journeyed to Minnesota with young naturalist Horace Mann, Jr. (son of educator Horace Mann) in the spring and summer of 1861. The trip did not stop the progress of his illness, however. Thoreau spent his final months in Concord editing and reworking his manuscripts. He died on May 6, 1862, at the age of forty-four. Originally buried in the New Hill Burying Ground, his body was later moved to Authors' Ridge in Sleepy Hollow Cemetery.

After Thoreau's death, over a period of years, Sophia Thoreau, Ellery Channing, Ralph Waldo Emerson, and Harrison Gray Otis Blake edited Thoreau's unpublished writings. Some important pieces first appeared in periodical form. "Walking," "Wild Apples," and "Life Without Principle" were published in *Atlantic Monthly*. Sophia Thoreau and Emerson edited the collection *Excursions*, published in 1863. *The Maine Woods, Cape Cod,* and *A Yankee in Canada, with Anti-Slavery and Reform Papers*, edited by Sophia Thoreau and Ellery Channing, appeared in 1864, 1865, and 1866, respectively. Emerson edited letters (*Letters to Various Persons*, 1865); Blake edited the four volumes organized by season from the journals (1881–1892); and Frank Sanborn and Thoreau biographer Henry Stephens Salt edited poems (*Poems of Nature*, 1895).

Thoreau enjoyed, at best, a modest reputation during his lifetime. Only with the passage of time has the broad relevance of his work been appreciated and his place as one of the most original and profound of American authors been recognized.

Introduction to Thoreau's Writing

Henry David Thoreau was an exacting practitioner of the art of writing. Although he exulted in the intuitive, creative genius that he felt within himself, throughout his life he was a disciplined craftsman who worked hard to revise and refine his material. As a writer, he drew strength from an understanding of the inseparability of his life and his art. Thoreau wrote of this unity in his journal (February 28, 1841), "Nothing goes by luck in composition. . . . The best you can write will be the best you are. Every sentence is the result of a long probation. The author's character is read from title-page to end." Thoreau intended his writing to be a fit expression of a life lived according to high ideals and aspirations, guided by integrity and morality, spent in pursuit of spiritual development, of the universal truth that lay behind the particular and the personal. He strove to convey transcendent meaning, the "oracular and fateful," in all that he wrote.

Thoreau saw his writing as a confluence of all his powers—physical, intellectual, and spiritual. He wrote in his journal entry for September 2, 1851:

> We cannot write well or truly but what we write with gusto. The body, the senses, must conspire with the mind. Expression is the act of the whole man, that our speech may be vascular.

He constantly revised his work not out of a fussy sense of perfectionism but because of the tremendous value that he placed on his writing as an embodiment of all that he was.

Style & Language

Thoreau was a versatile writer, capable of expressing stark reality in strong language and of conveying delicate detail and subtle nuance. His work is characterized both by directness of style and by the suggestion of far more than appears on the surface. He effectively employed a variety of techniques—paradox, exaggeration, and irony, for example—to create a penetrating prose. He brought considerable abilities and resources to his art—breadth of vision, closely examined personal experience, wide and deep reading, imagination, originality, a strong vocabulary and a facility for manipulating words (and even sometimes for minting new words to suit his purposes), an alertness to symbolic correspondences, and an aptitude for the figurative (simile, metaphor, allegory). He applied himself to translating what he observed of nature and humanity into words ("As you *see*, so at length will you *say*," he wrote in his journal on November 1, 1851). His writing, consequently, possesses immediacy.

Thoreau admired direct, vigorous, succinct, economical prose. For him, the importance of content far outweighed that of style. He avoided overemphasis on form at the expense of content. Romantic writer that he was, he cared little for observing the formalities of established literary genre. He wanted every word to be useful, to convey meaning, and he had no interest in the purely decorative. "As all things are significant," he wrote, "so all words should be significant." Thoreau felt that the very act of genuine expression elevated the written word: "A fact truly and absolutely stated is taken out of the region of common sense and acquires a mythologic or universal significance." Although Thoreau avoided obvious artifice, his highly crafted writing is anything but artless.

Thoreau's writing is full of mythological references and of illustrative passages from earlier authors with whom modern readers may not be familiar. Nevertheless, despite the obscurity of such allusions, it is hard even for those reading his work for the first time not to experience flashes of inspired understanding of his message. This is a tribute to Thoreau's effective use of language. He wrote carefully for an intelligent and thoughtful reader. His work appeals at least as much to such a reader today as it did in the nineteenth century. The lasting appeal of his work is due, too, to the breadth and timelessness of the major themes developed throughout his writings.

Thoreau put millions of words to paper over the course of his lifetime. He vacillated in the way he viewed and presented some of his themes in this massive body of his work. The reader of Thoreau must simply accept some degree of intellectual contradiction as evidence that the author was a complex man, constantly thinking and weighing ideas, open to a variety of interpretations, capable of accepting inconsistency. If Thoreau's thoughts on a subject did not always remain constant, at least there is coherence in his repeated exploration of certain basic themes throughout his writings.

The most central of Thoreau's themes is the idea that beyond reality—beyond nature and human existence—there is a higher truth operating in the universe. Reality—nature, in particular—symbolizes this higher truth, and, from its particulars, universal law may, to some degree, be comprehended. This idealism is consistent with the

Transcendental concept of the ultimate connectedness of God, man, and nature in the great oneness of the Oversoul, and with the optimistic Transcendental sense that the absolutes and the workings of the universe can be grasped by the human mind. Intuitive understanding rather than reason provides the means to such cosmic comprehension.

Thoreau expressed a clear vision of the unity of man, nature, and heaven. Following a description of moth cocoons resembling leaves suspended over the edge of the meadow and the river, he wrote in his journal entry for February 19, 1854:

> . . . it is startling to think that the inference has in this case been drawn by some mind that, as most other plants retain some leaves, the walker will suspect these also to. Each and all such disguises . . . remind us that not some poor worm's instinct merely, as we call it, but the mind of the universe rather, which we share, has been intended upon each particular object. All the wit in the world was brought to bear on each case to secure its end. It was long ago, in a full senate of all intellects, determined how cocoons had best be suspended,—kindred mind with mine that admires and approves decided it so.

This leap from the particular to the universal, from the mundane to the divine, is found throughout Thoreau's work.

Theme

Nature—its meaning and value—comprises one of the most pervasive themes in Thoreau's writings, expressed through both painstaking detail and broad generalization. Like Emerson, Thoreau saw an intimate and specific familiarity with the reality of nature as vital to understanding higher truth. Thoreau's Transcendental quest toward the universal drew him to immerse himself in nature at Walden Pond from 1845 to 1847. It led him to observe the natural world closely in order ultimately to "look through and beyond" nature, as he wrote in his journal on March 23, 1853. Thoreau's attraction to nature went far beyond emotional appreciation of its beauty; he embraced its harshness as well. Nature was, as he wrote in his essay "Walking," "a personality so vast and universal that we have never seen one of her features." There could be no "great awakening light" of understanding without knowledge of the manifestations of the universal in the observable world.

Thoreau was aware, however, that there was a fine line between inspiration through concrete knowledge of nature and fruitless preoccupation with masses of scientific detail. He saw that there was a danger of becoming "dissipated by so many observations" (journal entry, March 23, 1853), and recognized his own tendency to lose sight of the ultimate goal of higher understanding. On August 19, 1851, Thoreau wrote in his journal:

> I fear that the character of my knowledge is from year to year becoming more distinct and scientific; that, in exchange for views as wide as heaven's cope, I am being narrowed down to the field of the microscope. I see details, not wholes nor the shadow of the whole.

He perceived a world of difference between the natural philosopher and the more limited man of science.

Approached with a sense of wonder and of high purpose, nature provided Thoreau with a means of transcending the distractions of everyday life and of focusing on what was important. Thoreau's excursions in Concord and beyond were made through nature, toward loftier revelations. Nature, he felt, was a particular tonic to the human spirit in an age devoted to commerce, to politics, to the spread of dehumanizing industrialization and urbanization, to unfulfilling social interactions, and to the perpetuation of human institutions at best in need of change, at worst immoral. His essay "Walking" is a coherent expression of the power of nature—of "wildness," in which he found the "preservation of the world"—to enlarge man's vision. He wrote:

> If the heavens of America appear infinitely higher, and the stars brighter, I trust that these facts are symbolical of the height to which the philosophy and poetry and religion of her inhabitants may one day soar. At length, perchance, the immaterial heaven will appear as much higher to the American mind, and the intimations that star it as much brighter. For I believe that climate does thus react on man,—as there is something in the mountain-air that feeds the spirit and inspires. Will not man grow to greater perfection intellectually as well as physically under these influences? . . . I trust that we shall be more imaginative, that our thoughts will be clearer, fresher, and more ethereal, as our sky,—our understanding more comprehensive and broader, like our plains,—our intellect generally on a grander scale, like our thunder and lightning, our rivers and mountains and forests,—and our hearts shall even

correspond in breadth and depth and grandeur to our inland seas. Perchance there will appear to the traveler something, he knows not what, of *laeta* and *glabra*, of joyous and serene, in our very faces. Else to what end does the world go on, and why was America discovered?

But the broad patterns visible through nature provide an antidote to the shortcomings of human existence only if a man is open to them. The saunterer must "shake off the village" and throw himself into the woods on nature's terms, not his own.

Theme

Admiration for the primitive or simple man—a common theme in Romantic literature—is corollary to the significance of the natural world in Thoreau's work. Thoreau was fascinated by the American Indian, whom he described as "[a]nother species of mortal men, but little less wild to me than the musquash they hunted" (journal entry, March 19, 1842). His attraction was founded on the Native's closer relationship to nature than that of civilized man. He saw in the relics of Indian culture, which he found wherever he walked, evidence of the "eternity behind me as well as the eternity before." Although he could not fail to notice that the remaining local Indians of his time had been degraded, Thoreau was able to visualize through the Native an earlier connection between man and nature that had been lost in the evolution of civilization. He wrote in *The Maine Woods*:

> Thus a man shall lead his life away here on the edge of the wilderness, on Indian Millinocket stream, in a new world, far in the dark of a continent, . . . amid the howling of wolves; shall live, as it were, in the primitive age of the world, a primitive man. . . . Why read history then if the ages and the generations are now? He lives three thousand years deep in time, an age not yet described by poets. Can you well go further back in history than this? Ay! ay!—for there turns up but now into the mouth of Millinocket stream a still more ancient and primitive man, whose history is not brought down even to the former. . . . He glides up the Millinocket and is lost to my sight, as a more distant and misty cloud is seen flitting by behind a nearer, and is lost in space. So he goes about his destiny, the red face of man.

Thoreau wrote about the skillful Indian guide Joe Polis in *The Maine Woods*. He found characteristics of primitive man as a whole in the representative individual.

Thoreau also saw in other simple men who lived close to the woods and the earth a tacit understanding of the universal order that civilization obscured. In *Walden* ("Higher Laws"), he wrote of the following:

> Fishermen, hunters, woodchoppers, and others, spending their lives in the fields and woods, in a peculiar sense a part of Nature themselves, [who] are often in a more favorable mood for observing her . . . than philosophers or poets even, who approach her with expectation.

Such men knew important things "practically or instinctively," through direct, intuitive means. In the chapter of *Walden* titled "The Pond in Winter," Thoreau described fishermen as follows:

> . . . wild men, who instinctively follow other fashions and trust other authorities than their townsmen . . . as wise in natural lore as the citizen is in artificial. They never consulted with books, and know and can tell much less than they have done. . . . [The fisherman's] life itself passes deeper in Nature than the studies of the naturalist penetrate; himself a subject for the naturalist.

And the old Wellfleet oysterman in *Cape Cod*, whose only learning is what he had "got by natur [sic]," is presented as an archaic, bardic type.

Although Thoreau had mixed feelings regarding the farmer's capacity for higher understanding, he sometimes wrote in similar terms of those who cultivated the land. In his journal entry for January 20, 1852, Thoreau presented hauling muck, the most prosaic of farm chores, as analogous to his own literary activity:

> The scholar's and the farmer's work are strictly analogous. . . . When I see the farmer driving into his barn-yard with a load of muck, whose blackness contrasts strangely with the white snow, I have the thoughts which I have described. He is doing like myself. My barn-yard is my journal.

Moreover, Thoreau found in certain specific Concord farmers strong individuals who possessed an elemental connection with nature. He wrote in his journal about Cyrus Hubbard (December 1, 1856):

> . . . a man of a certain New England probity and worth, immortal and natural, like a natural product . . . a redeemer for me. . . . Moderate, natural, true, as if he were

made of earth, stone, wood, snow. I thus meet in this universe kindred of mine, composed of these elements.

Thoreau referred to George Minott, "the most poetical farmer," many times in his journals.

The importance of simplicity is another of Thoreau's recurrent themes. By keeping his needs and wants few, the individual may realize spiritual aims instead of devoting his energies to the material. Thoreau urged economy and self-reliance, the stripping away of luxuries and comforts down to the bare essentials. He wrote in "Economy," the first chapter of *Walden*, "Most of the luxuries, and many of the so called comforts of life, are not only not indispensable, but positive hindrances to the elevation of mankind." Thoreau deplored the "waste of life" through the brutalizing manual labor that was required to lay railroad tracks, operate mills, and accomplish the manufacture of items of questionable necessity. If a man spends all day in mind-numbing work, he has no life left for the pursuit of higher understanding. By doing for himself, the individual maintains his freedom to live deliberately, to cultivate himself, and to explore nature and divinity.

At Walden, Thoreau achieved the simplicity that allowed a rich and meaningful life:

> I went to the woods because I wished to live deliberately, to front only the essential facts of life, and see if I could not learn what it had to teach, and not, when I came to die, discover that I had not lived. I did not wish to live what was not life, living is so dear. . . . I wanted to live deep and suck out all the marrow of life. . . .

Just as Thoreau understood that living simply in nature allowed a man to live fully, he also recognized that society impeded both simplicity and the inner life.

In "Life Without Principle," Thoreau cautioned against the conventionalism of business, church, state, politics, government, law, even of established science and philosophy, all of which encroached upon individual freedom and the ability to think clearly for oneself. He exhorted, "Read not the Times. Read the Eternities. Conventionalities are at length as bad as impurities. . . . Knowledge . . . [comes] to us . . . in flashes of light from heaven." Civilized life not only creates artificial needs but also provides pat answers to questions that individuals should confront directly. Through simplicity and self-reliance, we may get beyond the conventional and come face-to-face with the universal. In "Walking," Thoreau pointed out the degeneracy of villagers, those who lived in the worldly commotion of town life: "They are wayworn by the travel that goes by and over them, without traveling themselves." Confined by social demands and strictures, they never seek the eternal. Thoreau himself assiduously avoided superficial social involvements and occupations, which he felt took "the edge off a man's thought."

Theme

The theme of travel is an important one in Thoreau's writings, operating on both literal and metaphorical levels, closely bound to the author's powerful sense of place. Thoreau took pains to emphasize that seeking exotic locations in pilgrimage toward higher understanding was unnecessary. He repeatedly focused attention on the inward rather than the outward nature of the journey that was most important in the life of a thinking man. He wrote in his journal (March 21, 1840), for example, "Let us migrate interiorly without intermission, and pitch our tent each day nearer the western horizon." He wrote in *Walden* that he had traveled "a good deal in Concord," meaning not just that he had explored every inch of the town but also that he had traveled inwardly toward higher reality there. Actual travel provided a change of circumstance, but the journey of the mind toward the universal could take place anywhere, and in fact more easily in familiar territory as in a faraway place that could be reached only through effort and expense.

Thoreau unquestionably felt a strong emotional attachment to his native town. He knew its landscape, its people, and its past intimately. He sometimes expressed his love of the place passionately and lyrically. His journal entry for September 4, 1841, reads:

> I think I could write a poem to be called "Concord." For argument I should have the River, the Woods, the Ponds, the Hills, the Fields, the Swamps and Meadows, the Streets and Buildings, and the Villagers. Then Morning, Noon, and Evening, Spring, Summer, Autumn, and Winter, Night, Indian Summer, and the Mountains in the Horizon.

Thoreau saw Concord as the place where he could best visualize and communicate the universals that transcend place precisely because it was the place he knew best. He wrote in his journal entry for November 20, 1857:

> If a man who has had deep experiences should endeavor to describe them in a book of travels, it would be to use the language of a wandering tribe instead of a universal language. . . . The man who is often thinking that it is better to be somewhere else than where he is excommunicates himself. If a man is rich and strong anywhere, it must be on his native soil. Here I have been these forty years learning the language of these fields that I may the better express myself. If I should travel to the prairies, I should much less understand them, and my past life would serve me but ill to describe them.

Thoreau also wrote of the tendency of travel away from the familiar to distract and dissipate the traveler.

But Concord was for Thoreau representative as well as concrete, and his sense of place in relation to Concord was generic as well as specific. In an undated journal entry recorded after July 29, 1850, he wrote:

> I, too, love Concord best, but I am glad when I discover, in oceans and wildernesses far away, the materials out of which a million Concords can be made,—indeed, unless I discover them, I am lost myself,—that there too I am at home.

The critical fact about place is how the individual internalizes and interprets the reality around him, no matter where he is.

And yet, seemingly inconsistently, Thoreau did travel some actual distances at various times in his life—up the Concord and Merrimack Rivers with his brother John, to New York, Maine, Cape Cod, Quebec, Mount Monadnock, the White Mountains, and Minnesota. Moreover, in keeping with the Romantic impulse to write about travel to faraway places, Thoreau incorporated into his work what he observed on his journeys. He traveled partly "to give our intellects an airing," partly to seek out locations possessing greater wildness than could be found in Concord. Moreover, he was interested in examining the particular relationship between a man and his environment, the affinity between man and place. In his travel narratives, Thoreau delineated certain individuals who seemed to have been organically shaped by landscape and occupation.

Transcendentalism incorporated the Romantic emphasis on the individual and the Unitarian belief in the goodness and perfectibility of man. These ideas are expressed throughout the writings of its proponents. The importance of the individual in relation to God, nature, and human institutions is at the heart of Thoreau's work. Thoreau wrote in his journal entry for August 24, 1841, for instance:

> Let us wander where we will, the universe is built round about us, and we are central still. By reason of this, if we look into the heavens, they are concave, and if we were to look into a gulf as bottomless, it would be concave also. The sky is curved downward to the earth in the horizon, because I stand in the plain. . . . The stars so low there seem loth to go away from me, but by a circuitous path to be remembering and returning to me.

Thoreau embraced the subjectivity of perception that followed from man's central position. He accepted that the individual's vantage point in some sense defined the universe.

If the individual enjoyed centrality in the cosmic view of things, however, Thoreau found him less fortunate in relation to human institutions. The author wrote in *Walden* of "an important distinction between the civilized man and the savage . . . in making the life of a civilized people an *institution*, in which the life of the individual is to a great extent absorbed." Thoreau distrusted all threats to individuality. He perceived that the community intruded upon the individual and, similarly, that the individual guided by principle and high purpose threatened community complacency. He felt that the individual's first duty was to himself—to know and to cultivate himself and to seek knowledge of how he fit into the universal picture. Solid citizens of the community, however, saw things otherwise. Thoreau spent his life living up to his responsibilities as he understood them. The judgment of the community mattered little to him. Thoreau was aware that some of his townsmen had no idea why he moved to Walden Pond in 1845, but their opinion did not deflect him.

Thoreau's antislavery and reform writings focus on the obligations of the individual in relation to society. A person was bound to observe a higher standard of morality when obedience to temporal law would diminish his integrity or that of others. Thoreau saw that the institutions of society tended to preserve the *status quo*, and so it fell to the individual to speak out against the shortcomings of human government and law. *Civil Disobedience*, first published in 1849, was written in response to his jailing in 1846 for nonpayment of the poll tax. Thoreau refused to support a government that he felt tolerated and abetted slavery, permitting the treatment of individuals as physical property, denying their humanity and spirituality. Although Thoreau disdained politics and was not inclined to take political action under ordinary circumstances, he could not overlook the immorality of slavery and of allowing slavery to continue. He wrote explicitly of the individual's authority at the end of *Civil Disobedience*:

> There will never be a really free and enlightened State, until the State comes to recognize the individual as a higher and independent power, from which all its own power and authority are derived, and treats him accordingly. I please myself with imagining a State at last which can afford to be just to all men, and to treat the individual with respect. . . .

Here and elsewhere in Thoreau's writings, the individual is paramount. Thoreau spoke out publicly in defense of John Brown, leader of the 1859 raid on the federal arsenal at Harper's Ferry, West Virginia. In his "A Plea for Captain John Brown," he again emphasized individual responsibility to higher law, asking "Is it not possible that an individual may be right and a government wrong?"

Thoreau wrote harshly of reform and reformers. However much he may have agreed with the principles behind particular movements, he believed that moral responsibility lay ultimately with the individual. Reform movements, like political affiliations, reduced the individual to membership in the group and restricted his freedom to make independent judgments. Thoreau felt that the reform of society would best be accomplished through the individual. He wrote in his journal on April 9, 1841, "I can do two thirds the reform of the world myself. . . . When an individual takes a sincere step, then all the gods attend. . . ." Thoreau was consummately Transcendental in his elevation of the individual.

Thoreau's writing presents a synthesis of optimistic idealism and earthy enjoyment of the here and now. He focused on ultimate meaning, but at the same time reveled in the sensuous details of nature and life as he lived it. Thoreau has sometimes been viewed as an ascetic who denied himself the pleasures of life, but his work does not bear out this judgment. Certainly, Thoreau was selective about the pleasures he chose to enjoy and to celebrate in words. But his writings reveal a healthy capacity to live joyfully in the moment. The endurance and increasing popularity of his work over time is due, in large part, to this ability to unify reality and idealism.

Selected Chronology of Thoreau's Writings

1827   Thoreau wrote student essay "The Seasons," his earliest known composition

1837   Thoreau began to keep a journal

First published piece, obituary notice of Anna Jones, appeared in Concord newspaper *Yeoman's Gazette*

1840   Published pieces in *The Dial* (poem "Sympathy"; essay "Aulus Perseus Flaccus")

1841   Published poetry in *The Dial* ("Stanzas," "Sic Vita," "Friendship")

1842   Published essay ("Natural History of Massachusetts") and poems (including "To the Maiden in the East") in *The Dial*

1843   Published in *Boston Miscellany* ("A Walk to Wachusett"), in *The United States Magazine and Democratic Review* (essay and book review), and in *The Dial* (poems, including "Smoke"; essays, including "A Winter Walk"; and selections in translation from Oriental literature and from Chaucer)

1844   Published lecture extracts ("Homer, Ossian, Chaucer"), essay ("Herald of Freedom"), and translations in *The Dial*

1845   Published letter ("Wendell Phillips Before the Concord Lyceum") in *The Liberator*

1847   Published "Thomas Carlyle and His Works" in *Graham's Magazine*

1848   Published "Ktaadn and the Maine Woods" in *The Union Magazine*

1849   *A Week on the Concord and Merrimack Rivers* appeared (Boston: James Munroe)

Published "Resistance to Civil Government" in Elizabeth Palmer Peabody's *Aesthetic Papers*

| 1852 | Published what would later be parts of *Walden* in *Sartain's Union Magazine* |

1852   Published what would later be parts of *Walden* in *Sartain's Union Magazine*

1853   Published "Excursions to Canada" in *Putnam's Monthly Magazine*

1854   Published in *New York Daily Tribune* (selections from soon-to-be-published *Walden*) and in *The Liberator* ("Slavery in Massachusetts")

       Walden; or, Life in the Woods appeared (Boston: Ticknor and Fields)

1855   Published "Cape Cod" in *Putnam's Monthly Magazine*

1858   Published "Chesuncook" in *Atlantic Monthly*

1860   Published in *The Liberator* ("The Last Days of John Brown") and in *New York Daily Tribune* ("The Succession of Forest Trees")

1862   "Walking," "Autumnal Tints," and "Wild Apples" published posthumously in *Atlantic Monthly*

1863   Previously unpublished pieces appeared in *The Commonwealth* and *Atlantic Monthly* ("Life Without Principle" and "Night and Moonlight," both in *Atlantic*)

       Excursions (edited by Sophia Thoreau and Emerson) appeared (Boston: Ticknor and Fields)

1864   Journal extracts published in *The Commonwealth*, "The Wellfleet Oysterman" and "The Highland Light" in *Atlantic Monthly*

       The Maine Woods (edited by Sophia Thoreau and Ellery Channing) appeared (Boston: Ticknor and Fields)

1865   *Cape Cod* (edited by Sophia Thoreau and Channing) appeared (Boston: Ticknor and Fields)

       Letters to Various Persons (edited by Emerson) appeared (Boston: Ticknor and Fields)

1866   *A Yankee in Canada, with Anti-Slavery and Reform Papers* (edited by Sophia Thoreau and Channing) appeared (Boston: Ticknor and Fields)

1878   Extracts from journals published in *Atlantic Monthly*

1881   *Early Spring in Massachusetts* (edited from journals by H.G.O. Blake) appeared (Boston: Houghton, Mifflin)

1884   *Summer* (edited by Blake from journals) appeared (Boston: Houghton, Mifflin)

1888   *Winter* (edited by Blake from journals) appeared (Boston: Houghton, Mifflin)

1892   *Autumn* (edited by Blake from journals) appeared (Boston: Houghton, Mifflin)

1894   *Familiar Letters of Henry David Thoreau* (edited by F.B. Sanborn) published (Cambridge: Riverside Press)

Riverside Edition of collected writings (11 volumes, including the 4 volumes from the journals as edited by Blake) published (Boston: Houghton, Mifflin)

1895   *Poems of Nature* (edited by Sanborn) published (London: John Lane; Boston and New York: Houghton, Mifflin)

1905   Journal extracts appeared in *Atlantic Monthly*

1906   Walden and Manuscript Editions of collected writings (20 volumes, including the 14-volume *Journal*) published (Boston: Houghton, Mifflin)

1971   First volume of "Princeton Edition" of collected writings published (publication ongoing to date)

Thoreau's Reputation and Influence

Thoreau is one of the most read and most influential of American authors, with a readership and a following around the world. His writings have been reprinted countless times, both in English and in translation into many foreign languages. His *Walden* is required reading in American literature courses at the college level. Much has been published about Thoreau's life and his work, both of which have been closely studied by scholars. The author himself has been idolized, and his image and quotations from his writings have been employed for a variety of purposes, including commercial use. In sharp contrast to his current popularity, during his lifetime there was only limited appreciation of Thoreau as a man and as a writer.

The way Thoreau was perceived by his contemporaries no doubt affected the reception of his work. Thoreau the man was easy to misunderstand. Even those who cared about him were conflicted in their feelings. He was not interested in making a good impression on others and did not care to correct false impressions. Thoreau's strong individualism, rejection of the conventions of society, and philosophical idealism all distanced him from others. He had no desire to meet external expectations if they varied from his own sense of how to live his life. Emerson, in his eulogy of Thoreau (printed in the August 1862 issue of *Atlantic Monthly*), wrote:

> Had his genius been only contemplative, he had been fitted to his life, but with his energy and practical ability he seemed born for great enterprise and for command; and I so much regret the loss of his rare powers of action, that I cannot help counting it a fault in him that he had no ambition. Wanting this, instead of engineering for all America, he was the captain of a huckleberry-party.

But ambition was a word little used in Thoreau's writings. At the end of *Walden* he wrote, "Why should we be in such desperate haste to succeed and in such desperate enterprises?"

There was no reason why the merchants, lawyers, and church-goers of Concord—those who formed the fabric of society—should sympathize with Thoreau's outlook. Not only did he dismiss their values, but he wrote about it, too. Moreover, Thoreau made no attempt to conciliate those who felt threatened by his disregard of community concerns. When, in 1844, Thoreau and Edward Hoar unintentionally set fire to the woods in Concord, the disapproval of men who regretted the loss of property in the form of standing and cut wood was aggravated by Thoreau's lack of repentance. "I have had nothing to say to any of them," he wrote in his journal.

And yet, Thoreau was pragmatic as well as idealistic. His useful skills appealed to practical men. Emerson commented in his eulogy:

> He grew to be revered and admired by his townsmen, who had at first known him only as an oddity. The farmers who employed him as a surveyor soon discovered his rare accuracy and skill, his knowledge of their lands, of trees, of birds, of Indian remains . . . which enabled him to tell every farmer more than he knew before of his own farm; so that he began to feel a little as if Mr. Thoreau had better rights in his land than he. They felt, too, the superiority of character which addressed all men with a native authority.

Emerson probably overstated the case in asserting the farmers' willingness to admit Thoreau's superior rights to their land. Nevertheless, through his residence in Concord from birth, his usefulness in his father's pencil business, and his range of skills as a handyman as well as a surveyor, Thoreau held a place in the community. And although he shunned superficial social connections (he referred to a party that he had attended as "a bad place to go"), he relished sympathetic companionship. He wrote in his journal entry for November 14, 1851, for example:

> . . . old Mr. Joseph Hosmer and I ate our luncheon of cracker and cheese together in the woods. I heard all he said, though it was not much, to be sure, and he could hear me. And then he talked out of such a glorious repose, taking a leisurely bite at the cracker and cheese between his words; and so some of him was communicated to me, and some of me to him. . . .

Thoreau clearly shared the common human craving for understanding.

Thoreau's idealism strained his relationships. Emerson wrote in his eulogy that "no equal companion stood in affectionate relations with one so pure and guileless," and went so far as to comment, "I think the severity of his ideal interfered to deprive him of a healthy sufficiency of human society." Moreover, there was an offputting thorniness to Thoreau's personality. Elizabeth Hoar said of him (as recorded in Emerson's journal and later incorporated into the eulogy), "I love Henry, but do not like him." Some of Thoreau's journal entries show a clear perception of the conflict between his need for friendship and closeness and his tendency toward disappointment with actual relationships. The fact that he never married (although he proposed once) likely indicates some level of understanding that his idealism worked against long-term intimacy.

Emerson wrote of Thoreau's combativeness in a June 1853 journal entry, later revised in the eulogy:

> There was somewhat military in his nature not to be subdued [the words "stubborn and implacable" are found in the journal entry]; always manly and able, but rarely tender, as if he did not feel himself except in opposition. He wanted a fallacy to expose, a blunder to pillory . . . a little sense of victory . . . to call his powers into full exercise. It cost him nothing to say No; indeed, he found it much

easier than to say Yes. It seemed as if his first instinct on hearing a proposition was to controvert it, so impatient was he of the limitations of our daily thought. This habit, of course, is a little chilling to the social affections. . . .

Emerson's comments cannot be accepted as unbiased. To some extent, they were written in an attempt to rationalize the failure of a friendship. Others were less harsh in their judgment of Thoreau. While living in the Old Manse in Concord (1842–1845), Nathaniel Hawthorne—no extrovert himself—enjoyed Thoreau's company. When Thoreau informed him of his plan to go to Staten Island in 1843, Hawthorne wrote in his journal (later published as *The American Notebooks*), "I should like to have him remain here." In "The Forester," Bronson Alcott called Thoreau "the most welcome of companions." But Emerson's assessment influenced opinion regarding Thoreau's character and, indirectly, his writings.

Other factors in addition to perceptions of Thoreau's personality—among them the realities of American literary publishing in the nineteenth century, the efforts of particular admirers, and changing cultural, political, and social values—have also affected the course of his reputation. His contemporary literary reputation began with the publication between 1840 and 1844 of some of his poetry, essays, and translations in the Transcendentalist periodical *The Dial*. Margaret Fuller edited *The Dial* from its inception until the spring of 1842, when Emerson took over from her. Frank in her criticism of what she did not like, Fuller did not accept all that Thoreau submitted to her. Emerson, then still Thoreau's literary advocate, published many more of Thoreau's pieces than had his predecessor. Emerson admired Thoreau's poetry as verse that "pleased, if not by beauty of particular lines, yet by the honest truth," as he wrote in his journal in November of 1842. Yet he also recognized the stylistic imperfection of Thoreau's poems: "Their fault is, that the gold does not yet flow pure, but is drossy and crude. The thyme and marjoram are not yet made into honey. . . ." Publication in *The Dial* identified Thoreau as a member of the Transcendental circle. However, it did not do much to establish a reputation beyond those directly involved with the magazine. The esoteric *Dial* had a very limited circulation.

Thoreau reached a broader audience through the more popular magazines that proliferated during the nineteenth century. Titles directed at the general reader—such as *Godey's*, *Graham's*, *Harper's Monthly*, *Harper's Weekly*, *Knickerbocker*, and *The United States Magazine and*

Democratic Review—gave considerable exposure to the work of many writers, Thoreau included. In 1843, Thoreau published "A Walk to Wachusett" in the *Boston Miscellany* and two pieces in *The United States Magazine and Democratic Review*. His article "Thomas Carlyle and His Works" was published in *Graham's Magazine* in 1847. Having delivered lyceum lectures based on his travels to various places, Thoreau knew that the popular appeal of such material was far greater than that of more abstract subjects. He consequently adapted his experience in the lecture hall to the literary world and submitted travel pieces to periodicals likely to publish them. His "Ktaadn and the Maine Woods" (initially presented in lecture form) appeared in *The Union Magazine* in 1848. Horace Greeley of the *New York Tribune*, whom Thoreau had met in New York in 1843, had taken a special interest in him and helped Thoreau to find a publisher for the piece. "Excursions to Canada" appeared in *Putnam's Monthly Magazine* in 1853, "Cape Cod" in *Putnam's* in 1855, and "Chesuncook" in *Atlantic Monthly* in 1858. Although the appearance of these pieces did not create great demand for Thoreau's work, the general magazines provided a venue that allowed him to write with reasonable expectation of seeing at least some of his material brought before an audience.

Even before the appearance of *A Week on the Concord and Merrimack Rivers*—his first book—in 1849, Thoreau's reputation as a writer suffered from his close connection with Emerson. Thoreau was sometimes presented as an imitator and a lesser version of Emerson. In his satirical *Fable for Critics* (1848), for instance, poet and literary critic James Russell Lowell lampooned Thoreau in verse:

There comes [Thoreau], for instance; to see him's rare sport,
Tread in Emerson's tracks with legs painfully short;
How he jumps, how he strains, and gets red in the face,
To keep step with the mystagogue's natural pace!
He follows as close as a stick to a rocket,
His fingers exploring the prophet's each pocket.
Fie, for shame, brother bard; with good fruit of your own,
Can't you let Neighbor Emerson's orchards alone?

Lowell did further damage after Thoreau's death with a piece published in the October 1865 issue of the *North American Review*. In reviewing the volume of Thoreau's letters edited by Emerson, he began his discussion of Thoreau's work by emphasizing Emerson's influence. He went on to charge Thoreau with "so high a conceit of himself that he accepted without questioning, and insisted on our accepting, his defects and weaknesses of character as virtues and powers peculiar to himself." He asserted that Thoreau had "no faculty of generalization from outside of himself"; that Thoreau condemned a world "he had never had the means of testing," had no active imagination, limited artistic control, and no sense of humor; and that he observed only what he wanted to see, grew cynical over time, was a sophist and a sentimentalizer, perverse and unhealthy in his thought. Whether any part of Lowell's harsh assessment of Thoreau was valid, it was strong criticism by an influential man, published in a respectable periodical. Lowell's words inevitably prejudiced readers, including potential readers of Thoreau's writings.

When *A Week on the Concord and Merrimack Rivers* appeared in 1849, it was not badly reviewed—even James Russell Lowell had some good things to say of it—but neither was it widely reviewed. Thoreau had assumed the cost of its publication. The publisher, James Munroe of Boston, did not promote it vigorously, and the book did not sell well. Its financial failure prompted Munroe to back out of an agreement to publish *Walden*. "Resistance to Civil Government" appeared at the same time as *A Week on the Concord and Merrimack Rivers*, in Elizabeth Peabody's *Aesthetic Papers*—an idealistic and short-lived venture that, like *The Dial*, had a limited readership. Ultimately one of Thoreau's most influential writings, "Resistance to Civil Government" did not create much of a ripple on its first publication.

Although Thoreau sometimes complained in his journals of the level of comprehension of his lecture audiences, he nevertheless continued to lecture and to work lecture material into publishable form. In the late 1840s and early 1850s, he was presenting material that would be incorporated into *Walden* (1854). In 1852, he published "The Iron Horse" and "A Poet Buying a Farm"—both of them parts of *Walden*—in two issues of *Sartain's Union Magazine*. When it finally appeared, then, *Walden* had already received what amounted to significant advance publicity.

The book was published in an edition of two thousand copies in August of 1854 by the Boston firm of Ticknor and Fields. As the premier literary publisher in America in the mid-nineteenth century, the company was in a position to see that Thoreau's work was well promoted and distributed. A sufficient number of notices and reviews appeared to assure broad interest in the book, which sold well. *Walden* was praised not only by those who knew Thoreau and his writings, but also in a variety of newspapers and magazines around the United States and in England. The Boston *Daily Bee* urged, "Get the book. You will like it. It is original and refreshing; and from the brain of a *live* man." Pieces about *Walden* were published in, among other publications, the Boston *Daily Journal* and *Daily Evening Traveller*; Concord's own *Monitor*; the New Bedford *Mercury*; *Dwight's Journal of Music*; the *Circular* of the community at Oneida; the Worcester *Palladium*; the Newark *Daily Advertiser*; the Cincinnati *Daily Gazette*; the New Orleans *Daily Picayune*; the Philadelphia *Register*; the *Daily Alta California*; the New York *Morning Express, Daily Tribune,* and *Times*; in *National Era, Putnam's Monthly, Knickerbocker,* and *Godey's*; and in the British periodicals *Westminster Review, Chamber's,* and *Critic.* This reception of the book gave Thoreau greater recognition as an author between 1854 and his death in 1862 than his earlier literary efforts had brought him.

Walden was the second and final of Thoreau's books published during his lifetime. He continued to lecture in the mid- to late-1850s and to prepare pieces for magazine publication. The publication of "Chesuncook" in *Atlantic Monthly,* which was aimed at an educated general audience, indicated the degree to the publication of *Walden* had elevated Thoreau's status as an author.

Thoreau prepared and revised his manuscript material up until his death. In the last months of his life, he was preparing "Walking," "Autumnal Tints," and "Wild Apples" for publication, but died before they appeared in *Atlantic Monthly.* They were printed in the June, October, and November issues, respectively. A number of obituaries appeared after the author's death. *Walden* and *A Week on the Concord and Merrimack Rivers* were soon reissued, and they were regularly reprinted after that. Sophia Thoreau, along with Emerson and Ellery Channing, undertook the job of editing her brother's unpublished material. *Excursions* appeared in 1863, followed in rapid succession by *The Maine Woods* in 1864, *Cape Cod* and *Letters to Various Persons* in 1865, and *A Yankee in Canada, with Anti-Slavery and Reform Papers* in 1866.

In 1894, Houghton, Mifflin (successor to Ticknor and Fields) issued the first collected edition of Thoreau's writings, the eleven-volume Riverside Edition, which included the four volumes edited by Blake from the journals. In 1906, Houghton, Mifflin published the twenty-volume Walden and Manuscript Editions, which included the *Journal* in fourteen volumes.

The spread of Thoreau's reputation after his death was aided by a handful of early admirers. His Worcester friend and correspondent Harrison Gray Otis Blake kept his memory alive through readings from the author's journals, which he had inherited from Sophia Thoreau; Blake also edited four volumes of selections from the journals. Other devotees of Thoreau included Alfred Winslow Hosmer of Concord and Dr. Samuel Arthur Jones of Ann Arbor, Michigan. Fred Hosmer, a storekeeper and photographer, gathered an important collection of books by and about Thoreau at a time when few others thought to do so. (His collection was given to the Concord Free Public Library in the twentieth century.) Hosmer photographed many Concord places associated with Thoreau and corresponded with others who shared his enthusiasm for the author. Henry Stephens Salt, the English biographer of Thoreau, was one of Hosmer's correspondents. Frank Sanborn, who edited and wrote about Thoreau, wished to be viewed as keeper of the author's reputation. In the long run, however, Sanborn's scholarly carelessness offset the value of his efforts in increasing interest in Thoreau.

By the late nineteenth century, the work of naturalists John Burroughs and John Muir—both influenced by Thoreau—drew attention to Thoreau as a nature writer. Beginning in 1899, photographer and environmentalist Herbert Wendell Gleason worked to popularize Thoreau by capturing images of the places that Thoreau had known and about which he had written. Gleason's photographs of Thoreau's world were used to illustrate the 1906 editions of Thoreau's collected writings; some of them appeared in *National Geographic*. Gleason also presented slide lectures on Thoreau for general audiences. From the late 1960s, the rise of environmentalism focused interest not only on Thoreau's writings but also on the work of Burroughs, Muir, and Gleason. Naturalist and Pulitzer Prize-winning author Edwin Way Teale helped to popularize Thoreau in the twentieth century.

The publication of Thoreau biographies began during the decade following the author's death and demonstrated growing interest in the man as well as his work. Ellery Channing's *Thoreau: The Poet-Naturalist* appeared in 1873 and was reprinted in 1902. *Thoreau: His Life and Aims*, by H.A. Page (a pseudonym for A.H. Japp) was published in London in 1877. Sanborn's *Henry D. Thoreau* appeared in 1882, *The Personality of Thoreau* in 1901, and *The Life of Henry David Thoreau* in 1917. *The Life of Henry David Thoreau* by British biographer Henry S. Salt was first published in 1890. (Thoreau's nineteenth century British following was reflected in the publication of *Walden* in

England in 1886 and of *A Week on the Concord and Merrimack Rivers* in 1889. His late nineteenth and early twentieth century recognition in England was promoted by the Labour Party, which found support in his social views.) Henry Seidel Canby's *Thoreau* (1939) was a popular success.

In the twentieth century, Thoreau's reputation—popular and academic—burgeoned. Interest in his work rose during the Great Depression of the 1930s, economic hardship made the philosophy of the simple life attractive, during the rebellion of the nonconformist "beat generation" in the 1950s, and during the social turmoil and Vietnam War protest of the late 1960s and early 1970s. During the 1930s, Thoreau also started to take on importance as a topic of academic study. The work of Raymond Adams from the 1930s and Walter Harding from the 1940s did much to enhance Thoreau's place in the study of American literature. In 1941, Harding played a key role in establishing the Thoreau Society, now affiliated with the Walden Woods Project (founded in 1990 to prevent development of the area near Walden Pond), both centered at the Thoreau Institute in Lincoln, Massachusetts. (The Society issues two periodical publications, the *Thoreau Society Bulletin* and *The Concord Saunterer*.) In 1971, the first volume of the authoritative "Princeton Edition" (now called the "Thoreau Edition") of Thoreau's collected writings appeared. The edition is ongoing today.

Thoreau's work is now available around the world. It has been translated into Dutch, French, German, Italian, Russian, Spanish, Greek, Portuguese, Hebrew, Arabic, Chinese, and Japanese, among other languages. It is much read and respected in Japan, which has its own Thoreau Society. The influence of Thoreau's work was expressed in Holland in the 1897 founding of the utopian community "Walden" and in Russia in the interest of Tolstoy and Chekov.

In "Civil Disobedience," Thoreau presented his ideas about the individual's responsibilities in relation to government. In the twentieth century, this work powerfully affected Mohandas Gandhi, who applied the principle of nonviolent resistance in the struggle for independence in India, and Dr. Martin Luther King, in his leadership of the American civil rights movement. If Thoreau could have foreseen the importance that his work would take on after his death, he probably would have been amazed at the size and range of his future audience. He might not have thought much of intensive scholarly dissection of his life and his writings. But he would likely have taken satisfaction in the translation of his ideals and ideas into constructive individual action.

A Week on the Concord and Merrimack Rivers

In 1840, Thoreau was recording journal entries about his 1839 trip with his brother John up the Concord and Merrimack Rivers. He started to think seriously of a book based on the trip after John's death in 1842. As he copied over journal entries relating to the trip, *A Week on the Concord and Merrimack Rivers* began to take shape in his mind. He was able to work his preliminary material into a first draft while living at Walden Pond; the second draft was completed in 1847. He continued to expand and revise the book until its publication in 1849. He first approached Ticknor & Company (predecessor of Ticknor and Fields) but, unable to obtain satisfactory terms, sent the manuscript to James Munroe and Company early in 1849. Munroe agreed to publish the book at the author's expense and issued it in an edition of 1,000 copies in May. In 1853, Munroe returned 706 unsold copies (256 bound, 450 in sheets) to the author. In 1862, just before Thoreau's death, Ticknor and Fields (publisher of *Walden* in 1854) bought the remaining 145 bound copies and the 450 unbound copies, which were reissued in 1862 with a new title page. A second edition, including revisions that Thoreau had made in his own copy of the first edition, was published by Ticknor and Fields in 1868, and later reissued several times. The first English edition appeared in 1889. *A Week on the Concord and Merrimack Rivers* was published as the first volume of the Riverside Edition of Thoreau's complete writings in 1894, as the first volume of the Walden and Manuscript Editions in 1906, and as the fifth volume of the Princeton Edition in 1980. Editions by a variety of publishers were issued in the twentieth century. Selections from *A Week on the Concord and Merrimack Rivers* were included in the Modern Library Edition of *Walden and Other Writings of Henry David Thoreau*, edited by Brooks Atkinson and first published in 1937. The essay on friendship from the chapter "Wednesday" has been separately printed a number of times.

Synopsis

Style & Language

Although its title suggests a travel narrative, *A Week on the Concord and Merrimack Rivers* focuses not so much on the actual two-week trip made by Henry and John Thoreau in 1839 (August 31 to September 13) as on journey into self, through nature, toward the infinite. It is an intensely cerebral, literary, metaphorical book, both long and dense.

It is divided into an opening chapter and a separate chapter for each day of the week, Saturday through Friday. Thoreau compresses and distills the two-week trip to provide a structure that clearly suggests the passage of time. Approaching its writing as a work of literature rather than a factual account, he incorporates material drawn from journal entries written well after the trip. Although the narrative sections of each chapter present the landscapes, the people, and the plant and animal life encountered along the actual journey, there is little uninterpreted description within the book. Moreover, Thoreau intersperses much information drawn from local histories (particularly regarding interactions between Native Americans and English settlers); references to and quotations from ancient, medieval, and modern authors; previously unpublished and published poems and essays of his own (for example, his "Aulus Persius Flaccus," published in *The Dial* in 1840, appears in "Thursday"; his poem "To the Maiden in the East," published in *The Dial* in 1842, appears in "Sunday"); and long philosophical explorations. These seeming digressions, connected to the narrative by thematic threads, are, in fact, integral to the meaning of the book. Only the reader willing to submit to the flow of the author's thoughts—as Thoreau surrenders himself to his journey on the rivers—can appreciate the richness and depth of *A Week*.

Theme

A Week on the Concord and Merrimack Rivers begins with an elegiac invocation to the muse of Thoreau's brother John. By maintaining John's presence throughout the book and exploring the themes of friendship, the passage of time, death, and immortality, Thoreau transforms personal grief into understanding and acceptance of loss within a larger philosophical framework.

Literary Device

In "Concord River," the opening chapter, Thoreau describes the river, evokes the Native Americans whose lives were intertwined with it long before the advent of English settlers, associates the Concord with the great rivers of this continent and others, and suggests the metaphorical nature of actual rivers as routes to the exploration of the unexplored territory in "the interior of continents." He places the Concord within a universal context as a symbol of the flow of time and life toward the eternal. He represents weeds on the bottom and objects floating by as "fulfilling their fate," and indicates his openness to what the river might teach in his resolution to "float whither it would bear me."

The brothers' journey begins in "Saturday." They depart from Concord, "a port of entry and departure for the bodies as well as the souls of men." On their first day, they travel as far as Billerica, Massachusetts. Thoreau describes what they see along the way, places the particular examples of humanity that they encounter within the all-encompassing scope of universal history, and likens life itself to a river, and the inevitable progress of a single life toward its absorption into infinity to the river's flow. The chapter contains a lengthy and detailed catalog of fishes. Despite the fragility and expendability of individual fishes, the race endures through the far-flung dissemination of its seeds. The lives of countless fishes are wasted as a matter of course, but there is a kind of virtue in their instinctive willingness to fulfill the role that nature has assigned them. The place where the brothers camp at night is described in classically sylvan terms. Past and present are intermingled throughout the chapter, and the specific employed to reveal universal significance. "Saturday" concludes with a discussion of night sounds, described as evidence of nature's health.

At the beginning of "Sunday," the dawn is described as dating from earlier than the fall of man and retaining a "heathenish integrity." This description sets the stage for Thoreau's later lengthy diatribe against established Christianity, prompted by the sight of people coming out of church on the Sabbath. Thoreau contrasts Christianity with the religion of nature. He refers to the displacement of the Indian by the English settler, and contrasts the wild life of the Indian with white man's civilization. The white man is described as "strong in community, yielding obedience to authority." Civilization lacks the "heroic spirit" and leads to the degeneration of man. The Indian—independent and aloof—preserves an integral relationship with his native gods and with nature. The sciences and arts do not affect us nearly as powerfully as more primal concerns—hunting, fishing, mythology, and fables. Mythology, "the most ancient history and biography," is explored, as is the poet's particular susceptibility to it. The ultimate passage of the works of man into nature is suggested by the canal at Billerica Falls. Thoreau urges a life embracing both spirit and matter (as nature demands) and discusses books, literature, and the fitness of poetry to treat nature and universal truth. He praises Homer and Shakespeare, dismisses the treatment of writing as a commodity, and likens writing to the river's flowing. He admires homeliness, simplicity, and a natural vigor in books. These qualities permit truthful and fresh expression even of topics that have been explored before. The brothers pitch their tent in Tyngsboro, Massachusetts, where, in contrast to the "Scythian vastness of the Billerica night," they are kept awake by raucous Irish laborers. One brother, visited by "Evil Destinies" in his dreams, is soothed by the other.

Literary Device

Thoreau begins "Monday" with reference to both the dawn of time and, in describing a ferryman on the river in the morning fog, to death. He alludes to the Styx (the ancient river of the underworld) and to Charon (the ferryman who transports souls across the Styx to the other world). He thus reinforces the imagery of the river as symbolic of universal history and the course of human life. In presenting the history of Tyngsboro, he again evokes the ever-present Indian and his extermination by the white settler. He pauses to reflect on "the lapse of the river and of human life" and on the permanence of the eternal despite the transitory nature of the particular, the individual. He urges seeking the larger principles of the universe as opposed to worldly wisdom, employing the imagery of seed that is present throughout the book. In questioning the value of reform, he presents society in general and the political state as institutions of the dead. Thoreau compares western with eastern religion. Eastern thought focuses on "loftier themes" than does western, and on contemplation—an element lacking in western religion—as well as action. He discusses history and its study, which should be more concerned with universals, more evocative of atmosphere, more vital than it is. History should distill and transcend facts and particulars, deal with the underlying connection between past and present, convey relevance to both the outward and inward life of man. Thoreau introduces the imagery of mountains in recalling a trip that he made to Mount Wachusett (in central Massachusetts). The distance of mountains from the daily life of men imparts to the traveler a broader perspective than is possible from the valleys below, allowing direct communication with nature and the infinite. A graveyard along the way prompts another consideration of death and life beyond death. Thoreau comments on the falseness of epitaphs, their failure to express what was important in a life, and presents the enrichment of the soil through the decay of the body as a more meaningful form of immortality than the monument over a grave. Like the previous two chapters, "Monday" concludes with a discussion of night sounds, which comprise sensual evidence of the health of the universe. He discusses music as "the sound of the universal laws promulgated." The brothers camp near Penichook (Pennichuck) Brook, on the outskirts of Nashua, New Hampshire.

Literary Device

Thoreau further develops the mountain imagery of *A Week* in "Tuesday," in which he describes his ascent, on another trip, of Mount Greylock ("Saddle-back Mountain") in western Massachusetts. He writes metaphorically of meeting and surmounting obstacles on such a journey, remarking that travelers frequently overestimate difficulties along the path. A person lost is not actually lost—he is simply where he is. Thoreau thus emphasizes the importance of openness to experience, observation, and understanding, of avoiding a predetermined route. He explores the subject of perspective in relation to mountains again, and—here and elsewhere in *A Week*—in relation to fog, mist, haze, and clouds. Mountain heights impart clarity; mist magnifies what is seen. Thoreau also develops the image of the all-encompassing river. Although it subsumes the tiny streams that empty into it, it nevertheless allows each to retain some of its own music, which remains audible as the river flows into the sea.

Character Insight

The local history of the region through which the brothers pass once again provides tales of Indian/white interaction. Thoreau is reminded by a "brawny New Hampshire man" of an earlier encounter, on another trip, with a "rather rude and uncivil man" named Rice. In his character sketch of Rice, he underscores the insignificance of what is commonly considered civility. Rice's character has grown naturally in the wild environment he inhabits. He is "as rude as a fabled satyr," direct, honest, and possesses a primal dignity and civility, as opposed to the acquired politeness of more civilized men. Back on the river, the sight of boatmen leads Thoreau into a discussion of the value of simple occupations. Resting at noontime, he takes up the *Travels and Adventures in Canada* by Alexander Henry, in whose life he finds a naturalness and lack of pretense and whose writing is characterized by directness, avoidance of exaggeration, and an abundance of natural fact. He finds that Henry's *Travels* express *"perennials"*—broad truth—beyond the straight historical fact of *"annals."* The two brothers kill, cook, and eat a pigeon, a small drama that causes some guilt, but that also prompts Thoreau to comment on the fulfillment of fate and on the detection of "the secret innocence of these incessant tragedies which Heaven allows." The chapter ends with a description of the "wild and solitary" landscape through which the travelers pass. They camp in Bedford, New Hampshire.

Thoreau begins "Wednesday" by contrasting roads (which "do some violence to Nature, and bring the traveller to stare at her") with the river (which "steals into the scenery it traverses without intrusion," creating and forming a part of the landscape, as well as providing an approach to it). In passing Indian burial sites, he revisits the subjects of death and rejuvenation. He comments on how "time is slowly crumbling the bones of a race." As the bones decay and become one with the earth, they fertilize the soil used to grow crops for the white man. Ever alert to microcosms of the universal, Thoreau returns to the theme of nature's enveloping scope in comparing even the smallest stream to a "*mediterranean* sea, a smaller ocean creek within the land." Thoreau describes the boats he viewed from Staten Island (where he lived in 1843). Through their great number and in the changing light of the day, these vessels lose their particularity and become increasingly generic. He attributes Arcadian and Oriental qualities to simple New England dwellings on the river, imagining the quiet, unhurried, pastoral life of their residents, and the mistress of one as "some Yankee-Hindoo woman."

At Manchester, the travelers approach the Amoskeag Falls, where they observe basins worn into rock by the falling water. Whereas the Native Americans understood that such basins were natural formations, members of the Royal Society described them in the eighteenth century as artificial. The Indian's native intuition is clearly portrayed as superior to the so-called knowledge of civilized man. Such natural formations, Thoreau writes, along with lichens, rocks, and other details of nature, form the antiquities of America, the stuff of our history. Unlike the remains of man-made objects, they do not return to dust. But nature incorporates evidence of past human life as well. Thoreau criticizes the distinction made by men and reflected in the practice of both religion and medicine, which regard matter as independent of spirit, and he asserts the inseparability of the physical and the spiritual in human life. As the brothers progress through New Hampshire from Manchester to Goffstown, Thoreau launches into the lengthy, idealistic, lyrical consideration of friendship that is central to the book. He reveals that his brother John is the friend of whom he writes in the moving passage, "My Friend is not of some other race or family of men, but flesh of my flesh, bone of my bone. He is my real brother." It is clear in this chapter that *A Week* represents Thoreau's attempt to work through his grief over John's death. Thoreau accepts that John has, in some way, been translated into nature and the eternal, and, moreover, that he will live in the spirit of those who cared for him. Thoreau writes affirmatively, "Even the death of Friends will inspire in us as much as their lives." The travelers camp in Hooksett. Thoreau considers the permanence of universal laws; the awakening within us, in serene moments, of all the eras of history; the world as "canvass to our imaginations"; the life of the mind, which craves expression; the fragility of human enterprise and aspiration; and the difficulty of achieving inner life in the normal course of human existence. The chapter closes with Thoreau's dream of a friend with whom he had had a "difference," which is resolved through the dream.

Literary
Device

"Thursday," opening with rain, brings the travelers to Concord, New Hampshire. In presenting the local history, Thoreau comments on the fact that geographical frontiers no longer exist, but adds that frontiers and wilderness endure "wherever a man *fronts* a fact." He discusses travel, metaphorically stating that continued travel is not productive—"True and sincere travelling is no pastime, but is as serious as the grave, or any other part of the human journey, and it requires a long probation to be broken into it." The wild country of the Pemigewasset and of Amonoosuck (Ammonoosuc)—the "Unappropriated Land"—is described. With a striking absence of detail about the ascent, Thoreau writes simply, "we were enabled to reach the summit of AGIOCO-CHOOK [Mount Washington]." All the remaining narrative relates to the trip back home to Concord, Massachusetts. Thoreau considers the swallowing up by nature of man's works; the innate refinement of the wildest nature; and the close relationship between nature and ideal art. But nature is God's art, which man's art can never match. Reaching a point at which the past almost seems to enter into the present, Thoreau tells the story of Hannah Dustan (also spelled elsewhere "Dustin" or "Duston"). A white woman taken and held captive by Indians, Dustan endured savagery in the wilderness. She and two other captives murdered their captors and escaped. Thoreau reflects on the great age of the world, and says that Hannah Dustan's story is, though relatively recent, nevertheless ancient. Universal history is thus expressed not just in ancient myth and history, but in events close to our own time as well. He writes about describing things as they are; considers Goethe, genius, and the artist; and reaffirms the importance of poetry—"atmospheric and irreducible"—as the "mysticism of mankind." He describes the power of composition as dangerous, possessing a certain savagery of its own. As the river flows on, he comments on the centrality of man in the universe. The travelers pitch camp at Merrimack, New Hampshire. Thoreau notes the difficulty of keeping a journal as a record of life while trying to live fully. The chapter ends with the sound of the blowing wind.

"Friday," the concluding chapter, celebrates the transition into fall, a new season, one to which Thoreau attributes qualities of regeneration rather than decline. He refers to the Concord Cattle Show, a seasonal festival of nature parallel to the great celebrations of antiquity. He discusses genius; the fact that genius and popular appreciation have nothing to do with one another; the poet—who possesses God within—and his rough, natural, truthful, penetrating strength; and the greatness of an artist, which lies in the degree to which his work expresses his life. He writes of the poet Ossian, of perspective and perception, of seeing things anew, and of permanence over the lapse of time. The "constant abrasion and decay of our lives" are presented as imparting new life—making "the soil of our future growth"—and the unity of body and spirit is restated.

Thoreau turns to mathematics and science, asserting that natural law, scientific truth, and moral law should not be considered separately from one another. He complains that the man of science does not approach the "central facts." Science will not be elevated until the scientist adopts a broader vision. Following qualified praise of Chaucer, Thoreau laments the decline of poetry from a ruder, more natural time, and discusses poets and poetry. He identifies two types of poets. One cultivates life, the other art. The former possesses genius and inspiration, the latter intellect and taste. He focuses again on the rough vigor of the work of genius. He returns to the river, and to nature's composition of an autumnal poem. Autumn is presented as a time of inner verdure and regeneration, possessing "ripe fruit" behind the sheaves and under the sod.

Literary Device

Thoreau urges man to spiritualize and naturalize so as to be open to the beauty of the world and to aspire to immortal existence, to conceive of a "better heaven." Temporal morality, he says, is petty beside pure, primeval nature. The seeking of nature beyond the ordinary is comparable to the discovery by Columbus of the New World. Thoreau metaphorically suggests that the world has many rings, that we live on the outermost, and that we must travel to the core. He urges the examination not of what was, but of what is, and optimistically states his hope that he will gain information on the "OTHER WORLD." Both science and poetry are "particles of information"; poets, philosophers, and spiritual men are "our astronomers." Thoreau advocates a radical, intuitive, expansive kind of thought, as opposed to a commonsensical, logical, narrow one. He points out the distance between what is and what appears to be. He quotes from Oriental literature on immortality and refers to the ways in which nature makes use of us without our knowledge (for instance, in the unintentional scattering of seeds as we walk). The book ends with a discussion of silence—presented as the ultimate refuge, a waiting for sound, and an openness to revelation. Thoreau refers indirectly to his hopes for his own earnest, reflective, suggestive book. And so the two travelers return to Concord, completing the circle of their journey.

Major Themes

Theme

The Journey Inward. *A Week on the Concord and Merrimack Rivers* is the record of Thoreau's journey inward toward an understanding of the universal and absolute. The actual journey described in the book provides a framework for Thoreau's many approaches to higher truth. The theme of inward journey is suggested by the book's structure, through imagery—particularly the image of the river as a stream of thought, by numerous passages throughout focusing on thought, the inner life, and the nature of exploration and discovery, and through reference to specific authors and books. Thoreau intimates the metaphorical nature of his journey at the beginning of *A Week*, in the chapter "Concord River":

> [Rivers] are the constant lure, when they flow by our doors, to distant enterprise and adventure, and, by a natural impulse, the dwellers on their banks will at length accompany their currents to the lowlands of the globe, or explore at their invitation the interior of continents.

Concord is Thoreau's own "port of entry and departure," both literally and spiritually. Throughout the book, he argues for the seeking of broad significance, of underlying principles as opposed to more limited worldly wisdom and particulate knowledge. His repeated praise of Oriental thought is based upon its focus on all-encompassing truth and on contemplation as well, in contrast with the western tendency toward busy, unexamined activity. Thoreau criticizes literature, religion, history, biography, medicine, and science as they exist because none is directed toward broad, transcendent vision. He emphasizes that the course of the journey inward is uncharted and unpredictable. The route is revealed along the way.

Thoreau affirms the reality and importance of the life of the mind in *A Week*. He writes in "Wednesday":

> This world is but canvass to our imaginations. I see men with infinite pains endeavoring to realize to their bodies, what I, with at least equal pains, would realize to my imagination,—its capacities. . . .

The inward journey through nature to higher understanding is serious and demanding. He writes in "Friday":

> It is easier to discover another such a new world as Columbus did, than to go within one fold of this which we appear to know so well; the land is lost sight of, the compass varies, and mankind mutiny; and still history accumulates like rubbish before the portals of nature.

He contrasts the disappearance of actual frontiers in his time with the persistence of the unexplored inner regions:

> But we found that the frontiers were not this way any longer. This generation has come into the world fatally late for some enterprises. Go where we will on the *surface* of things, men have been there before us. . . . But the lives of men, though more extended laterally in their range, are still as shallow as ever. . . . The frontiers are not east or west, north or south, but wherever a man *fronts* a fact, though that fact be his neighbor, there is an unsettled wilderness between him and Canada, between him and the setting sun, or, further still, between him and *it*.

Thoreau's ultimate optimism about the possibility of finding meaning through inward exploration is indicated by the two travelers' successful completion of their trip, literal and figurative, in *A Week*.

The Particular and the Universal. The purpose of the journey inward is to arrive at the universals revealed by particular expressions found in nature, history, and human character. The image of the all-encompassing river—composed of the many small streams flowing into it, all of them together emptying into the ocean—richly suggests the relationship between the particular and the universal. In *A Week*, Thoreau presents the comprehension of the divine and infinite as the object of all thought and activity. He writes in "Friday":

> Indeed, all that we call science, as well as all that we call poetry, is a particle of . . . information, accurate as far as it goes, though it be but to the confines of the truth. If we can reason so accurately, and with such wonderful confirmation of our reasoning, respecting so-called material objects and events infinitely removed beyond the range of our natural vision, so that the mind hesitates to trust its calculations even when they are confirmed by observation, why may not our speculations penetrate as far into the immaterial starry system, of which the former is but the outward and visible type?

Symbolic particulate information provides the evidence through which we understand the eternal. However, the accumulation of evidence will not by itself lead us to the universal. An alertness to revelation and a sense of vision—some degree of intuition—are required. We must be patient in waiting for insight.

Literary Device

Throughout *A Week*, Thoreau uses a number of specific examples to demonstrate the ways in which the universal is expressed through the particular. As the journey begins in "Saturday," he considers the place of the human life that he observes along the river within the context of universal history. In the same chapter, the specificity of his catalog of fishes threatens to overwhelm the reader until Thoreau places these creatures within the broad framework of nature's plan. Although there is a tremendous waste of individuals in the course of spawning and in the position of particular species within the food chain, the fishes comply with the role that nature has assigned them. In so doing, they thrive in the aggregate, despite the precariousness of the life of each one individually. In "Wednesday," he writes of watching the boats off Staten Island until they become generic rather than individual.

Thoreau finds little value in current science, history, and other disciplines that focus on the particular but stop short of broader perception. He looks more favorably on certain forms of expression—myth and fable, the literatures of ancient and more elemental times, Oriental scripture and literature, poetry, and music—that are not reducible into factual particulars and consequently allow a kind of direct perception of universals. Myth presents archetypal generalities of human experience rather than the biography of individual men. Poetry possesses a mystical, oracular quality. Music is "the sound of the universal laws promulgated." Fact and detail have their place but are only meaningful when interpreted by those with a larger sense of vision. Thoreau states his belief in the possibility that men of science and others devoted to the specific may achieve the perspective necessary to transform particular data into universal meaning.

Life, Death, and Regeneration. Life, death, and renewal are presented in various contexts throughout *A Week on the Concord and Merrimack Rivers.* The book opens with an invocation—tacitly a dedication—to John Thoreau, Thoreau's brother, traveling companion, and friend, whose death in 1842 provided the impetus behind the writing of *A Week.* Thoreau's discussion of fishes—individually transient, enduring as species—in "Saturday" focuses on both life and death. The passage of man's work into nature at Billerica Falls (in "Sunday") suggests impermanence and decay, and yet, at the same time, an absorption into something higher. "Monday" includes references to the Styx (ancient river of the underworld) and Charon (ferryman of the dead). A graveyard in "Monday" and Indian burial sites in "Wednesday" elicit comments on the enrichment of soil through decay of the bodies of the dead.

A Week is essentially an optimistic book in its treatment of death. Thoreau presents death not as an end but as part of larger natural and universal processes. Death not only results in the reabsorption of the body into the earth and into nature, but also in the transition of nature and the human soul into the infinity of the universe. The seed imagery throughout the book suggests constant regeneration even as individual lives pass away. The decay of Indian bones provides rich soil in which the food of later men may be grown. Thoreau's discussion of friendship in "Wednesday" ends with the confident assertion that "Friends have no place in the graveyard." A friend who dies will live on in the memories and hearts of those left behind. In "Friday," the final chapter, Thoreau lavishly develops the fall—often viewed as a time of decay and decline—as a vital season full of the promise of future growth.

The structure of *A Week* and the imagery of the river both powerfully suggest the passage of time. The journey takes place over the course of a week—a defined measure of time with a distinct beginning and end—and each chapter is organized around a single day. But time continues beyond the end of any measure of it. Moreover, there is optimism in the transition from summer to fall at the end of the book, and in the implicit anticipation of spring. And while the movement of the river toward the sea suggests the flow of time and life, the sea incorporates the river and the river lives on as part of something larger than itself. Eternity, a force present side by side with death throughout *A Week*, diminishes the significance of death.

Theme

Nature, Civilization, and the Human Spirit. *A Week on the Concord and Merrimack Rivers* is full of longing for and celebration of nature and wildness. Civilization and society, nature's foils, threaten man's communion with the wild. Human history has been destructive to wildness in both nature and man. From the beginning to the end of the book, the presence of the Native American in tales of local history constantly reminds the reader of civilization's incompatibility with nature. The story of Hannah Dustan in "Thursday" is a particularly powerful statement of the antagonism between civilization and the wild. Dustan, a New England folk heroine, experienced the full force of the wild in her captivity by Indians and in the murder of her infant. She escapes only by killing her captors—destroying the wild—but does so at a price to herself. As she proceeds down the river through the wilderness on her return to civilization, she is out of her element, silent and fearful. The woods are to her a "drear howling wilderness" to which she has no capacity to respond.

Character Insight

Thoreau finds a more positive example of man's ability to interact with nature in the person of the rough, rude, but innately civil man called Rice in "Tuesday." Like the Indian, Rice has grown naturally out of his wild environment. Above the meaningless niceties of society's standard of etiquette, Rice is naturally decent. Nature possesses its own refinement, Thoreau writes.

Thoreau denounces all of society's institutions in *A Week*. In "Sunday," he contrasts Christianity with the religion of nature, and the wildness of the Indian with the civilization of the white man, who is "strong in community, yielding in obedience to authority." Religion, political life, and society in general are presented as institutions of the dead, lacking both vitality and the heroic spirit. Man cannot heed the call of higher knowledge if he simply accepts conventional beliefs and definitions. Just as Thoreau travels against the current on the Merrimack River, he must go against the current of civilization and history in seeking the wild.

Literary Device

In "Thursday," the travelers pass into the Pemigewasset Wilderness. They climb Mount Washington, referred to only by its Indian name, "AGIOCOCHOOK." Although Thoreau describes the trek through the surrounding area, he is silent about the ascent. Silence is presented elsewhere in *A Week* as a listening for communication from nature and the divine. The lack of description and interpretation and the upper-casing of the mountain's name in the text suggest an experience too intense and mystical to be conveyed in words. At the end of the book, Thoreau exhorts his reader to become more natural and spiritual. The life of the spirit is not possible without openness to nature and the wild. Nature is essential to the inner voyage explored in *A Week*.

Theme

Inspiration and Writing. Thoreau's reading and his conscious consideration of writing are evident throughout *A Week*. The book includes quotations from a variety of authors, particularly ancient classical authors and archaic English writers, and poems and essays by Thoreau himself (some previously published). Moreover, many passages in *A Week* convey Thoreau's thoughts on the definition of powerful writing.

It is clear in *A Week* that Thoreau classes himself among poets. He did, in fact, write poetry, and published some of it in *The Dial* in the early 1840s. Some of his poetry remained in manuscript form, in his journal. Therefore, even though he is known primarily as a prose author, there is some literal truth to his defining himself as a poet. However, the word "poet" is used more broadly than in the literal sense of a writer of verse in *A Week*, as it is in the journal and elsewhere in Thoreau's writings. For Thoreau, the poet is an inspired writer with the ability to convey his life, the reality and significance of nature, and universal meaning. The poet is more than ordinarily susceptible to nature in all its forms, and preternaturally capable of expressing truth about the divine and the universal order. Thoreau respects myth, fable, and other primal forms that express the universal more than the narrowly cultural. As the "mysticism of mankind," poetry is close to myth and scripture. Thoreau also admires certain writers who possess vision and who treat broad and basic subjects. He writes in praise of Homer, Chaucer, Shakespeare, and Goethe, for example. He describes Alexander Henry's *Travels and Adventures in Canada* as natural, direct, rich in natural fact, lacking pretense and exaggeration. Although far from the standard definition of poetry, Henry's work transcends the narrowness of straight travel narrative and expresses "*perennials.*"

Thoreau distinguishes between two types of poets. The writer of genius and inspiration cultivates life and possesses God within. The writer of intellect and taste, more derivative than original, cultivates art. Thoreau states that true artistic greatness lies in the degree to which art expresses life. It is clear that he identifies his own efforts with the work of those poets who cultivate life. Interestingly, at the end of "Thursday," he writes of the difficulty of keeping a journal—the written record of life—while engaged in living the life that forms the subject matter of this record. Life and the art that reflects it may ideally be one, but in reality there is some distance between life and the written word.

Literary Device

Thoreau applies river imagery to writing as well as to life and the lapse of time in *A Week*. He likens writing to the flow of the river, thus endowing it with an organic, natural quality. He identifies homeliness, simplicity, vigor, and directness as virtues in poetry. Writing should be truthful, should describe things as they are. These fundamental qualities produce vital, fresh writing even when the subject matter is common. Originality rests in the treatment, not in the theme. Thoreau writes often of perception and perspective, of seeing things in a new light.

Poetry is appreciated in its irreducible integrity by "those for whom it was matured." But even early in his literary career, Thoreau understood that this audience was small. He indicates in "Friday" an awareness that there is not necessarily any connection between genius and appreciation. In "Sunday" and elsewhere, he disdains the approach to writing as a commodity. The actualities of the publishing world in the 1840s did not foster the sustained idealism necessary to create *A Week*.

Thoreau associates roughness and strength, even a certain violence, with meaningful writing. Just as nature possesses a savage and frightening aspect, so does composition. He writes in "Thursday": "The talent of composition is very dangerous,—the striking out the heart of life at a blow, as the Indian takes off a scalp. I feel as if my life had grown more outward when I can express it." And, as he perceives a loss of wildness to civilization over human history, so he observes a decline of poetry from a more natural age to the present.

Art and nature may exist in a kind of symbiosis. Thoreau writes in "Thursday":

> Art is not tame, and Nature is not wild, in the ordinary sense. A perfect work of man's art would also be wild or natural in a good sense. Man tames Nature only that he

may at last make her more free even than he found her, though he may never yet have succeeded.

The poet hopes to capture and transmit, and even enhance, the vitality of nature, his subject matter and his inspiration.

As he draws his book to a close in "Friday," Thoreau hopes for an audience sympathetic to his creative idealism, to his sense of writing as a medium for universal truth. He sees his proper audience as consisting of seekers after revelation and understanding such as he himself seeks: "A good book is the plectrum with which our else silent lyres are struck." He offers *A Week* as one of those good books that strike chords within the reader.

Theme

Friendship. The theme of friendship is implied throughout *A Week* in the companionship of the two travelers as they make their journey. John Thoreau, Henry's brother and the muse invoked at the beginning of the book, is never mentioned by name, nor is the depth of the emotional bond between the two referred to specifically and personally. The absence of comment on the relationship resembles Thoreau's silence regarding the ascent of Agiocochook. It suggests intensity of emotion, both private and deeply meaningful. The theme is explicitly developed in the long outpouring on friendship in "Wednesday." Thoreau's thoughts on the subject are highly idealistic and, the reader suspects, impossible to achieve and sustain outside of art. But the lyricism of this section is in keeping with Thoreau's idealism in presenting his other themes in *A Week*.

Neither the possibility of realizing the type of friendship that Thoreau extols nor his specific pronouncements on the nature of true friendship are as important as Thoreau's relationship with his brother, his sense of loss that must be worked through after John's death, and his writing the book to achieve some closure. Thoreau writes, "The only danger in Friendship is that it will end." He goes on to discuss the end of friendship through excessive criticism. Although he does not place the loss of a friend to death in the same category as loss through misunderstanding or failure of sympathy, either situation results in bereavement. He writes positively of the inspiration achieved through the death as well as the life of a friend. Because John's death did, in fact, inspire Thoreau to write *A Week*, the book itself affirms the endurance of friendship beyond death.

Civil Disobedience

Having spent one night in jail in July of 1846 for refusal to pay his poll tax in protest against slavery and the Mexican War, Thoreau lectured before the Concord Lyceum in January of 1848 on the subject "On the Relation of the Individual to the State." The lecture was published under the title "Resistance to Civil Government" in Elizabeth Peabody's *Aesthetic Papers*, in May 1849. It was included (as "Civil Disobedience") in Thoreau's *A Yankee in Canada, with Anti-Slavery and Reform Papers*, published in Boston in 1866 by Ticknor and Fields, and reprinted many times. The essay formed part of *Anti-Slavery and Reform Papers* as edited by British Thoreau biographer Henry S. Salt and issued in London in 1890. "Civil Disobedience" was included in the Riverside Edition of 1894 (in *Miscellanies*, the tenth volume), in the Walden and Manuscript Editions of 1906 (in *Cape Cod and Miscellanies*, the fourth volume), and in the Princeton Edition (in *Reform Papers*, the third volume) in 1973. One of Thoreau's most influential writings, it has been published separately many times (Walter Harding's *The Variorum Civil Disobedience*, for example, appeared in 1967), included in volumes of selections from Thoreau (among them the 1937 Modern Library Edition of *Walden and Other Writings of Henry David Thoreau*, edited by Brooks Atkinson), and translated into European and Asian languages.

Synopsis

Thoreau opens *Civil Disobedience* with the maxim "That government is best which governs least," and he speaks in favor of government that does not intrude upon men's lives. Government is only an expedient—a means of attaining an end. It exists because the people have chosen it to execute their will, but it is susceptible to misuse. The Mexican War is an example of a few people using the government as their tool. Thoreau asserts that government as an institution hinders the accomplishment of the work for which it was created. It exists for the sole purpose of ensuring individual freedom. Denying an interest in abolishing government, he states that he simply wants a better government. Majority rule is based on physical strength, not right and justice. Individual conscience should rule instead, and civil government should confine itself to those matters suited to decision by majority rule. He deplores the lack of judgment, moral sense, and conscience in the way men serve the state. A man cannot bow unquestioningly to the state's authority without disregarding himself.

Thoreau introduces the right of revolution, which all men recognize, and reflects on the American Revolution, the origins of which he finds less morally compelling than the issues at hand. Having developed the image of the government as a machine that may or may not do enough good to counterbalance what evil it commits, he urges rebellion. The opponents of reform, he recognizes, are not faraway politicians but ordinary people who cooperate with the system. The expression of opposition to slavery is meaningless. Only action—what you do about your objection—matters. Wrong will be redressed only by the individual, not through the mechanism of government. Although Thoreau asserts that a man has other, higher duties than eradicating institutional wrong, he must at least not be guilty through compliance. The individual must not support the structure of government, must act with principle, must break the law if necessary.

Abolition can be achieved by withdrawing support from the government, which may be accomplished practically through the non-payment of taxes. If imprisonment is the result, there is no shame in it—prison is the best place for a just man in an unjust society. In the current state of affairs, payment of taxes is violent and bloody. Non-payment constitutes a "peaceable revolution." Thoreau comments on the corrupting influence of money and property, and urges a simple, self-reliant lifestyle as a means of maintaining individual freedom. He describes his experience in the Concord Jail in some detail, commenting upon the folly of the state's treatment of a man as if he were a physical entity only, rather than an intellectual and moral one. A man can be compelled only by one who possesses greater morality. In *Civil Disobedience* as throughout his other writings, Thoreau focuses on the individual's ultimate responsibility to live deliberately and to extract meaning from his own life; overseeing the machinery of society is secondary.

Thoreau asserts that he does not want to quarrel or to feel superior to others. He wants to conform to the laws of the land, but current laws are not honorable from a higher point of view. Politics and politicians act as though the universe were ruled by expediency. In the progression from absolute monarchy to limited monarchy to democracy, Thoreau observes an evolution in government toward greater expression of the consent of the governed. He notes that democracy may not be the final stage in the process. His emphasis at the end of the essay is firmly on respect for the individual. There will never be a "really free and enlightened State" until the state recognizes the preeminence of the individual.

Major Themes

Theme

Civil Government and Higher Law. In *Civil Disobedience*, Thoreau's basic premise is that a higher law than civil law demands the obedience of the individual. Human law and government are subordinate. In cases where the two are at odds with one another, the individual must follow his conscience and, if necessary, disregard human law.

Thoreau prepared his lecture and essay on resistance to civil government in response to a specific event—the Mexican War, which was declared in May of 1846, and which was expected to result in the expansion of slave territory. He was not particularly inclined to devote much thought to political theory and reform. He writes in *Civil Disobedience*:

> . . . the government does not concern me much, and I shall bestow the fewest possible thoughts on it. It is not many moments that I live under a government, even in this world. If a man is thought-free [free in his thinking], fancy-free, imagination-free, that which *is not* never for a long time appearing *to be* to him, unwise rulers or reformers cannot fatally interrupt him.

The search for understanding of universal laws forms the proper use of a man's time, energy, and intellect. Thoreau writes dismissively of conscious reform: "I have other affairs to attend to. I came into this world, not chiefly to make this a good place to live in, but to live in it, be it good or bad." However, circumstances make it impossible to live life as usual without damage to morality and conscience:

> It is not a man's duty, as a matter of course, to devote himself to the eradication of any, even the most enormous wrong; he may still properly have other concerns to engage him; but it is his duty, at least, to wash his hands of it, and, if he gives it no thought longer, not to give it practically his support. If I devote myself to other pursuits and contemplations, I must first see, at least, that I do not pursue them sitting upon another man's shoulders. I must get off him first, that he may pursue his contemplations too.

Thoreau's antislavery and reform pieces do not diminish the significance of Transcendental exploration and discovery. They are specific reactions to what he sees as extreme events. They form an acknowledgment that inner exploration loses meaning if matters of conscience are overlooked in the process.

Government enforces civil law by physical means, which are ineffectual in relation to moral issues. When the man of conscience is at variance with the state, he is punished by physical confinement, a type of force, which accomplishes nothing. Thoreau comments, "They only can force me who obey a higher law than I do. They force me to become like themselves. I do not hear of *men* being *forced* to live this way or that by masses of men." The laws that apply in matters of conscience belong to a different sphere than those (like the building of roads) that can be decided by majority rule. In fact, government oversteps its authority when it becomes involved in moral issues.

Theme

Government and the Individual. Thoreau writes of government as "an expedient by which men would fain succeed in letting one another alone." It exists by consent of the governed to ensure the individual freedom that allows the pursuit of deep living and high thinking. Although it is liable to abuse, Thoreau nevertheless concedes that it is necessary: "But it is not the less necessary for [its shortcomings]; for the people must have some complicated machinery or other . . . to satisfy that idea of government which they have." Powerful statement though it is, *Civil Disobedience* is written in a relatively measured tone. Despite popular misinterpretation, Thoreau does not advocate the dissolution of government in it. He asks "not at once for no government, but *at once* a better government."

However, Thoreau does call for a government limited to decide those issues that it is fitted to consider:

> . . . a government in which the majority rule in all cases cannot be based on justice, even as far as men understand it. Can there not be a government in which majorities do not virtually decide right and wrong, but conscience?— in which majorities decide only those questions to which the rule of expediency is applicable? Must the citizen ever for a moment, or in the least degree, resign his conscience to the legislator?

Moral issues must be decided by the individual and his conscience, not by the majority through government. The Mexican War, which Thoreau believes must be stopped, may be halted by individual action, but not through the political process. *Civil Disobedience* is a call for limited government. Through nonpayment of taxes (the withholding of support from a government that commits immoral acts), the individual protests the government's involvement in issues over which it has no proper jurisdiction. This constitutes a "peaceable revolution," not a violent one. Thoreau is still able to accept that government has its place: "In fact, I quietly declare war with the State, after my fashion, though I will still make what use and get what advantage of her I can. . . ."

Throughout *Civil Disobedience*, Thoreau presents government as useless in relation to moral issues. Voting is but an expression of majority sentiment, and lacks the power of timely action possessed by the individual. The political process results in the election of those who hold office—available men, who accept the process but are not necessarily guided by principle. Thus, the system perpetuates itself and degenerates over time.

Thoreau underscores the power of the individual to effect reform. He says of the government at the beginning of the *Civil Disobedience*, "It has not the vitality and force of a single living man. . . ." Later, he urges individuals to fulfill their moral responsibility by taking the action that most would prefer to relegate to external forces:

> Some are petitioning the State to dissolve the Union, to disregard the requisitions of the President. Why do they not dissolve it themselves,—the union between themselves and the State,—and refuse to pay their quota into its treasury? Do they not stand in the same relation to the State, that the State does to the Union? And have not the same reasons prevented the State from resisting the Union, which have prevented them from resisting the State?

Reform will come only through the individual. Moral issues are the individual's concern. The individual's obligation is "to do at any time what [he thinks] right."

Thoreau expresses qualified optimism at the end of the essay, in his presentation of the evolution of government from absolute to limited monarchy to democracy, and in his suggestion that there may yet be a better form of government:

> There will never be a really free and enlightened State, until the State comes to recognize the individual as a higher and independent power, from which all its own power and authority are derived, and treats him accordingly. I please myself with imagining a State at last which can afford to be just to all men, and to treat the individual with respect as a neighbor. . . . A State which bore this

fruit . . . would prepare the way for a still more perfect and glorious State, which also I have imagined, but not yet anywhere seen.

Although non-government may constitute this "more perfect and glorious State," Thoreau recognizes that the time has not come for its realization.

On July 4, 1854, in the wake of the failure of an attempt to prevent the return of fugitive slave Anthony Burns to his master in accordance with the Fugitive Slave Law of 1850, Thoreau delivered "Slavery in Massachusetts" before an abolitionist audience in Framingham, Massachusetts. Although based upon the ideas expressed in *Civil Disobedience* about the nature and authority of government and about the individual's obligations in relation to both civil and higher law, "Slavery in Massachusetts" is a far more impassioned statement. As the abolitionist struggle became more desperate, Thoreau's willingness to demand radical and violent measures grew, and was more forcefully expressed. In "Slavery in Massachusetts," he calls for the government of Massachusetts to resist federal might through military means. His "Plea for Captain John Brown," delivered in Concord on October 30, 1859, following Brown's arrest for attempting to incite a slave rebellion through his attack on the federal arsenal at Harper's Ferry, is also based on the ideology presented in *Civil Disobedience*, and goes even farther in advocating whatever steps are necessary to stop government injustice. Thoreau writes in "A Plea": "I do not wish to kill nor to be killed, but I can foresee circumstances in which both these things would be by me unavoidable." Thoreau's vision of the relationship between man, God, and the state did not change, but his sense of the way in which individuals must resist institutionalized injustice evolved in response to specific national and local events.

Materialism and the Simple Life. Thoreau writes in *Civil Disobedience* of corrupting materialism and of the simple life as its antidote. He states that those who "assert the purest right, and consequently are most dangerous to a corrupt State, commonly have not spent much time in accumulating property." The upright man is thus typically untainted by money. Thoreau presents the level of a man's virtue as proportionate to how much money he possesses—"the more money, the less virtue." Money makes difficult choices and the consideration of priorities unnecessary. It takes the "moral ground . . . from under [a man's] feet." As means increase, the opportunity to live meaningfully decreases. The rich man, Thoreau writes, "is always sold to the institution which makes him rich." There is a close connection between the rich and the government that their taxes support.

Thoreau comments on the difficulty of trying to live "honestly and at the same time comfortably in outward respects." It is pointless to accumulate property. He suggests that it is better "to hire or squat somewhere, and raise but a small crop, and eat that soon. You must live within yourself, and depend upon yourself, always tucked up and ready for a start, and not have many affairs." In this emphasis on shunning materialism and living self-sufficiently, he foreshadows a major theme of *Walden* (1854).

Walden

While Thoreau lived at Walden (July 4, 1845–September 6, 1847), he wrote journal entries and prepared lyceum lectures on his experiment in living at the pond. By 1847, he had begun to set his first draft of *Walden* down on paper. After leaving Walden, he expanded and reworked his material repeatedly until the spring of 1854, producing a total of eight versions of the book. James Munroe, publisher of *A Week on the Concord and Merrimack Rivers* (1849), originally intended to publish *Walden* as well. However, with the failure of *A Week*, Munroe backed out of the agreement. In 1852, two parts of what would be *Walden* were published in *Sartain's Union Magazine* ("The Iron Horse" in July, "A Poet Buys A Farm" in August). Six selections from the book (under the title "A Massachusetts Hermit") appeared in advance of publication in the March 29, 1854 issue of the *New York Daily Tribune*. Ticknor and Fields published *Walden; or, Life in the Woods* in Boston in an edition of 2,000 copies on August 9, 1854. A second printing was issued in 1862, with multiple printings from the same stereotyped plates issued between that time and 1890. A second American edition (from a new setting of type) was published in 1889 by Houghton, Mifflin, in two volumes, the first English edition in 1886. In 1894, *Walden* was included as the second volume of the Riverside Edition of Thoreau's collected writings, in 1906 as the second volume of the Walden and Manuscript Editions. In 1971, it was issued as the first volume of the Princeton Edition.

Since the nineteenth century, *Walden* has been reprinted many times, in a variety of formats. It has been issued in its entirety and in abridged or selected form, by itself and in combination with other writings by Thoreau, in English and in many European and some Asian languages, in popular and scholarly versions, in inexpensive printings, and in limited fine press editions. A number of editions have been illustrated with artwork or photographs. Some individual chapters have been published separately.

Some of the well-known twentieth century editions of or including *Walden* are: the 1937 Modern Library Edition, edited by Brooks Atkinson; the 1939 Penguin Books edition; the 1946 edition with photographs, introduction, and commentary by Edwin Way Teale; the 1946 edition of selections, with photographs, by Henry Bugbee Kane; the 1947 *Portable Thoreau*, edited by Carl Bode; the 1962 *Variorum Walden*, edited by Walter Harding; and the 1970 *Annotated Walden* (a facsimile reprint of the first edition, with illustrations and notes), edited by Philip Van Doren Stern.

Synopsis

Although Thoreau actually lived at Walden for two years, *Walden* is a narrative of his life at the pond compressed into the cycle of a single year, from spring to spring. The book is presented in eighteen chapters.

Thoreau opens with the chapter "Economy." He sets forth the basic principles that guided his experiment in living, and urges his reader to aim higher than the values of society, to spiritualize. He explains that he writes in response to the curiosity of his townsmen, and draws attention to the fact that *Walden* is a first-person account. He writes of himself, the subject he knows best. Through his story, he hopes to tell his readers something of their own condition and how to improve it. Perceiving widespread anxiety and dissatisfaction with modern civilized life, he writes for the discontented, the mass of men who "lead lives of quiet desperation." Distinguishing between the outer and the inner man, he emphasizes the corrosiveness of materialism and constant labor to the individual's humanity and spiritual development. Thoreau encourages his readers to seek the divinity within, to throw off resignation to the status quo, to be satisfied with less materially, to embrace independence, self-reliance, and simplicity of life. In identifying necessities—food, shelter, clothing, and fuel—and detailing specifically the costs of his experiment, he points out that many so-called necessities are, in fact, luxuries that contribute to spiritual stagnation. Technological progress, moreover, has not truly enhanced quality of life or the condition of mankind. Comparing civilized and primitive man, Thoreau observes that civilization has institutionalized life and absorbed the individual. He writes of living fully in the present. He stresses that going to Walden was not a statement of economic protest, but an attempt to overcome society's obstacles to transacting his "private business." He does not suggest that anyone else should follow his particular course of action. Each man must find and follow his own path in understanding reality and seeking higher truth. Discussing philanthropy and reform, Thoreau highlights the importance of individual self-realization. Society will be reformed through reform of the individual, not through the development and refinement of institutions.

Literary Device

In "Where I Lived, and What I Lived For," Thoreau recounts his near-purchase of the Hollowell farm in Concord, which he ultimately did not buy. He remains unencumbered, able to enjoy all the benefits of the landscape without the burdens of property ownership. He becomes a homeowner instead at Walden, moving in, significantly, on July 4, 1845—his personal Independence Day, as well as the nation's. He casts himself as a chanticleer—a rooster—and *Walden*—his account of his experience—as the lusty crowing that wakes men up in the morning. More than the details of his situation at the pond, he relates the spiritual exhilaration of his going there, an experience surpassing the limitations of place and time. He writes of the morning hours as a daily opportunity to reaffirm his life in nature, a time of heightened awareness. To be awake—to be intellectually and spiritually alert—is to be alive. He states his purpose in going to Walden: to live deliberately, to confront the essentials, and to extract the meaning of life as it is, good or bad. He exhorts his readers to simplify, and points out our reluctance to alter the course of our lives. He again disputes the value of modern improvements, the railroad in particular. Our proper business is to seek the reality—the absolute—beyond what we think we know. This higher truth may be sought in the here and now—in the world we inhabit. Our existence forms a part of time, which flows into eternity, and affords access to the universal.

In the chapter "Reading," Thoreau discusses literature and books—a valuable inheritance from the past, useful to the individual in his quest for higher understanding. True works of literature convey significant, universal meaning to all generations. Such classics must be read as deliberately as they were written. He complains of current taste, and of the prevailing inability to read in a "high sense." Instead of reading the best, we choose the mediocre, which dulls our perception. Good books help us to throw off narrowness and ignorance, and serve as powerful catalysts to provoke change within.

Literary Device

In "Sounds," Thoreau turns from books to reality. He advises alertness to all that can be observed, coupled with an Oriental contemplation that allows assimilation of experience. As he describes what he hears and sees of nature through his window, his reverie is interrupted by the noise of the passing train. At first, he responds to the train—symbol of nineteenth century commerce and progress—with admiration for its almost mythical power. He then focuses on its inexorability and on the fact that as some things thrive, so others decline—the trees around the pond, for instance, which are cut and transported by train, or animals carried in the railroad cars. His comments on the railroad end on a note of disgust and dismissal, and he returns to his solitude and the sounds of the woods and the nearby community—church bells on Sundays, echoes, the call of the whippoorwill, the scream of the screech owl (indicative of the dark side of nature) and the cry of the hoot owl. The noise of the owls suggests a "vast and undeveloped nature which men have not recognized . . . the stark twilight and unsatisfied thoughts which all have." Sounds, in other words, express the reality of nature in its full complexity, and our longing to connect with it. He builds on his earlier image of himself as a crowing rooster through playful discussion of an imagined wild rooster in the woods, and closes the chapter with reference to the lack of domestic sounds at his Walden home. Nature, not the incidental noise of living, fills his senses.

Literary Device

Thoreau opens "Solitude" with a lyrical expression of his pleasure in and sympathy with nature. When he returns to his house after walking in the evening, he finds that visitors have stopped by, which prompts him to comment both on his literal distance from others while at the pond and on the figurative space between men. There is intimacy in his connection with nature, which provides sufficient companionship and precludes the possibility of loneliness. The vastness of the universe puts the space between men in perspective. Thoreau points out that if we attain a greater closeness to nature and the divine, we will not require physical proximity to others in the "depot, the post-office, the bar-room, the meeting-house, the school-house"—places that offer the kind of company that distracts and dissipates. He comments on man's dual nature as a physical entity and as an intellectual spectator within his own body, which separates a person from himself and adds further perspective to his distance from others. Moreover, a man is always alone when thinking and working. He concludes the chapter by referring to metaphorical visitors who represent God and nature, to his own oneness with nature, and to the health and vitality that nature imparts.

Character Insight

Thoreau asserts in "Visitors" that he is no hermit and that he enjoys the society of worthwhile people as much as any man does. He comments on the difficulty of maintaining sufficient space between himself and others to discuss significant subjects, and suggests that meaningful intimacy—intellectual communion—allows and requires silence (the opportunity to ponder and absorb what has been said) and distance (a suspension of interest in temporal and trivial personal matters). True companionship has nothing to do with the trappings of conventional hospitality. He writes at length of one of his favorite visitors, a French Canadian woodchopper, a simple, natural, direct man, skillful, quiet, solitary, humble, and contented, possessed of a well-developed animal nature but a spiritual nature only rudimentary, at best. As much as Thoreau appreciates the woodchopper's character and perceives that he has some ability to think for himself, he recognizes that the man accepts the human situation as it is and has no desire to improve himself. Thoreau mentions other visitors—half-wits, runaway slaves, and those who do not recognize when they have worn out their welcome. Visiting girls, boys, and young women seem able to respond to nature, whereas men of business, farmers, and others cannot leave their preoccupations behind. Reformers—"the greatest bores of all"— are most unwelcome guests, but Thoreau enjoys the company of children, railroad men taking a holiday, fishermen, poets, philosophers—all of whom can leave the village temporarily behind and immerse themselves in the woods.

Literary Device

In "The Bean-Field," Thoreau describes his experience of farming while living at Walden. His bean-field offers reality in the forms of physical labor and closeness to nature. He writes of turning up Indian arrowheads as he hoes and plants, suggesting that his use of the land is only one phase in the history of man's relation to the natural world. His bean-field is real enough, but it also metaphorically represents the field of inner self that must be carefully tended to produce a crop. Thoreau comments on the position of his bean-field between the wild and the cultivated—a position not unlike that which he himself occupies at the pond. He recalls the sights and sounds encountered while hoeing, focusing on the noise of town celebrations and military training, and cannot resist satirically underscoring the vainglory of the participants. He notes that he tends his beans while his contemporaries study art in Boston and Rome, or engage in contemplation and trade in faraway places, but in no way suggests that his efforts are inferior. Thoreau has no interest in beans per se, but rather in their symbolic meaning, which he as a writer will later be able to draw upon. He vows that in the future he will not sow beans but rather the seeds of "sincerity, truth, simplicity, faith, innocence, and the like." He expands upon seed imagery in referring to planting the seeds of new men. Lamenting a decline in farming from ancient times, he points out that agriculture is now a commercial enterprise, that the farmer has lost his integral relationship with nature. The true husbandman will cease to worry about the size of the crop and the gain to be had from it and will pay attention only to the work that is particularly his in making the land fruitful.

Thoreau begins "The Village" by remarking that he visits town every day or two to catch up on the news and to observe the villagers in their habitat as he does birds and squirrels in nature. But the town, full of idle curiosity and materialism, threatens independence and simplicity of life. He resists the shops on Concord's Mill Dam and makes his escape from the beckoning houses, and returns to the woods. He writes of going back to Walden at night and discusses the value of occasionally becoming lost in the dark or in a snowstorm. Sometimes a person lost is so disoriented that he begins to appreciate nature anew. Fresh perception of the familiar offers a different perspective, allowing us "to find ourselves, and realize where we are and the infinite extent of our relations." He refers to his overnight jailing in 1846 for refusal to pay his poll tax in protest against slavery and the Mexican War, and comments on the insistent intrusion of institutions upon men's lives.

Literary Device

Turning from his experience in town, Thoreau refers in the opening of "The Ponds" to his occasional ramblings "farther westward . . . into yet more unfrequented parts of the town." Throughout his writings, the west represents the unexplored in the wild and in the inner regions of man. In *Walden*, these regions are explored by the author through the pond. He writes of fishing on the pond by moonlight, his mind wandering into philosophical and universal realms, and of feeling the jerk of a fish on his line, which links him again to the reality of nature. He thus presents concrete reality and the spiritual element as opposing forces. He goes on to suggest that through his life at the pond, he has found a means of reconciling these forces.

Literary Device

Walden is presented in a variety of metaphorical ways in this chapter. Believed by many to be bottomless, it is emblematic of the mystery of the universe. As the "earth's eye," through which the "beholder measures the depth of his own nature," it reflects aspects of the narrator himself. As "a perfect forest mirror" on a September or October day, Walden is a "field of water" that "betrays the spirit that is in the air . . . continually receiving new life and motion from above"—a direct conduit between the divine and the beholder, embodying the workings of God and stimulating the narrator's receptivity and faculties. Walden is ancient, having existed perhaps from before the fall of man in the Garden of Eden. At the same time, it is perennially young. It possesses and imparts innocence. Its waters, remarkably transparent and pure, serve as a catalyst to revelation, understanding, and vision. Thoreau refers to talk of piping water from Walden into town and to the fact that the railroad and woodcutters have affected the surrounding area. And yet, the pond is eternal. It endures despite all of man's activities on and around it. In this chapter, Thoreau also writes of the other bodies of water that form his "lake country" (an indirect reference to English Romantic poets Coleridge and Wordsworth)—Goose Pond, Flint's Pond, Fair Haven Bay on the Sudbury River, and White Pond (Walden's "lesser twin"). He concludes "The Ponds" reproachfully, commenting that man does not sufficiently appreciate nature. Like Walden, she flourishes alone, away from the towns of men.

Style & Language

In "Baker Farm," Thoreau presents a study in contrasts between himself and John Field, a man unable to rise above his animal nature and material values. The chapter begins with lush natural detail. A worshipper of nature absorbed in reverie and aglow with perception, Thoreau visits pine groves reminiscent of ancient temples. He calls upon particular familiar trees. He describes once standing "in the very abutment of a rainbow's arch," bathed briefly and joyfully in a lake of light, "like a dolphin." The scene changes when, to escape a rain shower, he visits the squalid home of Irishman John Field. Field came to America to advance his material condition. The meanness of his life is compounded by his belief in the necessity of coffee, tea, butter, milk, and beef—all luxuries to Thoreau. Thoreau talks to Field as if he were a philosopher, urging him to simplify, but his words fall on uncomprehending ears. Exultant in his own joy in nature and aspiration toward meaning and understanding, Thoreau runs "down the hill toward the reddening west, with the rainbow over my shoulder," the "Good Genius" within urging him to "fish and hunt far and wide day by day," to remember God, to grow wild, to shun trade, to enjoy the land but not own it. The last paragraph is about John Field, by comparison with Thoreau "a poor man, born to be poor . . . not to rise in this world"—a man impoverished spiritually as well as materially.

In "Higher Laws," Thoreau deals with the conflict between two instincts that coexist side by side within himself—the hunger for wildness (expressed in his desire to seize and devour a woodchuck raw) and the drive toward a higher spiritual life. In discussing hunting and fishing (occupations that foster involvement with nature and that constitute the closest connection that many have with the woods), he suggests that all men are hunters and fishermen at a certain stage of development. Although most don't advance beyond this stage, if a man has the "seeds of better life in him," he may evolve to understanding nature as a poet or naturalist and may ultimately comprehend higher truth. Thoreau says that he himself has lost the desire to fish, but admits that if he lived in the wilderness, he would be tempted to take up hunting and fishing again. A man can't deny either his animal or his spiritual side. In discussing vegetarian diet and moderation in eating, sobriety, and chastity, he advocates both accepting and subordinating the physical appetites, but not disregarding them. The chapter concludes with reference to a generic John Farmer who, sitting at his door one September evening, despite himself is gradually induced to put aside his mundane thoughts and to consider practicing "some new austerity, to let his mind descend into his body and redeem it, and treat himself with ever increasing respect."

Literary Device

Continuing the theme developed in "Higher Laws," "Brute Neighbors" opens with a dialogue between Hermit and Poet, who epitomize polarized aspects of the author himself (animal nature and the yearning to transcend it). Through the rest of the chapter, he focuses his thoughts on the varieties of animal life—mice, phoebes, raccoons, woodchucks, turtle doves, red squirrels, ants, loons, and others—that parade before him at Walden. He provides context for his observations by posing the question of why man has "just these species of animals for his neighbors." He answers that they are "all beasts of burden, in a sense, made to carry some portion of our thoughts," thus imparting these animals with symbolic meaning as representations of something broader and higher. Several animals (the partridge and the "winged cat") are developed in such a way as to suggest a synthesis of animal and spiritual qualities. Thoreau devotes pages to describing a mock-heroic battle of ants, compared to the Concord Fight of 1775 and presented in straightforward annalistic style as having taken place "in the Presidency of Polk, five years before the passage of Webster's Fugitive-Slave Bill." He thus ironically undercuts the significance of human history and politics. The battle of the ants is every bit as dramatic as any human saga, and there is no reason that we should perceive it as less meaningful than events on the human stage. The image of the loon is also developed at length. Diving into the depths of the pond, the loon suggests the seeker of spiritual truth. It also represents the dark, mysterious aspect of nature. Thoreau thus uses the animal world to present the unity of animal and human life and to emphasize nature's complexity.

Literary Device

The narrative moves decisively into fall in the chapter "House-Warming." Thoreau praises the ground-nut, an indigenous and almost exterminated plant, which yet may demonstrate the vigor of the wild by outlasting cultivated crops. He describes the turning of the leaves, the movement of wasps into his house, and the building of his chimney. Described as an "independent structure, standing on the ground and rising through the house to the heavens," the chimney clearly represents the author himself, grounded in this world but striving for universal truth. The pond cools and begins to freeze, and Thoreau withdraws both into his house, which he has plastered, and into his soul as well. He continues his spiritual quest indoors, and dreams of a more metaphorical house, cavernous, open to the heavens, requiring no housekeeping. He regrets the superficiality of hospitality as we know it, which does not permit real communion between host and guest. He writes of gathering wood for fuel, of his woodpile, and of the moles in his cellar, enjoying the perpetual summer maintained inside even in the middle of winter. Winter makes Thoreau lethargic, but the atmosphere of the house revives him and prolongs his spiritual life through the season. He is now prepared for physical and spiritual winter.

Thoreau begins "Former Inhabitants; and Winter Visitors" by recalling cheerful winter evenings spent by the fireside. But winter is quiet—even the owl is hushed—and his thoughts turn to past inhabitants of the Walden Woods. He writes of Cato Ingraham (a former slave), the black woman Zilpha (who led a "hard and inhumane" life), Brister

Freeman (another slave) and his wife Fenda (a fortune-teller), the Stratton and Breed families, Wyman (a potter), and Hugh Quoil—all people on the margin of society, whose social isolation matches the isolation of their life near the pond. Thoreau ponders why Walden's "small village, germ of something more" failed, while Concord thrives, and comments on how little the former inhabitants have affected the landscape. The past failed to realize the promise of Walden, but perhaps Thoreau himself will do so. He observes that nobody has previously built on the spot he now occupies—that is, he does not labor under the burden of the past. He has few visitors in winter, but no lack of society nevertheless. He still goes into town (where he visits Emerson, who is referred to but not mentioned by name), and receives a few welcome visitors (none of them named specifically)—a "long-headed farmer" (Edmund Hosmer), a poet (Ellery Channing), and a philosopher (Bronson Alcott). He waits for the mysterious "Visitor who never comes."

Thoreau again takes up the subject of fresh perspective on the familiar in "Winter Animals." He examines the landscape from frozen Flint's Pond, and comments on how wide and strange it appears. He writes of winter sounds—of the hoot owl, of ice on the pond, of the ground cracking, of wild animals, of a hunter and his hounds. He describes a pathetic, trembling hare that shows surprising energy as it leaps away, demonstrating the "vigor and dignity of Nature."

At the beginning of "The Pond in Winter," Thoreau awakens with a vague impression that he has been asked a question that he has been trying unsuccessfully to answer. But he looks out upon nature, itself "an answered question," and into the daylight, and his anxiety is quelled. The darkness and dormancy of winter may slow down spiritual processes, but the dawn of each day provides a new beginning. In search of water, Thoreau takes an axe to the pond's frozen surface and, looking into the window he cuts in the ice, sees life below despite its apparent absence from above. The workings of God in nature are present even where we don't expect them. He writes of the fishermen who come to the pond, simple men, but wiser than they know, wild, who pay little attention to society's dictates and whims. He describes surveying the bottom of Walden in 1846, and is able to assure his reader that Walden is, in fact, not bottomless. There is a need for mystery, however, and as long as there are believers in the infinite, some ponds will be bottomless. In probing the depths of bodies of water, imagination dives down deeper than nature's reality. Thoreau expresses the Transcendental notion that if we knew all the laws of nature, one natural fact or phenomenon would allow us to infer the whole. But our knowledge of nature's laws is imperfect. He extrapolates from the pond to humankind, suggesting the scientific calculation of a man's height or depth of character from his exterior and his circumstances. The pond and the individual are both microcosms. Thoreau describes commercial ice-cutting at Walden Pond. Despite what might at first seem a violation of the pond's integrity, Walden is unchanged and unharmed. Moreover, ice from the pond is shipped far and wide, even to India, where others thus drink from Thoreau's spiritual well. Walden water mixes with Ganges water, while Thoreau bathes his intellect "in the stupendous and cosmogonal philosophy of the Bhagvat Geeta"—no doubt an even exchange, in Thoreau's mind.

Literary Device

"Spring" brings the breaking up of the ice on Walden Pond and a celebration of the rebirth of both nature and the spirit. Thoreau again presents the pond as a microcosm, remarking, "The phenomena of the year take place every day in a pond on a small scale." He revels in listening and watching for evidence of spring, and describes in great detail the "sand foliage" (patterns made by thawing sand and clay flowing down a bank of earth in the railroad cut near Walden), an early sign of spring that presages the verdant foliage to come. In its similarity to real foliage, the sand foliage demonstrates that nothing is inorganic, and that the earth is not an artifact of dead history. It is, rather, living poetry, compared with which human art and institutions are insignificant. The chapter is rich with expressions of vitality, expansion, exhilaration, and joy. Thoreau focuses on the details of nature that mark the awakening of spring. He asks what meaning chronologies, traditions, and written revelations have at such a time. Rebirth after death suggests immortality. Walden has seemingly died, and yet now, in the spring, reasserts its vigor and endurance. The narrator, too, is reinvigorated, becomes "elastic" again. A man's thoughts improve in spring, and his ability to forgive and forget the shortcomings of his fellows—to start afresh—increases. Thoreau states the need for the "tonic of wildness," noting that life would stagnate without it. He comments also on the duality of our need to explore and explain things and our simultaneous longing for the mysterious. Taking either approach, we can never have enough of nature—it is a source of strength and proof of a more lasting life beyond our limited human span. Thoreau refers to the passage of time, to the seasons "rolling on into summer," and abruptly ends the narrative. He compresses his entire second year at the pond into the half-sentence, "and the second year was similar to it." The last sentence records his departure from the pond on September 6, 1847.

Literary Device

In his "Conclusion," Thoreau again exhorts his reader to begin a new, higher life. He points out that we restrict ourselves and our view of the universe by accepting externally imposed limits, and urges us to make life's journey deliberately, to look inward and to make the interior voyage of discovery. Evoking the great explorers Mungo Park, Lewis and Clark, Frobisher, and Columbus, he presents inner exploration as comparable to the exploration of the North American continent. Thoreau explains that he left the woods for the same reason that he went there, and that he must move on to new endeavors. There is danger even in a new enterprise of falling into a pattern of tradition and conformity. One must move forward optimistically toward his dream, leaving some things behind and gaining awareness of others. A man will replace his former thoughts and conventional common sense with a new, broader understanding, thereby putting a solid foundation under his aspirations. Thoreau expresses unqualified confidence that man's dreams are achievable, and that his experiment at Walden successfully demonstrates this. The experience and truth to which a man attains cannot be adequately conveyed in ordinary language, must be "translated" through a more expressive, suggestive, figurative language. Thoreau entreats his readers to accept and make the most of what we are, to "mind our business," not somebody else's idea of what our business should be. He presents the parable of the artist of Kouroo, who strove for perfection and whose singleness of purpose endowed him with perennial youth. Transcending time and the decay of civilization, the artist endures, creates true art, and achieves perfection. This parable demonstrates the endurance of truth. Thoreau again urges us to face life as it is, to reject materialism, to embrace simplicity, serenely to cultivate self, and to understand the difference between the temporal and the permanent. He ends *Walden* with an affirmation of resurrection and immortality through the quest for higher truth. One last time, he uses the morning imagery that throughout the book signifies new beginnings and heightened perception: "Only that day dawns to which we are awake. There is more day to dawn. The sun is but a morning star."

Major Themes

Theme

The Spiritual Journey. *Walden* is, above all, the account of Thoreau's own exploration of his capabilities and his search for spiritual understanding. Thoreau recounts his personal quest to demonstrate to his readers the possibility of surmounting the obstacles that materialistic society places in the path of the individual. He does not—cannot—spell out for the reader the spiritual truth that lies at the end of the journey. He focuses on the search itself and the compelling need to make it. *Walden* chronicles spiritual growth, but the progress of this growth is not linear. It has peaks and valleys, periods of latency as well as of inspired perception.

In "Economy," Thoreau explains his purpose in going to live at the pond. He distinguishes between the outer man—the ephemeral physical being that "is soon ploughed into the soil for compost," and the inner man. He points out the forces that dull and subjugate the inner man, materialism and constant labor in particular. He recognizes the pervasive malaise that results from society's suppression of what we might be—the "stereotyped but unconscious despair . . . concealed even under what are called the games and amusements of mankind." In "Where I Lived, and What I Lived For," he advises self-improvement, the cultivation of our intellectual and spiritual needs:

> We must learn to reawaken and keep ourselves awake . . .
> by an infinite expectation of the dawn, which does not
> forsake us in our soundest sleep. I know of no more
> encouraging fact than the unquestionable ability of man
> to elevate his life by a conscious endeavor.

The ultimate goal of the author's experiment at Walden is not to prove the economic advantage of living simply, but rather to nurture understanding of self and of the universe.

Literary
Device

In the "Conclusion," Thoreau urges us to seek "our own interior . . . on the chart," regardless of whether it proves to be good or bad, to investigate the "continents and seas in the moral world to which every man is an isthmus or an inlet." Actual voyages of exploration and discovery pale by comparison to the journey inward and upward. He encourages the reader to begin right now. We tend to "esteem truth remote, in the outskirts of the system, behind the farthest star." But, as the author writes in "Where I Lived, and What I Lived For":

> . . . all these times and places and occasions are now and
> here. God himself culminates in the present moment,
> and will never be more divine in the lapse of all the
> ages. And we are enabled to apprehend at all what is sub-
> lime and noble only by the perpetual instilling and drench-
> ing of the reality which surrounds us.

Our existence occupies one moment in the continuity of time ("Time
is but the stream I go a-fishing in," Thoreau writes at the end of "Where
I Lived . . ."). From any particular point of existence, the universal is
accessible. By living deliberately, self-reliantly, and independently in the
present, we may transcend the limits of time, "walk with the Builder of
the universe . . . not . . . live in this restless, nervous, bustling, trivial
Nineteenth Century, but stand or sit thoughtfully while it goes by" (as
Thoreau writes in his "Conclusion").

Life at Walden Pond provides Thoreau with the opportunity to journey into himself, into nature, and into the divine, but other men may
have approaches of their own, reflecting their particular conditions and
circumstances. Even for Thoreau, his Walden experiment is only one
expression of the spiritual impulse. As he explains in the "Conclusion,"
he leaves Walden because he has "several more lives to live," and can
spare no more time for the one he has so fully described in his book.
He does not prescribe living at Walden as a remedy for the spiritual ills
of others; he offers it only as an example.

**Literary
Device**

Thoreau uses an astonishing range of metaphors to characterize the spiritual quest. Walden Pond itself, where Thoreau's own journey unfolds,
is both real and symbolic. It represents the reality of nature, an expression of the divine, human potential for clear perception and understanding, and the mystery of the universe, which, although vast, may
nevertheless be approached and understood. Thoreau's bean-field symbolizes the author's inner field, which must be planted, hoed, and tended.
Others cultivate themselves by studying art in Boston or Rome, but
Thoreau's Transcendental self-culture takes place in the bean-field.
Described in "House-Warming" as "an independent structure, standing
on the ground and rising through the house to the heavens," Thoreau's
chimney symbolizes individual aspiration toward the spiritual and infinite. As it dives into Walden's depths, the loon that shows up repeatedly
in the book stands for man in search of higher understanding. The
imagery of morning and light in *Walden* suggests increased perception,
insight, and inspiration. And the sand foliage in "Spring" represents the
work of the creator, evident to man through nature.

Literary
Device

Thoreau presents the spiritual journey of *Walden* in relation to the cycle of the seasons. The book is structured around the advancing seasons of a single year, beginning with the author's preparing to build his house in the spring, proceeding through fall and winter, and ending with the return of spring. The two years of his actual stay at Walden are compressed into a single year to provide narrative coherence and movement and to build toward the presentation of rebirth in "Spring." The narrator expresses optimism and anxiety at different phases of his spiritual journey. His mood is integrally connected to season. Winter, a time of spiritual dormancy, slows the journey. At the beginning of "The Pond in Winter," he awakens in a state of anxiety, with "the impression that some question has been put to me, which I have been endeavoring in vain to answer in my sleep." If winter delays the processes of perception and understanding, the arrival of spring brings celebration of the divine in nature, exuberant reawakening of all the narrator's faculties, and a renewed sense of spiritual possibility.

Character
Insight

There are seasons in the development of individual men and mankind as a whole, as well as in nature. In "Higher Laws," Thoreau discusses preoccupation with hunting and fishing as one stage in the evolution toward spiritual consciousness. Hunting and fishing, expressions of man's animal aspect, comprise one form of intense involvement with nature. The man who has "seeds of a better life in him" may progress to a broader, more poetic understanding of the natural world, and ultimately achieve true spirituality. Thoreau observes in certain individuals—fishermen, hunters, and woodchoppers—the ability to perceive the reality of nature clearly, and evidence of higher capacities as well. Openness to change and to new perspectives is necessary to elevate the rudimentary link with nature to a higher plane of awareness and understanding. As Thoreau writes in "The Village," we need to be lost to "appreciate the vastness and strangeness of Nature," to "begin to find ourselves, and realize where we are and the infinite extent of our relations." Not many men can make the leap from hunting and fishing to higher pursuits. And many, like the Irishman John Field in "Baker Farm" and most of Thoreau's contemporaries in the village, are essentially disconnected from nature. Field cannot decide whether he wants to go fishing. When he actually makes up his mind to do so, he proves a poor fisherman. He cannot even begin the spiritual journey at the most elemental level.

Theme

Duality of Man and of Nature. Thoreau's appeal to the readers of *Walden* to spiritualize is predicated on the recognition of two sides of human nature—the animal and the spiritual—and upon his conviction that man must acknowledge and in some way reconcile these opposing tendencies. In "Economy," he discusses the physical necessities of life—food, shelter, clothing, and fuel. Until these needs are met, a person cannot rise above them. After he has taken care of the essentials, however, "there is another alternative than to obtain the superfluities; and that is, to adventure on life now, his vacation from humbler toil having commenced," and ultimately to turn his thoughts "into the heavens above."

All men have both animal instincts and higher capacities. Thoreau underscores this coexistence of animal and higher qualities in "Solitude," in which he describes man as simultaneously a physical entity and as an intellectual spectator within his own body. Some men show intelligence, perception, and a relation to nature. A few actually embark upon the spiritual quest. Those who are comfortable in nature—even if they do not actively seek to understand natural laws—and who are willing to think for themselves may progress from living in reality to a more spiritual life.

Character Insight

Thoreau is fascinated by simple men who live close to nature, and particularly by the French Canadian woodchopper (Alek Therien, unnamed in *Walden*). He describes the woodchopper in "Visitors" as a true "Homeric or Paphlagonian man," who appreciates epic poetry in his own way. He is both stout and a "great consumer of meat." He is deliberate and unhurried in his actions, good at his work, quiet, solitary, and happy. Thoreau writes, "In him the animal man chiefly was developed. . . . But the intellectual and what is called spiritual man in him were slumbering as in an infant." He is humble, reverent, respectful of his betters, and accepts life as it is. Thoreau detects in him a "man whom I had not seen before, and I did not know whether he was as wise as Shakespeare or as simply ignorant as a child." He approaches things with practical intelligence, displays an almost philosophical outlook, has a certain "positive originality," and is capable of "thinking for himself and expressing his own opinion." But Thoreau cannot move the woodcutter to "take the spiritual view of things." Thoreau suspects that there are unexplored depths of intellect and spirituality within this man:

He suggested that there might be men of genius in the lowest grades of life, however humble and illiterate, who take their own view always, or do not pretend to see at all; who are as bottomless even as Walden Pond was thought to be, though they may be dark and muddy.

But the woodcutter resists rising beyond his animal nature, and consequently offers no insight into the integration of man's animal and spiritual sides.

Thoreau considers man's dual nature—animal and spiritual—in "Higher Laws." He writes of his own urge to gobble down a raw woodchuck as an expression of animal impulse that is as much a part of him as of any man. Throughout the chapter, he writes of subduing the appetites, of subordinating the animal to the higher instincts. In writing of hunting and fishing, Thoreau writes that he himself, formerly a fisherman, no longer has a taste for fishing: "There is unquestionably this instinct in me which belongs to the lower orders of creation; yet with every year I am less a fisherman . . . at present I am no fisherman at all." In stating that if he lived in the wilderness he would be tempted "to become a fisher and hunter in earnest," Thoreau acknowledges that no matter how well developed a man is intellectually and spiritually, the animal is always present within. The individual's awareness of self, of nature, and of higher purpose provides the key to surpassing animal nature. The reconciliation of animal and spiritual—if sublimation can be considered reconciliation—takes place through human understanding.

Literary Device

Nature, too, has its duality in *Walden*. Thoreau clearly perceives and enjoys nature as reality. He writes at the beginning of "Sounds" of the "language which all things and events speak without metaphor." And yet, throughout the book, he repeatedly uses objects and creatures in the natural world—Walden Pond, his bean-field, and the loon, among others—metaphorically. He clearly shares Emerson's Transcendental understanding of nature (expressed in *Nature* in 1836) as symbolic of spirit. Thoreau writes that he values the very real beans in his bean-field not merely as beans, but as "tropes and expression, to serve a parable-maker one day." And in discussing just why particular species, and only those species, exist in nature, Thoreau comments that "they are all beasts of burden, in a sense, made to carry some portion of our thoughts."

Literary
Device

In the chapter "The Ponds," Thoreau suggests integration of nature as reality and nature as symbol. He writes of fishing on the pond at night:

> It was very queer, especially in dark nights, when your thoughts had wandered to vast and cosmogonal themes in other spheres, to feel this faint jerk, which came to interrupt your dreams and link you to Nature again. It seemed as if I might next cast my line upward into the air, as well as downward into this element which was scarcely more dense. Thus I caught two fishes as it were with one hook.

The thinking man is thus abruptly brought back from the spiritual realm to reality. The pond is the work of the divine creator, a point of access to the universal for the alert seeker. Through the pond, through nature, man sits at the gateway between earth and heaven. The physical pond can be surveyed. But the symbolic pond seems bottomless to some men, and will continue to be so perceived as long as men need to believe in the infinite. Man (as Thoreau writes in "Spring") wants to understand things, and yet, at the same time, craves the inexplicable. Such synthesis as is possible between the reality and symbolism of nature takes place within the mind of the observer, through flashes of intuition, inspiration, and imagination.

Theme

Growth, Change, and Renewal. *Walden* is Thoreau's entreaty to his reader to begin a new life. The book affirms change over stasis, present over past, vitality over stagnation, life over death. It celebrates renewal, even immortality. In writing *Walden*, Thoreau tells of the course of his own spiritualization—a process of intense change and development—and counsels the reader on how to elevate. Optimism about change is evident in his own story and implicit in his advice to the reader.

Transformation and inertia are presented as conflicting forces, balanced against one another in a kind of universal tension. The individual changes biologically as well as intellectually and spiritually, but his physical progression from youth to old age follows a path more or less set by nature. Nature itself changes cyclically, but the cycle of the seasons—the cycle of life—is repeated over and over. The classics of literature possess permanence in their expression of universal meaning, their relevance to men in all times. They simultaneously have the life-altering power to change a man. Higher laws and divinity are absolute, but they are transformative for the man sensitive to the meanings of nature. Society, institutions, and the traditions of the past—expressions

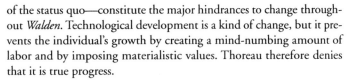

of the status quo—constitute the major hindrances to change through-out *Walden*. Technological development is a kind of change, but it pre-vents the individual's growth by creating a mind-numbing amount of labor and by imposing materialistic values. Thoreau therefore denies that it is true progress.

Literary Device

As a manifestation of vigorous nature and of God's work, Walden is eternal. It transcends time and change. Thoreau writes in "The Ponds":

> . . . of all the characters I have known, perhaps Walden wears best, and best preserves its purity. . . . Though the woodchoppers have laid bare first this shore and then that, and the Irish have built their sties by it, and the railroad has infringed on its border, and the ice-men have skimmed it once, it is itself unchanged, the same water which my youthful eyes fell on; all the change is in me. . . . It is perennially young. . . . Why, here is Walden, the same woodland lake that I discovered so many years ago; where a forest was cut down last winter another is springing up by its shore as lustily as ever; the same thought is welling up to its surface that was then; it is the same liquid joy and happiness to itself and its Maker, ay, and it *may* be to me. It is the work of a brave man surely. . . .

The degree to which an individual may spiritualize, may comprehend divinity, depends on his ability to differentiate between permanent and transient values and his persistence in seeking the permanent, the absolute and ideal. Thoreau's spiritual journey provides one example of striving toward the absolute. The story of the artist of Kouroo, who aspired to perfection and, in the process of single-mindedly achieving it, transcended time and mortality, provides another.

Vitality and the ability to change are bound up with perception throughout *Walden*. The light of each new day brings fresh opportu-nity for understanding. Thoreau refers often to vision and to perception-enhancing experience. He writes in "The Village" of being lost in a snowstorm, which bestows a heightened appreciation of nature and an ability to see familiar things anew. At the beginning of "Winter Animals," he describes looking at the landscape from the frozen surface of Flint's Pond and marveling at the sensation of never having seen it before. Openness to taking new perspectives is essential to individual change.

In "Spring," the process of rebirth, the leap from death to life, represents radical change. Thoreau writes that Walden was dead, and is now alive again. The chapter concludes with the seasons "rolling on into summer" in a predictable cycle of endless change. The narrative of *Walden* thus ends with the integration of transience and permanence, of change and constancy.

Theme

The Individual—Centrality and Independence. As the story of Thoreau's own spiritual journey, *Walden* elevates the individual in a personal way. The experience of the author himself is central to the book. Thoreau emphasizes the first-person nature of his narrative in "Economy": "In most books, the *I*, or first person, is omitted. . . . We commonly do not remember that it is, after all, always the first person that is speaking. I should not talk so much about myself if there were any body else whom I knew as well." He requires not only of himself but of every writer "a simple and sincere account of his own life." His life validates the narrator's work and confers the right to advise others. Thoreau emphasizes the fact that he proclaims his own experience through the image of himself as Chanticleer, the fabled rooster, in "Where I Lived, and What I Lived For": ". . . I do not propose to write an ode to dejection, but to brag as lustily as chanticleer in the morning, standing on his roost, if only to wake my neighbors up."

Literary Device

In *Walden*, as throughout Thoreau's writings, anything that encourages individual conformity to the status quo—society, institutions, the historical past—is criticized. In "Economy," Thoreau compares primitive and civilized life: "[T]his points to an important distinction between the civilized man and the savage . . . the life of a civilized people [is made] an *institution*, in which the life of the individual is to a great extent absorbed." Thoreau stresses how costly this assimilation is. Institutions—church, the marketplace, government, the political arena—impose their own values and curtail the individual's freedom to think independently. The village is full of shops that beckon to the passerby, but their materialistic appeal distracts a man from the pursuit of nature and spirit. In "The Bean-Field," the noisy members of the military training band (ironically described as keepers of "the liberties of Massachusetts and of our fatherland") blur into an indistinct, humming swarm. In "Economy," the train—regarded by most as progress—transports the products of trade and commerce, metaphorically running over most of those who rush to board it. When Thoreau describes his July 1846 arrest in the village for refusing to pay his poll tax, his freedom to protest slavery and the Mexican War is compromised by government as personified in the jailer (Sam Staples, unnamed in *Walden*). Government infringes upon the "virtues of a superior man." Wherever the individual goes, "men will pursue and paw him with their dirty institutions and, if they can, constrain him to belong to their desperate odd-fellow society." The thinking man is necessarily opposed to the social structure. In *Walden*, Thoreau exalts the change required for individual spiritualization. Society and its institutions are conservative, inertial forces, obstacles to transformation.

Thoreau writes disparagingly of organized reform in *Walden*, particularly at the end of "Economy": "If I knew for a certainty that a man was coming to my house with the conscious design of doing me good, I should run for my life. . . ." The reform of society rests within the individual. Each man is a microcosm. If he works at improving himself, he reforms the world more effectively than can any philanthropic scheme or organization. Thoreau perceives in the externally-directed reformer "not his sympathy with his fellows in distress, but . . . his private ail." He adds, "Let this be righted, let the spring come to him, the morning rise over his couch, and he will forsake his generous companions without apology." The man who minds his own business—tends to his own spiritual health—is the true reformer of society. The individual alone is capable of meaningful, far-reaching change.

Literary Device

Thoreau emphasizes the individual's need to maintain independence. Independence of thought requires self-reliance and some degree of separation from others. Significantly, he moves into his house at Walden Pond on July 4, 1845—more than a literal Independence Day. His chimney, symbol of the narrator himself in "House-Warming," is described as an independent structure. As he points out in "Solitude," a man thinking and a man working are always alone. Thoreau distinguishes between solitude and loneliness. In solitude, there is a sufficiency of companionship in self and nature, and the possibility of spiritual understanding. Loneliness is not a consideration. Men should stay away from the busy places where crowds congregate, and seek instead "the perennial source of life." Meaningful interaction with others—when companions begin "to utter big thoughts in big words," as he writes in "Visitors"—must allow both distance and silence, which impart perspective. Physical and intellectual independence from narrowing influences protect the individual's ability to make the spiritual journey.

The Simple Life. In "Where I Lived, and What I Lived For," Thoreau urges, "Simplicity, simplicity, simplicity! I say, let your affairs be as two or three, and not a hundred or a thousand; instead of a million count half a dozen, and keep your accounts on your thumb nail." This passage is one of the most frequently quoted from all of Thoreau's writings. Throughout *Walden*, Thoreau devotes considerable attention to the subject of the simple life. In "Economy," he presents the details of his simple, efficient, self-reliant life at Walden Pond, calculating the costs of shelter, food, clothing, and other necessities to the half penny. He is so specific and precise that many readers have approached *Walden* as a manifesto of particular social, economic, and political points of view, in the process sometimes overlooking Thoreau's larger purpose in describing his life at the pond.

Thoreau emphasizes the crushing, numbing effect of materialism and commercialism on the individual's life. Property ownership and technological progress consume men before they have a chance to consider how they might live. The author encourages his contemporaries to be content with less materially. In "Where I Lived, and What I Lived For," he tells how he himself came close to purchasing the Hollowell place (a Concord farm), but in the end did not. He thus remains able to enjoy the landscape without obligating himself and giving up his freedom. In "The Bean-Field," he laments the commercialization of agriculture, which has lost its archaic dignity. In "The Village," he exposes the at once comic and grotesque seductiveness of the shops on Concord's Mill Dam, and describes his own hasty escape from town. In "Baker Farm," he sketches the character of John Field, a poor man who regards as necessities tea, coffee, meat, and other dispensables that are obtained only at the cost of precluding higher life. Thoreau's own simple lifestyle contrasts throughout with the multiple, insistent expressions of society's materialism.

But never in *Walden* does Thoreau suggest that every man should move to Walden Pond, bake his own bread, and grow beans. His experiment in simplicity is but a means to the end of self-realization and spiritualization—not the end itself. He stresses that there may be as many ways of transcending worldly values as there are men. He writes in "Economy":

> . . . I would have each one be very careful to find out and pursue *his own* way, and not his father's or his mother's or his neighbor's instead. The youth may build or plant or

sail, only let him not be hindered from doing that which he tells me he would like to do.

There are other approaches than Thoreau's own to the dilemmas that society creates.

At the end of "The Pond in Winter," Thoreau provides a suggestive example of the translation of commercial enterprise into the spiritual realm. He writes of the shipment of Walden ice to Madras, Bombay, and Calcutta, enabling others to drink from his own spiritual well, while at Walden he immerses himself in the Bhagavad Gita. This perfect turning of the tables on materialism underscores that Thoreau's equation of the simple life with the spiritual quest is more subtle than a straightforward correspondence of the two.

"Walking"

Thoreau's essay "Walking" grew out of journal entries developed in 1851 into two lectures, "Walking" and "The Wild," which were delivered in 1851 and 1852, and again in 1856 and 1857. Thoreau combined the lectures, separated them in 1854, and worked them together again for publication in 1862, as he was dying. "Walking" was first published just after the author's death, in the June 1862 issue of *Atlantic Monthly*. (The manuscript that Thoreau prepared for the publisher has been held by the Concord Free Public Library since 1873.) "Walking" was included in the collection *Excursions*, first issued in Boston by Ticknor and Fields in 1863 and reprinted a number of times from the Ticknor and Fields plates until the publication of the Riverside Edition of Thoreau's writings in 1894. It appeared in the version of *Excursions* reorganized for and printed as the ninth volume of the Riverside Edition, and in the fifth volume (*Excursions and Poems*) of the 1906 Walden and Manuscript Editions. It has been printed in a number of selected editions, among them: *Essays and Other Writings of Henry Thoreau*, edited by Will H. Dircks (London, 1891); *Selections from Thoreau*, edited by Henry S. Salt (London, 1895); the Modern Library Edition of *Walden and Other Writings of Henry David Thoreau*, edited by Brooks Atkinson (first published in New York in 1937); *The Portable Thoreau*, edited by Carl Bode (New York, 1957); *Thoreau: The Major Essays*, edited by Jeffrey L. Duncan (New York, 1972); and *The Natural History Essays*, edited by Robert Sattelmeyer (Salt Lake City, 1980). "Walking" has also been printed separately, both in its entirety and in excerpted form.

Synopsis

Thoreau declares in the first sentence of "Walking":

> I wish to speak a word for Nature, for absolute freedom
> and wildness, as contrasted with a freedom and culture
> merely civil,—to regard man as an inhabitant, or a part
> and parcel of Nature, rather than a member of society.

The entire essay is an expansion upon the ideas expressed in this opening sentence. Thoreau explores the etymology of the word "saunter," which he believes may come from the French "*Sainte-Terre*" (Holy Land) or from the French "*sans terre*" (without land). Either derivation applies to walking as he knows it, but he prefers the former. True walking is not directionless wandering about the countryside, nor is it physical exercise. It is a crusade "to go forth and reconquer this Holy Land from the hands of the Infidels." Although he admits that his own walks bring him back to home and hearth at the end of the day, the walking to which he aspires demands that the walker leave his life behind in the "spirit of undying adventure, never to return." The "Walker, Errant" is in a category by himself, "a sort of fourth estate, outside of Church and State and People." But many of Thoreau's townsmen are too tied to society and daily life to walk in the proper spirit. Walking leads naturally to the fields and woods, and away from the village—scene of much busy coming and going, accessed by established roads, which Thoreau avoids. He suggests the degeneracy of the village by exploring the etymology of the word "village," connecting it to the Latin words for "road" and for "vile."

Thoreau's neighborhood offers the possibility of good walks, which he has not yet exhausted. He refers to the new perspective that even a familiar walk can provide. He deplores man's attempts to bound the landscape with fences and stakes, placed by the "Prince of Darkness" as surveyor. He contrasts the hurried walking undertaken in conducting the business of life with that made "out into a Nature such as the old prophets and poets, Menu, Moses, Homer, Chaucer, walked in"—a kind of exploration very different from that of Vespucci or Columbus. Thoreau's walking explores a territory better expressed by mythology than history. He conveys some urgency to walk by stating that, although the landscape is not owned at present, he foresees a time when property ownership may prevail over it.

Thoreau refers to the difficulty of choosing the direction of a walk, asserting that there is a "right way" but that we often choose the wrong.

The walk we should take "is perfectly symbolical of the path which we love to travel in the interior and ideal world"—a path difficult to determine because it does not yet "exist distinctly in our idea." Thoreau's own natural tendency is to head west, where the earth is "more unexhausted and richer," toward wildness and freedom. The east leads to the past—the history, art, and literature of the Old World; the west to the forest and to the future, to enterprise and the adventure of the New World. As a nation, we tend toward the west, and the particular (in the form of the individual) reflects the general tendency. Thoreau believes that physical environment inspires man and that the vast, untamed grandeur of the American wilderness is "symbolical of the height to which the philosophy and poetry and religion of [America's] inhabitants may one day soar." He expands upon the evidence of history in Europe as reflective of the past. America, whose landscape has not yet been completely civilized, suggests "more of the future than of the past or present." The author sees in the promise of wild America "*the heroic age itself.*"

Thoreau takes up the subject of the wild (synonymous with the west), in which he finds "the preservation of the World." The legend of Romulus and Remus (founders of Rome, who as infants were suckled by a wolf) demonstrates that civilization has drawn strength from the wild. He writes of the wildness of primitive people, of his own yearning for "wild lands where no settler has squatted," and of his hope that each man may be "a part and parcel of Nature" (the phrase repeated from the beginning of the essay), exuding sensory evidence of his connection with her. He equates wildness with life and strength. He himself prefers the wild vigor of the swamp, a place where one can "recreate" oneself, to the cultivated garden. The wild confers health on both the individual and society. "A township where one primitive forest waves above while another . . . rots below" nurtures poets and philosophers. Thoreau perceives agriculture as an occupation that makes the farmer stronger and more natural, and the wild and free in literature as that which most appeals to the reader. Genius is an uncivilized force, like lightning, not a "taper lighted at the hearthstone of the race." Thoreau calls for a literature that truly expresses nature. Although no literature has yet adequately done so, mythology is more satisfactory. The west—the American continent—"is preparing to add its fables to those of the East," and there will be an American mythology to inspire poets everywhere.

Thoreau finds truth in "the wildest dreams of wild men," even though these truths defy common sense. He is drawn to "wild fancies, which transcend the order of time and development." All good things, he declares, are wild and free. He rejoices that civilized men, like domestic animals, retain some measure of their innate wildness. Some men possess it to a greater degree than others. All men can fulfill low purposes. Only some—those who are not as suited to civilization as others—can fulfill higher purposes and should not be tamed. Whether or not we acknowledge it, there is a savage in all of us, even the most civilized, and that primal nature will show itself in impassioned or inspired moments. Civilization pulls us from nature—"this vast, savage, howling mother of ours"—and allows only social relations, "interaction man on man." Civilized life produces a hasty, rushed maturation of the individual, but does not allow the latent development that comes in periods of dormancy.

Not every man should be cultivated, nor every part of one man. Thoreau writes that "the greater part will be meadow and forest, not only serving an immediate use, but preparing a mould against a distant future, by the annual decay of the vegetation which it supports." Man needs "wild and dusky knowledge" more than lettered learning. Thoreau undercuts the notion of "Useful Knowledge," which may preclude higher understanding, preferring instead "Useful Ignorance" or "Beautiful Knowledge." His own desire for knowledge is intermittent, but his "desire to bathe my head in atmospheres unknown to my feet is perennial and constant." He encourages not the seeking of knowledge per se but rather of "Sympathy with Intellect." Our understanding cannot encompass the magnitude of nature and the universal. Thoreau writes that in his own relationship with nature he lives "a sort of border life, on the confines of a world into which I make occasional and transient forays only." Even Thoreau—a man who has devoted his life to higher pursuit—cannot grasp the full meaning of nature. When we are successful in beginning to approach the universal through our experience of nature, our glimpses of understanding are fleeting and evanescent. Imperfect though our comprehension is, however, we must elevate, must seek those places that offer broader perspective. Thoreau employs the image of the rooster—crowing confidently to inspire others to alertness and awareness, expressing the "health and soundness of Nature"—used in *Walden*. "Walking" ends with Thoreau rhapsodically recalling a moving sunset he had earlier seen, conveying a powerful and optimistic longing for inspired understanding. In the last paragraph of the essay, Thoreau refers again to sauntering toward the Holy Land, until "one day the sun shall shine more brightly than ever he has done, shall perchance shine into our minds and hearts, and light up our whole lives with a great awakening light, as warm and serene and golden as on a bankside in autumn."

Major Themes

Theme

The Pursuit and Comprehension of the Wild. Thoreau prepared the essay "Walking" for publication during his final months. It forms part of a cluster of natural history writings that he worked on late in his life. (Among the others, "Autumnal Tints" and "Wild Apples" were, like "Walking," published in *Atlantic Monthly* in 1862, after Thoreau's death.) "Walking" represents a final statement of Thoreau's understanding of nature. It contains ideas expressed in his earlier writings, presented imperatively. Its tone is visionary. Although the essay resulted from the union of two lectures prepared in 1851, it is difficult not to think of it as a deathbed communication, an ultimate, emphatic reiteration and extension of themes developed throughout Thoreau's writings, a final exhortation to the reader to be alert to nature.

Style &
Language

Thoreau makes clear in the first sentence of "Walking" that nature in its most intense form—"absolute freedom and wildness"—is his subject. Throughout the essay, he exalts unconfined wildness in both nature and man, and rejects the forces (the past, society, and the materialistic values of the present) that inhibit the full experience of nature and that limit thought and expression. The heightened, unrestrained, frequently impassioned rhetoric of the piece stylistically reinforces Thoreau's message.

Literary
Device

In defining all that he means by wildness, or "the Wild," Thoreau develops the metaphor of "the West." The west, the direction in which he prefers to walk, evokes the American frontier and the vast, unexplored, wild landscape beyond it, and at the same time suggests the uncharted, boundless, as yet unrealized possibility of man. His discussion of the west reveals the powerful fascination that westward expansion held for Thoreau.

Although territorial acquisition as supported by the doctrine of Manifest Destiny had, in the spread of slavery, consequences Thoreau found unacceptable, the symbolic west in "Walking" possesses a mythological significance. The west represents health, vigor, new ventures with unknown outcomes, and the future. The west is full of promise:

> . . . I saw that [the west] was a Rhine stream of a different kind; that the foundations of castles were yet to be laid, and the famous bridges were yet to be thrown over the river; and I felt that *this was the heroic age itself,* though we know it not. . . .

Thoreau prophesies an American mythology based on the potential of the west. In contrast, the east, where lies the Old World, represents the history, art, and literature of the past.

In "Walking" as elsewhere in his writings, Thoreau explores the idea of a fit expression of wildness, an expression not achieved by English literature nor by any poetry yet written. He writes:

> I walk out into a Nature such as the old prophets and poets, Menu, Moses, Homer, Chaucer, walked in. You name it America, but it is not America. . . . There is a truer account of it in mythology than in any history of America, so called, that I have seen.

In Atlantis and the Hesperides, the ancients had their own "Great West, enveloped in mystery and poetry," which can be recaptured each time we look "into the sunset sky." Thoreau refers to Romulus and Remus, who were suckled by a she-wolf and went on to achieve greatness through the founding of Rome. He finds in this ancient Roman legend an elemental recognition of man's connection to the strength-giving wild. The story contains a truth that transcends what we narrowly think of as reality: "The story of Romulus and Remus being suckled by a wolf is not a meaningless fable." Mythology is a form unbounded by the limitations of fact and common sense. It exists independent of time and place in its relevance as a universal statement.

Literary Device

Walking as presented in the essay is man's attempt to seek and to understand the wild, to confront it directly, on its own terms, outside of ordinary life and of what we think we know to be reality. It is a deliberate journey away from the business of life, as is the river trip described in *A Week on the Concord and Merrimack Rivers* and Thoreau's removal to the pond in *Walden*. The metaphor of the walker as a crusader to the Holy Land elevates walking to a spiritual quest. Thoreau reinforces the metaphor by placing the devil himself in opposition to the freedom and wildness that the walker craves. The "Prince of Darkness" is the surveyor who places the stakes that keep the walker away from the landscape. The "Evil One" cries "Whoa!" to the wildness of mankind. In "Walking," Thoreau more starkly depicts the polarization of nature and civilization as a struggle between the forces of good and evil than he does in *A Week* or *Walden*.

Proper walking, or sauntering, requires that the walker leave everything behind and submit fully to the experience of the walk, forgetting the town and avoiding the narrowly constricted path afforded by the well-defined road. The walker naturally chooses a route outwardly symbolic of "the path which we love to travel in the interior and ideal world," into the wild. In thus heading both outward and inward into the wild, we ensure not only our own health and well-being, but the very preservation of the world as well. We ignore our need to acknowledge and explore the real and metaphorical wild at peril to ourselves as individuals and as a civilization.

Thoreau examines our openness to the wild while walking by contrasting the "wildest dreams of wild men" with the common sense that prevails in society, "Useful Knowledge" with "Useful Ignorance" or "Beautiful Knowledge." The walker surrenders himself to the experience of nature and thus gains an inspired insight unobtainable through the facts and skills accumulated through traditional learning. He seeks an elusive kind of knowledge, one that is not easy to obtain and that is granted unpredictably. Thoreau admits that his own comprehension of the meaning of nature is imperfect, and that man's ability to perceive the universal laws behind nature may not be fully equal to the task. He writes that knowledge is the "lighting up of the mist by the sun," and that "with respect to knowledge, we are all children of the mist." Only by recognizing, accepting, and celebrating the wild reality in nature and beyond the veneer of civilized life will we see through the mist. This process will be unsettling. The primitive within man is deep and savage in some respects. Walking requires a willingness to embrace "a wildness whose glance no civilization can endure,—as if we lived on the marrow of koodoos devoured raw." The best that we can do is to remain alert to evidence of this possibly unfathomable knowledge. Thoreau writes: "My desire for knowledge is intermittent; but my desire to bathe my head in atmospheres unknown to my feet is perennial and constant. The highest that we can attain is not Knowledge, but Sympathy with Intelligence." As in *A Week* and *Walden*, he repeatedly deals with the subjects of perception and perspective, with the heightened, unbounded consciousness necessary for the intuition of universal law—perhaps the most important theme of "Walking."

In many ways, "Walking" seems both a distillation of and an expansion upon *Walden*. Because Thoreau was preparing the lectures that he combined to form "Walking" simultaneously with *Walden*, it is natural that there is a particular correspondence between the two. The major themes of *Walden* are the major themes of "Walking," presented more urgently and dramatically in the essay than in the book. The end of "Walking" is especially reminiscent of *Walden*. As he does in *Walden*, Thoreau uses the image of the rooster as the crowing, bragging "expression of the health and soundness of Nature," rousing men to wakefulness and perception, to "a pure morning joy." Moreover, Thoreau concludes both *Walden* and "Walking" with the imagery of the powerful, inspiring light of alert understanding. But the light at the end of "Walking" is presented in far greater detail and far more lyrically than that of dawn and the sun as a morning star at the conclusion of *Walden*. He writes in "Walking" of the "glory and splendor" of a particular November sunset:

> We walked in so pure and bright a light, gilding the withered grass and leaves, so softly and serenely bright, I thought I had never bathed in such a golden flood, without a ripple or a murmur to it. The west side of every wood and rising ground gleamed like the boundary of Elysium, and the sun on our backs seemed like a gentle herdsman driving us home at evening.

Indeed, the relationship of theme and image between "Walking" and *Walden* suggests one important reason for Thoreau's powerful continuing appeal, beyond the relevance of his message to our own time. Although his major ideas are presented in different ways and with varying degrees of emphasis throughout his work, his writings possess a satisfying aesthetic coherence.

CliffsNotes Review

Use this CliffsNotes Review to test your understanding of the original text, and reinforce what you've learned in this book. After you work through the essay questions, reading and research topics, and the fun and useful practice projects, you're well on your way to understanding a comprehensive and meaningful interpretation of Thoreau, Emerson, and Transcendentalism.

Essay Questions

1. Compare and contrast the views on nature expressed in Emerson's *Nature* and in Thoreau's "Walking."

2. Examine the attitudes toward reform expressed in Emerson's "Divinity School Address" and "Experience" and in Thoreau's *Civil Disobedience*.

3. Discuss the significance of perception and perspective as developed in the writings of Emerson and Thoreau.

4. Compare and contrast Emerson's and Thoreau's attitudes toward society as expressed in their lives and writings.

5. Examine and discuss Thoreau's views on technological progress as expressed in *Walden*. Refer specifically to his presentation of the railroad.

6. Discuss, with specific reference to Emerson's writings, the following Transcendental concepts: the Oversoul; correspondence; intuition ("reason" as opposed to "understanding"); perfectibility; and self-reliance.

7. Discuss the circle imagery in Emerson's *Nature*.

8. Transcendentalist Elizabeth Palmer Peabody wrote in her 1858 piece "Egotheism, the Atheism of To-Day" (reprinted in 1886 in her *Last Evening with Allston*):

> . . . when faith stagnates in the mere affirmation of the spiritual, men deify their own conceptions; i.e., they say that their conception of God is all that men can ever know of God. In short, faith commits suicide . . . at the summit of the moral life, and the next step to this is necessarily EGOTHEISM, which denies other self-consciousness to God than our own subjective consciousness;—not

recognizing that there is, beyond our conception, inconceivable Power, Wisdom, and Love,—of the immanence of whose substantial being within us our best conception is but a transient form. Thus Egotheism, in the last analysis, is Atheism; and we find this "latest form of infidelity," as the understanding has rather blindly denominated it,—though not without a degree of religious instinct,—in the science, philosophy, and politics of the age,—at once glorifying it and saddening its poetry;—for man proves but a melancholy God."

Is Miss Peabody's criticism applicable to ideas expressed in Emerson's *Nature* and "Divinity School Address"?

9. Discuss the image of the river in Thoreau's *A Week on the Concord and Merrimack Rivers.*

10. Discuss Thoreau's presentation of the Hannah Dustan story in the chapter "Thursday" in *A Week on the Concord and Merrimack Rivers,* and the story's connection to the major themes of the book.

11. Choose a symbol from Thoreau's *Walden* (the rooster, loon, chimney, pond, sand foliage, for example), and explain its development and significance.

12. Comment on the battle of the ants in "Brute Neighbors" in Thoreau's *Walden.* What does Thoreau say in it of the relationship between man and nature?

13. Comment on the dialogue between "Hermit" and "Poet" at the beginning of "Brute Neighbors" in *Walden.* How does it relate to themes explored in the book as a whole?

14. Discuss Thoreau's thoughts on poetry and writing.

Extended Reading and Research Topics

1. Read Emerson's "American Scholar" and compare it with his "Divinity School Address."

2. Read Emerson's essay "History." Compare the view of history expressed in it with that in the poem "Hamatreya."

3. Read and analyze Emerson's poem "Each and All," or some other Emerson poem of your choice. Discuss the poem in relation to Emerson's Transcendental philosophy, as expressed elsewhere in his writings.

4. Read Emerson's "Historic Notes of Life and Letters in New England." How does this retrospective assessment compare with the expression of Transcendentalism in Emerson's life and writings, or in Thoreau's?

5. Read Coleridge's *Aids to Reflection* and discuss its influence on Emerson and on Transcendentalism.

6. Read Elizabeth Palmer Peabody's essay "Language" (available in the 1975 AMS Press facsimile reprint of her *Last Evening with Allston*). Compare what she writes on the subject with what Emerson writes in "Language" (Chapter IV of his *Nature*).

7. Read Theodore Parker's "A Discourse of the Transient and Permanent in Christianity" (printed in Perry Miller's anthology *The Transcendentalists*), and compare it with Emerson's "Divinity School Address."

8. Research Bronson Alcott's Fruitlands or George Ripley's Brook Farm. Consider the ways in which Transcendental idealism was expressed in the utopian community you choose.

9. Research the educational philosophy of Bronson Alcott or Elizabeth Palmer Peabody, and discuss how it reflected Transcendental concerns and ideas.

10. Research the life of one Transcendental thinker aside from Emerson and Thoreau—Bronson Alcott, Margaret Fuller, Elizabeth Peabody, or another of your own choice—and discuss it in relation to the development and expression of Transcendental thought.

11. Research the history of environmentalism in the United States. How has Thoreau's thought influenced it? Specifically, explore Thoreau's influence on John Muir.

12. Research and discuss the influence of Thoreau on Gandhi and on Martin Luther King, Jr.

Practice Projects

1. You are the book reviewer for a major urban newspaper in 1836. You are assigned to write a review of a book titled *Nature*, by Ralph Waldo Emerson. Striving for objectivity, write a balanced review that expresses both the strengths and weaknesses of the book. (Alternatively, you are the same reviewer in 1854, assigned to write a review of Thoreau's *Walden*.)

2. You are a citizen of Concord, walking down Main Street in September 1846. You bump into Henry David Thoreau, whom you know only slightly. Curious about what he is doing at Walden Pond, you question him about his life there, and about the night he recently spent in jail. Record the dialogue that you have with him.

3. Consider the current emphasis on personal health and fitness as Emerson might have regarded it. Write an essay on the subject from Emerson's point of view. Alternatively, consider and write about the Unification Church of Sun Myung Moon from an Emersonian point of view, or about the New Age Movement.

4. As a group project, construct a Web site that presents the major concepts of Transcendental philosophy and related topics through quotations from Emerson, Thoreau, and other Transcendental authors. Begin by determining the concepts and topics you will present. You might choose to include the Oversoul, correspondence, intuition ("reason" versus "understanding"), perfectability, self-reliance, nature, reform, religion, progress, science and scientists, and poets and poetry, among other topics.

The site should consist of a main page with links to separate pages for each topic or concept presented. The main page should include a summary definition of Transcendentalism, and each linked page a summary definition or brief discussion of the particular concept or topic presented.

Quotations from authors other than Emerson and Thoreau may be drawn from Perry Miller's *The Transcendentalists: An Anthology*, if separate editions are not readily available. The work of searching texts for appropriate quotations should be divided up among class members, either by topic or by author.

If possible, provide an appropriate photograph or illustration for the home page and for each linked page.

CliffsNotes Resource Center

The learning doesn't need to stop here. CliffsNotes Resource Center shows you the best of the best—links to the best information in print and online about the authors and/or related works. And don't think that this is all we've prepared for you; we've put all kinds of pertinent information at www.cliffsnotes.com. Look for all the terrific resources at your favorite bookstore or local library and on the Internet. When you're online, make your first stop www.cliffsnotes.com where you'll find more incredibly useful information about Thoreau, Emerson, and Transcendentalism.

Books

This CliffsNotes book provides a meaningful interpretation of Thoreau, Emerson, and Transcendentalism, published by Wiley Publishing, Inc. If you are looking for information about Thoreau and Emerson and/or related works, check out these other publications:

American Transcendentalism: An Anthology of Criticism, edited by Brian M. Barbour, includes essays by various writers, some approaching Transcendentalism broadly, some focusing on particular aspects of it (religious, philosophical, political, social), some specifically on Emerson. Also includes a selected bibliography and an index. Notre Dame, Indiana: University of Notre Dame Press, 1973.

American Transcendentalism, 1830–1860: An Intellectual Inquiry, by Paul F. Boller, Jr., offers a broad approach, containing chapters on religious radicalism, intuitional philosophy, Transcendental idealism, social reform, cosmic optimism, and transience and permanence. Includes suggestions for further reading and an index. New York: Putnam, 1974.

Biographical Dictionary of Transcendentalism, edited by Wesley T. Mott, offers succinct entries on each of the Transcendentalists (major and minor), their contemporaries and associates, and those they influenced. Volume includes references for each entry, and a bibliographical essay and an index to the whole. Especially useful for the student beginning research on a figure connected with the movement. Westport, Connecticut: Greenwood Press, 1996.

The Cambridge Companion to Henry David Thoreau, edited by Joel Myerson, includes thirteen essays by various writers on a range of topics, including Thoreau's reputation, his connection with Concord, his relationship with Emerson, Thoreau as a poet, individual writings by Thoreau, his attitude toward the natural environment, and his attitude toward reform. Includes a chronology, a bibliography for further reading, and an index. New York: Cambridge University Press, 1995.

The Cambridge Companion to Ralph Waldo Emerson, edited by Joel Porte and Saundra Morris, includes twelve essays by various contributors, on Transcendentalism and aspects of Emerson's life, thought, writings, and influence. Includes a bibliography and an index. New York: Cambridge University Press, 1999.

The Days of Henry Thoreau, by Walter Harding, is a major biography reflecting the author's extensive familiarity with primary sources relating to Thoreau. Includes illustrations and an index. Princeton: Princeton University Press, 1982.

Emerson Among the Eccentrics: A Group Portrait, by Carlos Baker, is a biography placing Emerson in the context of his friends and associates. Deals with Emerson's relationships with his brothers; his aunt Mary Moody Emerson; his wife Lidian and their children; Bronson Alcott; Margaret Fuller; Jones Very; Ellery Channing; Nathaniel Hawthorne; Theodore Parker; Walt Whitman; John Brown; and others. Includes illustrations, bibliography, and index. New York: Viking, 1996.

Emerson and Thoreau: The Contemporary Reviews, edited by Joel Myerson, offers a good selection of contemporary reactions to all major works by Emerson and Thoreau, providing insight into the early reception and reputation of these authors. Includes an index. New York: Cambridge University Press, 1992.

Emerson as Poet, by Hyatt H. Waggoner, is a comprehensive examination of Emerson's poems, both individually and in the context of the full range of his writings. Discusses technical as well as thematic aspects of the poetry. Includes an index. Princeton, New Jersey: Princeton University Press, 1974.

Emerson Handbook, by Frederic Ives Carpenter, is a comprehensive handbook, still useful for student purposes, presenting Emerson's life, writings, ideas, sources, and influence. Includes sections on his reform and antislavery involvements and on Emerson biography. Also includes bibliographies and an index. New York: Hendricks House, 1953.

Encyclopedia of Transcendentalism, edited by Wesley T. Mott, is, as described in the preface, "a comprehensive guide to the major philosophical concepts, antecedents, genres, institutions, organizations, movements, periodicals, events, and places associated with Transcendentalism in the United States." Includes references for each entry, and a bibliography and an index to the whole. Like its companion (*Biographical Dictionary of Transcendentalism*), the title is a good starting point for student research. Westport, Connecticut: Greenwood Press, 1996.

German Literary Influences on the American Transcendentalists, by Stanley M. Vogel, is a detailed study presented in two parts, "German Scholarship Outside the Transcendental Circle," and "German Scholarship Among the Transcendentalists." Includes a summary; appendices on German material in the Boston area, on books of German interest in Emerson's personal library, and on Emerson's German reading; a bibliography of manuscripts; and an index. New Haven, Connecticut: Yale University Press, 1955.

Henry David Thoreau: A Descriptive Bibliography, by Raymond R. Borst, comprehensively lists Thoreau's writings, including separate publications, collected works, first-appearance contributions to books and pamphlets, first-appearance contributions to magazines and newspapers, collections, principal works about Thoreau, and an index. Pittsburgh, Pennsylvania: University of Pittsburgh Press, 1982.

Henry Thoreau: A Life of the Mind, by Robert D. Richardson, Jr., is an intellectual biography of Thoreau's development as a thinker, writer, and naturalist from his college graduation in 1837 until his death in 1862. Includes a listing of sources, notes, and an index. Berkeley: University of California Press, 1986.

A Historical Guide to Ralph Waldo Emerson, edited by Joel Myerson, is a collection of essays by seven contributors, placing Emerson within the context of his time. Includes a lengthy biographical essay; pieces on Emerson and individualism; and pieces on Emerson's approach to nature and natural science, to religion, to the antislavery movement, and to the women's rights movement. Also includes a chronology, a piece on biographical treatments of Emerson, a bibliographical essay, illustrations, and an index. New York: Oxford University Press, 2000.

The Life of Ralph Waldo Emerson, by Ralph L. Rusk, is a major biography based on the author's thorough knowledge of Emerson's writings and a comprehensive understanding of the source material. Includes extensive references and an index. Still essential, although published over half a century ago. New York: Charles Scribner's Sons, 1949.

The New England Transcendentalists and the Dial: *A History of the Magazine and Its Contributors,* by Joel Myerson, includes four chapters on the history of and thirty-six chapters on contributors to the periodical. Also includes illustrations and a listing of contents of and contributors to each issue, a bibliography, and an index. Rutherford, New Jersey: Fairleigh Dickinson University Press, 1980.

The New Thoreau Handbook, by Walter Harding and Michael Meyer, is a useful resource dealing comprehensively with Thoreau's life, work, sources, ideas, artistry, and reputation. Includes a chronology, bibliography, and index. New York: New York University Press, 1980.

The Orient in American Transcendentalism: A Study of Emerson, Thoreau, and Alcott, by Arthur Christy, offers an in-depth study of the specific Eastern influences on the thought and work of the Transcendentalists. Includes an appendix of Oriental and related texts familiar to Emerson, Thoreau, and Alcott, bibliographical references and explanatory notes, and an index. New York: Columbia University Press, 1932.

Ralph Waldo Emerson: A Descriptive Bibliography, by Joel Myerson, provides a comprehensive listing of Emerson's writings, including separate publications, collected editions, miscellaneous collections, first-appearance contributions to books and pamphlets, first-appearance contributions to magazines and newspapers, books edited by Emerson, reprinted material in books and pamphlets, material attributed to Emerson, principal works about Emerson, and an index. Pittsburgh, Pennsylvania: University of Pittsburgh Press, 1982.

A Thoreau Profile, by Milton Meltzer and Walter Harding, is a highly readable and informative topical introduction to Thoreau's life and writings, drawing heavily on the author's own words. Includes illustrations, a chronology, a list of first editions, a section on Thoreau collections around the country, and an index. New York: Crowell, 1962.

Transcendentalism in New England: A History, by Octavius Brooks Frothingham, is the earliest full-scale historical treatment of Transcendentalism and is still a valuable source. Examines German, French, and English philosophical, religious, and literary influences on the development of American Transcendentalism, its forms of expression, and its proponents (Emerson, Alcott, Fuller, Parker, Ripley, and others). Includes an index. New York: G.P. Putnam's Sons, 1876 (facsimile edition: Glouster, Massachusetts: Peter Smith, 1965).

The Transcendentalists: An Anthology, edited by Perry Miller, is a useful anthology including selected writings by minor as well as major figures among the Transcendentalists. Also includes contemporary reactions to and assessments of the movement and an index. Frequently reprinted and widely available. Cambridge, Massachusetts: Harvard University Press, 1950.

It's easy to find books published by Wiley Publishing, Inc. You'll find them in your favorite bookstores (on the Internet and at a store near you). We also have three Web sites that you can use to read about all the books we publish:

■ www.cliffsnotes.com

■ www.dummies.com

■ www.wiley.com

Internet

Check out these Web resources for more information about Thoreau, Emerson, and Transcendentalism:

American Transcendentalism Web, www.vcu.edu/engweb/transweb — includes pages providing an overview of Transcendentalism, discussing its roots and influences, the Transcendental philosophy of education, authors, literary works, the philosophy of nature, aesthetics and the vocation of writing, religion, and social and political reform. Also includes bibliographies and links. Site features essays, student papers, literary texts, and images.

Concord Free Public Library Special Collections Home Page,
198.112.12.245/cfpl/scollect/scoll.html —
includes information on archival, manuscript, printed, photographic,
and other holdings relating to Emerson, Thoreau, Transcendentalism, and nineteenth-century Concord.

The Concord Magazine, www.concordma.com/magazine — an
electronic journal including articles on Concord history, life, literature, and people of all periods.

CyberSaunter, usmh12.usmd.edu/thoreau/ — contains information on Thoreau's life and work, as well as links to sites relating to
Transcendentalism and Unitarian Universalism.

Henry David Thoreau, www.geocities.com/~freereligion/
1thorea.html — includes essays, images, online texts of writings by Thoreau, listings of books and other materials on or by
Thoreau, Thoreau quotations, many links, and searching information.

**PAL: Perspectives in American Literature: A Research and Reference
Guide, Chapter 4: Early Nineteenth Century: American
Transcendentalism,** www.csustan.edu/english/reuben/
pal/chap4/CHAP4.HTML — includes a bibliography, an introduction, and pages on several movements (antislavery, utopian,
women's rights) and many figures connected to or contemporary
with the movement. Separate pages include essays, bibliographies,
study questions, and links.

Ralph Waldo Emerson, www.geocities.com/freereligion/
1emerson.html — includes general information, a biographical
sketch, a chronology, genealogical information, literary texts, a resource
listing, images, searching information, and many links to sites on Transcendentalism, Unitarian Universalism, and other topics.

**A Student's History of American Literature, Chapter IV: Philosophy
and   Romance,**
www.bibliomania.com/Reference/Simonds/
SHAL/p1-chap4.html — an exclusively textual site. Includes a
page with information on the literary development of New England, the Unitarian movement, the Reverend William Ellery Channing, Transcendentalism, *The Dial*, Brook Farm, Emerson, the
Alcotts, and Margaret Fuller, as well as pages on Emerson, Thoreau,

Hawthorne, and Poe.

Thoreau, Walden, and the Environment: The Thoreau Home Page, www.walden.org — the combined Web sites of the Walden Woods Project, the Thoreau Society, and the Thoreau Institute. Provides access to information on Thoreau, Emerson, and other nineteenth-century authors; on Transcendentalism and the Transcendentalists; on environmental issues; and on other related topics. Includes online concordance to Emerson's essays.

The Transcendentalists, www.geocities.com/freereligion/ — includes essays, articles, separate pages for individual authors, book lists, literary texts, and many links to other sites on a variety of topics (for example, on the Reverend William Ellery Channing, on individual Transcendentalists and other nineteenth century thinkers and authors, and on those people whom the Transcendentalists influenced).

Next time you're on the Internet, don't forget to drop by www.cliffs notes.com. We created an online Resource Center that you can use today, tomorrow, and beyond.

Magazines and Journals

Check out these magazines and journals for more information on Thoreau, Emerson, and Transcendentalism. (Quoted narrative descriptions are taken from within the periodicals themselves.)

ATQ. 1–62 (1969–1986); new series 1:1–[ongoing] (1987–[present]). Numbers 1–62 published under title *American Transcendental Quarterly*. "... a quarterly journal of 19th-century American literature and culture. Studies of literary works and authors, as well as non-technical articles on all other aspects of 19th-century American culture and society" are included.

The Concord Saunterer. 1–20 (1966–1988); new series 1:1–[ongoing] (Fall 1993–[present]). "... an annual publication of The Thoreau Society, [containing] biographical, historical, textual, bibliographical, and interpretive articles relating to Henry Thoreau and his associates, Concord, and Transcendentalism."

Emerson Society Papers. 1:1–[ongoing] (1990–[present]). Published twice yearly, this newsletter of the Ralph Waldo Emerson Society includes "information about editions, publications, and research in progress on Emerson and his circle; queries and requests for information in aid of research in these fields; and significant news... of Emersonian scholars. . . .[A]lso notes and short articles . . . on subjects of interest to [its] membership."

ESQ: A Journal of the American Renaissance. 1–[ongoing] (1955–[present]). Numbers 1–53 published under title *Emerson Society Quarterly.* New series numbering added to old in 1982. ". . . devoted to the study of nineteenth-century American literature. It focuses upon all aspects—literary, religious, philosophical, and historic—of the romantic transcendental tradition emanating from New England, of which Emerson is a principal figure. *ESQ*'s coverage, however, encompasses influences upon and responses to midcentury romanticism generally. . . . Critical essays, source and influence studies, and biographical studies of all figures in the century are [included], as well as more general discussions of literary theory, literary history, and the history of ideas."

Studies in the American Renaissance. 1–20 (1977–1996). Volume 20 includes twenty-year index. An annual publication containing pieces on "the lives and works of mid-nineteenth-century American authors and the circumstances in which they wrote, published, and were received. [Includes] biographical, historical, and bibliographical articles on the literature, history, philosophy, art, religion, and general culture of America during the period 1830–1860."

The Thoreau Quarterly. 1–17 (1969–1985). Volumes 1–13 published under title *Thoreau Journal Quarterly.* ". . . devoted to literary and philosophical studies. [Includes pieces] focused directly on the writings of Thoreau or on themes and problems he addressed. . . . [S]tudies of topics concerning the American Renaissance, the New England Transcendentalists, or American philosophy are [included], as are many other studies."

These specialized journals are not likely to be available through any but the largest public libraries. They are, however, widely available in college and university libraries. Specific articles located through standard indexes may frequently be requested via interlibrary loan. Consult your local reference librarian for assistance.

Index

Stäel, Madame de, 9
Stowe, Harriet Beecher, 23
Stuart, Moses, 9
Student's History of American Literature
Web site, 220
Studies in the American Renaissance, 222
style and language
Civil Disobedience (Thoreau), 180
Emerson's, 63, 64
"Hamatreya" (Emerson), 121–123
Thoreau's, 137, 138
Walden (Thoreau), 187, 188
"Walking" (Thoreau), 207
A Week on the Concord and Merrimack
Rivers (Thoreau), 159, 160
Supreme Court decision, Dred Scott
case, 16, 17

T

temperance, 23
tenets of Transcendentalism, 7
Oversoul, 5, 64, 67, 91, 100, 104, 139
relationship with God and nature, 4
territorial exploration and expansion, 14
Texas, freedom of/from Mexico, 16
textile industry, 7
themes
A Week on the Concord and Merrimack
Rivers (Thoreau), 160, 167, 168,
170–172, 174
accessibility of universal understanding
(Nature), 90, 91
attributes of individuals (Emerson),
65, 66
Civil Disobedience (Thoreau), 177–181
difficulty of reconciling philosophy
("Experience"), 113
exaltation of the individual, 66, 67
exploration by individuals of self, 17
function of the preacher ("Divinity
School Address"), 107, 108
human history versus universal history
("Hamatreya"), 123
in Romantic literature, 36, 141
influence of the divine, 66
inherited versus intuited religion
("Divinity School Address"), 106
intuition, 67, 68
intuitive process (Emerson), 68, 69
man as outlet to the divine ("Divinity
School Address"), 104, 105

man's position in the universe
(Emerson), 67
material versus spiritual ("Hamatreya"),
120
matter and spirit (Nature), 97–99
Nature (Emerson), 64–67
perspective and insight ("Experience"),
115–118
philosophy versus experience of life,
70, 71
poems, spiritual origin of, 70
reality versus illusion, 121
reason and understanding (Nature), 93,
94, 95
reconciling material and spiritual, 69, 70
relationship of man and nature (Nature),
95–97
separateness versus unity
("Hamatreya"), 122
Thoreau's, 138–148
transience versus permanence
("Hamatreya"), 122
unity of God, man, and nature
(Nature), 91–93
unity of man and nature, 100
universal unity, 89
Walden (Thoreau), 196, 198–200,
202, 203
"Hamatreya" (Emerson), 120–123
"Walking" (Thoreau), 207
theory of labor, 26
Thoreau Profile, A (Meltzer and
Harding), 218
Thoreau Quarterly, 222
Thoreau, Henry David
A Week on the Concord and Merrimack
Rivers, 159
antislavery position, 18, 132, 135
arrest of, 132, 133, 176
career, 129, 131, 133
chronology of writings, 148–150
Civil Disobedience, 18, 175, 176
death, 136
early career, 128
early life, 126
education, 127, 128, 130
family of origin, 126, 127
friendship with Emerson, 58, 130,
133, 135
interest in exploration, 17
introduction to writings, 137–148
journals, 128, 136

continued

CliffsNotes

LITERATURE NOTES

Absalom, Absalom!
The Aeneid
Agamemnon
Alice in Wonderland
All the King's Men
All the Pretty Horses
All Quiet on the
    Western Front
All's Well &
    Merry Wives
American Poets of the
    20th Century
American Tragedy
Animal Farm
Anna Karenina
Anthem
Antony and Cleopatra
Aristotle's Ethics
As I Lay Dying
The Assistant
As You Like It
Atlas Shrugged
Autobiography of
    Ben Franklin
Autobiography of
    Malcolm X
The Awakening
Babbit
Bartleby & Benito
    Cereno
The Bean Trees
The Bear
The Bell Jar
Beloved
Beowulf
The Bible
Billy Budd & Typee
Black Boy
Black Like Me
Bleak House
Bless Me, Ultima
The Bluest Eye & Sula
Brave New World
The Brothers Karamazov

The Call of the Wild &
    White Fang
Candide
The Canterbury Tales
Catch-22
Catcher in the Rye
The Chosen
The Color Purple
Comedy of Errors...
Connecticut Yankee
The Contender
The Count of
    Monte Cristo
Crime and Punishment
The Crucible
Cry, the Beloved
    Country
Cyrano de Bergerac
Daisy Miller &
    Turn...Screw
David Copperfield
Death of a Salesman
The Deerslayer
Diary of Anne Frank
Divine Comedy-I.
    Inferno
Divine Comedy-II.
    Purgatorio
Divine Comedy-III.
    Paradiso
Doctor Faustus
Dr. Jekyll and Mr. Hyde
Don Juan
Don Quixote
Dracula
Electra & Medea
Emerson's Essays
Emily Dickinson Poems
Emma
Ethan Frome
The Faerie Queene
Fahrenheit 451
Far from the Madding
    Crowd
A Farewell to Arms
Farewell to Manzanar
Fathers and Sons
Faulkner's Short Stories

Faust Pt. I & Pt. II
The Federalist
Flowers for Algernon
For Whom the Bell Tolls
The Fountainhead
Frankenstein
The French
    Lieutenant's Woman
The Giver
Glass Menagerie &
    Streetcar
Go Down, Moses
The Good Earth
The Grapes of Wrath
Great Expectations
The Great Gatsby
Greek Classics
Gulliver's Travels
Hamlet
The Handmaid's Tale
Hard Times
Heart of Darkness &
    Secret Sharer
Hemingway's
    Short Stories
Henry IV Part 1
Henry IV Part 2
Henry V
House Made of Dawn
The House of the
    Seven Gables
Huckleberry Finn
I Know Why the
    Caged Bird Sings
Ibsen's Plays I
Ibsen's Plays II
The Idiot
Idylls of the King
The Iliad
Incidents in the Life of
    a Slave Girl
Inherit the Wind
Invisible Man
Ivanhoe
Jane Eyre
Joseph Andrews
The Joy Luck Club
Jude the Obscure

Julius Caesar
The Jungle
Kafka's Short Stories
Keats & Shelley
The Killer Angels
King Lear
The Kitchen God's Wife
The Last of the
    Mohicans
Le Morte d'Arthur
Leaves of Grass
Les Miserables
A Lesson Before Dying
Light in August
The Light in the Forest
Lord Jim
Lord of the Flies
The Lord of the Rings
Lost Horizon
Lysistrata & Other
    Comedies
Macbeth
Madame Bovary
Main Street
The Mayor of
    Casterbridge
Measure for Measure
The Merchant
    of Venice
Middlemarch
A Midsummer Night's
    Dream
The Mill on the Floss
Moby-Dick
Moll Flanders
Mrs. Dalloway
Much Ado About
    Nothing
My Ántonia
Mythology
Narr. ...Frederick
    Douglass
Native Son
New Testament
Night
1984
Notes from the
    Underground

CliffsNotes™
@ cliffsnotes.com

The Odyssey
Oedipus Trilogy
Of Human Bondage
Of Mice and Men
The Old Man and
the Sea
Old Testament
Oliver Twist
The Once and
Future King
One Day in the Life of
Ivan Denisovich
One Flew Over the
Cuckoo's Nest
100 Years of Solitude
O'Neill's Plays
Othello
Our Town
The Outsiders
The Ox Bow Incident
Paradise Lost
A Passage to India
The Pearl
The Pickwick Papers
The Picture of
Dorian Gray
Pilgrim's Progress
The Plague
Plato's Euthyphro...
Plato's The Republic
Poe's Short Stories
A Portrait of the
Artist...
The Portrait of a Lady
The Power and
the Glory
Pride and Prejudice
The Prince
The Prince and
the Pauper
A Raisin in the Sun
The Red Badge of
Courage
The Red Pony
The Return of the
Native
Richard II
Richard III

The Rise of
Silas Lapham
Robinson Crusoe
Roman Classics
Romeo and Juliet
The Scarlet Letter
A Separate Peace
Shakespeare's
Comedies
Shakespeare's Histories
Shakespeare's
Minor Plays
Shakespeare's Sonnets
Shakespeare's Tragedies
Shaw's Pygmalion &
Arms...
Silas Marner
Sir Gawain...Green
Knight
Sister Carrie
Slaughterhouse-five
Snow Falling on Cedars
Song of Solomon
Sons and Lovers
The Sound and the Fury
Steppenwolf &
Siddhartha
The Stranger
The Sun Also Rises
T.S. Eliot's Poems &
Plays
A Tale of Two Cities
The Taming of the
Shrew
Tartuffe, Misanthrope...
The Tempest
Tender Is the Night
Tess of the D'Urbervilles
Their Eyes Were
Watching God
Things Fall Apart
The Three Musketeers
To Kill a Mockingbird
Tom Jones
Tom Sawyer
Treasure Island &
Kidnapped
The Trial

Tristram Shandy
Troilus and Cressida
Twelfth Night
Ulysses
Uncle Tom's Cabin
The Unvanquished
Utopia
Vanity Fair
Vonnegut's Works
Waiting for Godot
Walden
Walden Two
War and Peace
Who's Afraid of
Virginia...
Winesburg, Ohio
The Winter's Tale
The Woman Warrior
Worldly Philosophers
Wuthering Heights
A Yellow Raft in
Blue Water

Check Out the All-New CliffsNotes Guides

TECHNOLOGY TOPICS
Balancing Your Check-
book with Quicken
Buying and Selling
on eBay
Buying Your First PC
Creating a Winning
PowerPoint 2000
Presentation
Creating Web Pages
with HTML
Creating Your First
Web Page
Exploring the World
with Yahoo!
Getting on the Internet
Going Online with AOL
Making Windows 98
Work for You

Setting Up a
Windows 98
Home Network
Shopping Online Safely
Upgrading and
Repairing Your PC
Using Your First iMac
Using Your First PC
Writing Your First
Computer Program

PERSONAL FINANCE TOPICS
Budgeting & Saving
Your Money
Getting a Loan
Getting Out of Debt
Investing for the
First Time
Investing in
401(k) Plans
Investing in IRAs
Investing in
Mutual Funds
Investing in the
Stock Market
Managing Your Money
Planning Your
Retirement
Understanding
Health Insurance
Understanding
Life Insurance

CAREER TOPICS
Delivering a Winning
Job Interview
Finding a Job
on the Web
Getting a Job
Writing a Great Resume

CPSIA information can be obtained at www.ICGtesting.com
Printed in the USA
LVOW08s2159060414

380579LV00001B/80/P